SCANDAL

BRANDON ROTTINGHAUS

SCANDAL

Why Politicians Survive Controversy in a Partisan Era

Columbia University Press / *New York*

Columbia University Press
Publishers Since 1893
New York Chichester, West Sussex

Library of Congress Cataloging-in-Publication Data

Names: Rottinghaus, Brandon, 1977– author
Title: Scandal : why politicians survive controversy in a partisan era / Brandon Rottinghaus.
Description: New York : Columbia University Press, 2026. | Includes bibliographical references and index.
Identifiers: LCCN 2025023799 (print) | LCCN 2025023800 (ebook) | ISBN 9780231218818 hardback | ISBN 9780231218825 trade paperback | ISBN 9780231562447 ebook
Subjects: LCSH: Political culture—United States | Polarization (Social sciences)—Political aspects—United States | Scandals—Political aspects—United States | Political corruption—United States | United States—Politics and government—20th century | United States—Politics and government—21st century
Classification: LCC JK1726 .R744 2026 (print) | LCC JK1726 (ebook)

Cover design: Elliott S. Cairns
Cover image: AP Photo / J. Scott Applewhite

GPSR Authorized Representative: Easy Access System Europe, Mustamäe tee 50, 10621 Tallinn, Estonia, gpsr.requests@easproject.com

To my mentors

CONTENTS

ACKNOWLEDGMENTS

My interest in studying scandals began in 2003 when the mayor of the city where we were living was nabbed in an online sting by the local newspaper alleging he offered internships to young gay men in high school on the website Gay.com. The irony was that the mayor admitted to homosexual behavior with adults despite supporting and promoting "anti-gay" legislation—he made his political career on restricting rights to this community. Although he was never charged, despite allegations of past abuse, the local story quickly went national. The city council, in a unanimous resolution, asked for his resignation, as did the local and state Republican Party. But he refused to resign. Only a recall election eventually removed him from office.

His efforts to survive—and his ultimate inability to do so—struck me is interesting and telling. Scandals strike in the most unusual and unpredictable ways for politicians. The ways they deal with them, and the ways the political system treats the aftermath, are a check engine light on American democracy. This book is an outgrowth of those observations.

This book would not have "survived" without help from several people. Special thanks to my research assistant Lucas Lothamer, now himself a faculty member, for expert help on a survey experiment. Thanks also to my University of Houston colleague Jason Casellas and former student Matthew Ward for letting me tag along on a survey they were doing. Finally, thanks to my home department at the University of Houston, which gave me a research leave to finish this project.

Big thanks to Stephen Wesley and the entire team at Columbia University Press, who could not have made this process easier. Two reviewers aided in making the manuscript stronger. CUP's deft touch throughout the process made publishing this book as easy as any I have written.

Finally, to my family, who endured many bizarre tales of scandalous misdeeds during the writing of this book, I owe a lifetime of gratitude.

INTRODUCTION

The Death of Scandal?

I could stand in the middle of Fifth Avenue and shoot somebody, and I wouldn't lose any voters, OK? It's, like, incredible.

—DONALD TRUMP

If Watergate happened in 2024, there's every chance Nixon would have hung in there.

— ZACHARY BASU, *AXIOS* JOURNALIST

Donald Trump, the forty-fifth president of the United States, faced scandal after scandal involving himself, his cabinet, his staff, and even his family throughout his tumultuous presidential run and first term in the White House. He is the only president in American history impeached twice for high crimes and misdemeanors, the only president ever indicted on criminal charges, and the only president to be convicted of a felony (thirty-four, in fact). He survived (although not all of his compatriots did). Indeed, upon reelection in 2024, he "not only survived but thrived," even hanging a framed photo of his mug shot outside the Oval Office.[1]

He is not alone. The list of politicians snared in the net of scandal—sometimes of their own making, sometimes because of outside circumstances—is long. When it was revealed, in February 2019, that the white Democratic governor of Virginia, Ralph Northam, had donned blackface during medical school in the 1980s, his political career was presumed dead. But he held on, serving out his term. Democratic New Jersey senator Bob Menendez—already a target of the law because of a prior scandal—was caught with gold bars at his home, which he claimed his wife had inherited, and was accused of taking bribes from the Egyptian government. He argued he was a target because of political persecution by his enemies. He was convicted of bribery in 2024, and while he decided not to run for reelection, he held onto his seat until his conviction was final, about a month before the election. Post-conviction, an elementary school named in his honor changed its name. Former disgraced Republican Missouri governor Eric Greitens, who resigned in 2018 following a sexual assault and campaign finance allegations, announced he would run again for the U.S. Senate in 2020 (he lost in the primary). The list goes on and on.

Surviving scandal seems the norm now. It was apparent to everyone, but when George Santos admitted he was a "terrible liar," his misdeeds all came into obvious focus. Santos, the embattled Republican congressman from New York who fabricated large chunks of his résumé, publicly admitted he lied about, well, just about everything. His fabrications included "claiming to be Jewish, graduating from college, working at finance giants Citigroup and Goldman Sachs, and that his mother was in the World Trade Center during the Al-Qaida terrorist attack on 11 September 2001."[2] These were the first prevarications. As the media and partisan opponents probed, they found he had lied about where he went to high school, stolen the identity of donors' credit cards (some money ended up in his bank account and was used to make purchases at Hermes and OnlyFans), used campaign money for personal travel and Botox treatments, fraudulently collected $24,000 in unemployment benefits, and claimed that his niece was kidnapped by two Chinese men from a Queens playground.[3] And more! Santos faced calls to resign almost immediately, but he initially refused. Instead he doubled down, announcing he would run for reelection in 2024 (he eventually dropped the bid).

Why did he not resign right away? Prolonging his time definitely did not provide effective representation for his district, and the extended disgrace burned allies' support. The "scandal penalty," the loss of support an incumbent party gets in a district following a scandal, would likely be severe.[4] But holding onto the office was politically beneficial. Staying in office may have been a bargaining chip for a plea deal for criminal charges he faced (both federal and local investigations into his campaign finance reports led initially to a not guilty plea to wire fraud and aggravated identity theft)—or he might win reelection. "If the field is crowded enough and Santos keeps running to the right, it's possible he could skate by with a plurality," said Gavin Wax, president of the New York Young Republicans who backed Santos's 2022 campaign. "He needs to build a cult following and continue to humanize himself."[5] Holding on following scandal is more common now. According to a National Public Radio headline, "when politicians have no shame, the old rules don't apply." Perhaps the biggest reason, according to one longtime (retiring) senator, "The fact that he [Santos] is still here is a product of this time," Patrick Leahy of Vermont said. "When I came here, Republican or Democrat, his own party would tell him you have to go."[6] Following a damning ethics report, the House voted 311 to 104 to expel him from Congress, the first member to be expelled since 2002.

In a polarized world where affective polarization (dislike of partisan opponents) is high, trust in media is low, and partisanship shapes news attention, do scandals matter in politics anymore? This book explores this simple question. The short answer is that in a polarized political world, political scandals are less likely to have much effect on politicians' approval, survival in office, or political ambitions. Why? Scholars have explored several possible reasons, but no one work examines them collectively. This book uses extensive survey data over several years, an elite expert survey, an experimental survey design, and a natural experiment, harnessing fifty years of verified political scandals from 1972 to 2021 to illuminate findings on partisan polarization, affective partisanship, conspiracy theories, and trust in media to examine the impact of scandal in a polarized America. The result is a broad indictment of conventional political wisdom that suggests scandals are debilitating for elected officials. Although historically scandals have been bad omens for political careers, the politics of scandals has changed—this book charts those changes from Watergate to the present.

Although varying by time period, political institution, and survey respondent, it is clear from the findings in this book that the political impact of scandals is smaller now than years ago. Politicians survive longer in office following scandals, partisan politics minimizes the importance of scandals for voters, and political legacies are only modestly affected by scandals. Simply put, scandals do not hit the way they used to—and politicians know it. These results help clarify the conventional wisdom about how politicians survive (or do not) scandals while in office and whether these trends are exacerbated by the political climate of several distinct eras. This book finds that scandals still matter under the right conditions, but the impact is lessened in our polarized environment. Indeed, it is clear that extreme partisanship and affective polarization result in accepting (and even embracing) scandals from fellow in-partisans and reveling in scandals affecting out-partisans. The book also speaks to the role of media distrust and the spread of misinformation, both of which affect the way the partisan impact of scandal falls differently on some citizens than on others.

Nevertheless, voters can still spot scoundrels, especially when opponents point out ulterior motives for a politician's actions. Obviously not all politicians survive scandal—every year scandals fell politicians of every stripe. While it is too early to proclaim the death of scandals' impact on politicians, this book explores how and when scandals still matter in a polarized America. Importantly, this book also illuminates the ways in which scandals undermine democratic accountability. Scandals are like canaries in the coal mine—an early warning system that there is trouble. Losing the punch of scandals creates accountability problems for American politics—and, too often, lets politicians get away with bad behavior.

WHY DO WE CARE ABOUT SCANDAL?

Scandals have given an avenue to the venom in partisan politics for a generation since Watergate.[7] Scandal is one facet of modern contentious American political life and a big factor in the growth of the "public integrity war."[8] It is argued that scandals are on the rise because the media are more invasive, communications technology is more pervasive, and political opponents thrive by using these events as political weapons.[9] Assertions of "gotcha" politics have become predominant in shaping American political culture, changing how the media and other political actors relate to the political system.[10] Politicians are susceptible to the perceived growing tide of scandal as their political fortunes are arguably linked to such events.[11] Scandals are more than just moral transgressions or illegal activities: the impact of scandals may lead to a cynical "burn it down" mentality in which politicians snared in scandals lash out, using confusion, suspicion, and fear as means of misdirection from their misdeeds.[12]

In fact, scandals are a good thing, and not just for shitposting on social media or punch lines for jokes. There are practical benefits to scandals that help the system correct itself, reshaping ethics laws, expunging wayward politicians, and improving accountability. Scholarship outlines the health benefits of scandals in American political life. Being exposed to scandalous information helps voters remember the campaign's policy issues, so scandals may even improve elections' quality.[13] Scandals cause voters to sharpen their exposure to information about a candidate, both good and bad, honing their choices.[14] Even small scandals can spur reform efforts.[15] Investigations may scrutinize public officials' wrongdoing, holding them accountable, and can prompt broader change when the issue can be connected to misdeeds or systemic problems.[16] Scandals can also prompt more internal investigations inside the executive branch.[17] Such efforts can help push changes in political norms.

DO SCANDALS MATTER?

There is debate about this question. One body of work suggests scandals have negative political consequences. Although conditioned by candidate characteristics, prior attitudes, and context, scandals "generally reveal negative evaluative effects for politicians."[18] A less partisan public will see past political arguments used to justify scandals.[19] Negative framing of an event, called negativity bias, may initially characterize a scandal as problematic, fixing the public against the action or individual.[20] Lazarus showed that scandal-tainted incumbents were more likely to face opposition in both their primary and general elections and were more likely to face challengers with electoral experience. Scholars have found that politicians were reelected at lower rates following scandals.[21] This is in part because scandals strangle political fundraising for some candidates.[22] Drawing on real-world judicial scandals, scholars find that controversies involving judges hurt support for individual judicial actors but not necessarily for the system.[23] Political cynicism toward elected officials resulting from scandals affects how individuals interpret information about future political scandals.[24] These "spillover" effects can be pernicious and affect public officials—and the political system—beyond just the politicians involved.[25]

The type of scandal, the frame of the scandal in the media, and even the attractiveness of the candidate all contribute to the political impact of a scandal.[26] Allegations of wrongdoing leveled at elected officials at several levels can hurt them politically. Congressional investigations depress presidential approval ratings, and investigations into congressional members' campaign finance violations hurt them in subsequent elections. State judicial scandals depress vote share for incumbents, especially when jurists face quality challengers.[27] The political damage from scandals also affects state legislators, especially leaders who face high scrutiny while in office. Lower legislative chamber leaders in Missouri, Kentucky, Ohio, Tennessee, Texas, and Illinois have all come under scrutiny in the past decade, leading to resignations of the Missouri House Speaker in 2015, after sending sexually explicit messages to a college student intern; the Kentucky House Speaker in 2018, over a sexual harassment scandal; the Ohio Speaker of the House in 2018, over allegations of misusing public funds for travel and using a donor's luxury condo; the Tennessee Speaker of the House in 2019, for texting sexually explicit pictures; the Texas Speaker of the House, for damaging private conversations excoriating allies; and the former Illinois Speaker, who controlled much of the state's agenda for four decades, who resigned after facing a federal bribery investigation.[28]

Not surprisingly, politicians snared in scandals often lose, or at least take a political hit, when running again. Members of Congress who had one or more of their actions referred to the House Ethics Committee—the committee that adjudicates potential wrongdoing by House members—were less likely to be reelected (49 percent) than those members who did not have a case referred (87 percent).[29] Members involved in scandals were also significantly more likely to be defeated in a primary (14 percent) than those not involved (4 percent). Basinger also found that the specific type of scandal matters: corruption scandals led to an 8 percent reduction in vote share; sex and financial scandals led to a 5 percent reduction in vote share.[30] In special elections where an incumbent was removed because of scandal, a candidate from the scandalized party performs 9 percent worse, the so-called scandal penalty.[31] Losing is one thing; the longevity of a politician's career beyond a scandal is another. Paschall, Sulkin, and Bernard present compelling evidence that a Congress member's legislative effectiveness and their upward trajectory in committee assignments and leadership positions are blunted by scandals.[32]

In the long term, political scandals undermine the public's trust in government, especially when a scandal involves political accountability.[33] Allegations of corruption may decrease turnout.[34] In the short run, politicians, especially presidents, must grapple with the political fallout of scandal allegations, pushing them off message and encouraging political enemies who smell blood in the water to attack. Fousek and Wasserman cite "the rapid decline of public support for presidents whose leadership appears ethically compromised."[35] A scandal might diminish a president's ability to enact legislation.[36] A poorly handled scandal may also lead to policy paralysis or, even worse, more partisanship.[37]

Another body of scholarship, however, suggests that in a polarized political world, scandals may *not* have a large effect on incumbent political officials. A polarized America means scandals matter less to partisan voters. Scandals are not necessarily "dealbreakers" for many voters.[38] Williams laments that "there is no obvious correspondence between the degree of controversy generated by scandals and the gravity of the alleged misdeeds. Some of those involved in scandals pay a heavy price: resignation, disgrace, and even imprisonment. Others, who seem equally culpable, escape conviction and retire with dignity."[39] What gives? Simply put, partisanship limits the negative impact of scandals.[40] Partisans stress different messages about scandals based upon partisanship and may rake in additional campaign contributions from party faithful.[41] Scrutiny should help in the democratic monitoring process, but it does not always do so. More media coverage may simply generate "white noise" that the public ignores or ambivalent reactions that "all politicians do it."[42] Voters simply throw up their hands.

DO SCANDALS *STILL* MATTER?

Scandals have certainly killed political careers, and those even scandals that have not killed careers have permanently wounded them. But this is less true than before.

The political world is different in modern partisan times. Elites are more polarized, leading to a more divided political environment that intensifies the impact of party endorsements on preferences and decreases the import of substantive information.[43] This polarization makes policy positions clearer but also fosters a unified front when politicians of the same party are confronted with scandal.[44] Partisans protect their own, and voters follow. Cues from elites allow partisan leaders to shield fellow partisans even through serious controversies, such as Donald Trump's efforts to "scandal-proof" his cabinet nominees in his transition to a second term.[45] Motivated reasoning, in which individuals interpret information through the lens of party commitment, is the direct result of elite fragmentation.[46] This is a key factor in how voters assess scandals.

Indeed, while some scandals are a liability, others are not.[47] Nyhan found that there were more scandals when government was divided, suggesting a polarized effect of scandals that are weaponized politically. This can lead to voters discounting scandals. The effects of scandal on candidate approval is short-lived and dissipate quickly.[48] Scholars find that, because of accessibility bias, the electoral consequences of scandal fade quickly, and only controversies in election years systematically affect vote share of incumbents, although media coverage of moral scandals may have larger impacts.[49] The intense volume of information is too much for voters: too many social media reports of scandals (of a fictional candidate) has a diminishing return on scandals. While support for a scandal-ridden politician drops with a single scandal, there is no additional punishment for candidates involved in many scandals.[50] Voters rate scandal-plagued politicians more negatively than other politicians but still prefer ideologically proximate candidates, in terms of partisanship and shared political views, despite scandal.[51] Perception of politicians and their susceptibility to corruption also affects the impact of scandals. Barnes, Beaulieu, and Saxton find people are less skeptical of politicians' misdeeds when there is a greater potential for institutional sanction.[52] In other words, "the system will fix it." This is not always the case, however, especially in the modern political climate.

The type of scandal matters as well. People respond more negatively to financial scandals than to moral scandals that do not involve abuses of power.[53] Corruption and sex scandals tend to be more damaging to reelection prospects than political scandals.[54] Other scandals of a personal nature do not hit the way they might have years ago, despite changing racial and gender norms and "today's polarized world of instant cancellation." As mentioned previously, Virginia governor Ralph Northam weathered calls for his resignation after photos of him in blackface from his medical school yearbook page popped up on the internet. It gets worse: he was standing next to another student in a Ku Klux Klan robe. The governor and his staff were inundated for weeks with letters, emails, and calls to resign. But Virginia senator Tim Kaine, a fellow Democrat who initially joined the chorus of calls for Northam to resign, called him the most consequential Virginia governor of the modern era, leading policy changes to "abolish the death penalty, expand access to the vote, legalize marijuana and pass a long list of other changes, large and small." How did he survive? Black Virginians—facilitated by an apology tour around the state—gave the governor a second chance, and he "used that opportunity for good."[55] He also had a sympathetic legislature and lots of political friends.

Of course, not all public officials face the same scrutiny; some have it worse. Some candidates—women, nonwhite, and gay political figures especially—face steeper electoral penalties for the same behavior as their white male counterparts. Women involved in sex scandals activate traditional gender norms and provoke hostility; falling short of being "pure and moral," they are more likely to be hurt by scandals.[56] Male politicians involved in traditionally "female" transgressions (hiring an illegal immigrant for domestic work or having sex with a superior) are not damaged as much as female politicians in the same scenarios.[57] Sexism conditions the severity of male politicians' scandals in the MeToo movement, where respondents who have more sexist attitudes are more forgiving of scandals like malfeasance, making sexist jokes, or sexual assault.[58] Punishment varies by partisanship too. Liberals are more forgiving of sex scandals but not corruption, and conservatives punish women more than men for both sex and corruption scandals.[59]

If scandals are a breach of the public trust, why do some not have a strong negative political impact? Although scandals tend to hurt the approval ratings of a politician, the public can distinguish between behavior it believes central to the actor's job and those it considers private. In isolated instances, presidents may actually maintain or even expand their popularity, depending on the specific conditions.[60] Prior approval of a politician and perceptions of the importance of the scandal also shape public attitudes. In the case of President Clinton during the Lewinsky scandal, citizens constructed "seemingly reasonable justifications" for what they believed and wanted to continue to believe: that the president was an effective leader.[61] The public may respond to formal investigations rather than informal charges: Kriner and Schickler found that congressional committee investigations have a greater negative influence on presidential approval than identical charges not attributed to institutional authority.[62]

A POLARIZED AMERICA MUTES THE IMPACT OF SCANDALS

Do scandals still matter in a polarized political environment? The literature is mixed but leads to one clear expectation: politicians in contemporary political times are more likely to survive scandal. Why?

PARTISANSHIP HAS HARDENED POLITICAL PREFERENCES

Scandals affect partisan identifiers differently than others. As a result, political circumstances insulate some politicians from the otherwise deleterious effects of political scandals. Partisan politics produces fertile soil for scandals. Partisanship, rather than moral foundations, drives most of U.S. voters' responses to violations by politicians, such as transgressions of moral foundations like care, fairness, and loyalty. But these indiscretions are malleable when partisan actors are involved: respondents of both parties express greater negativity when a politician of the other party violates a moral foundation.[63] Affective polarization—the tendency of Democrats and Republicans to dislike and distrust one another—is also to blame.[64] This concept highlights partisanship as an identity, an identity that is hard to shake. The animosity between parties portrays the "other" party and its acolytes as selfish, closed-minded, and, well, just wrong.[65] The phenomenon is often associated with perceptions of elites but is increasingly consequential to voters and to how people perceive reality.

A good example is NFL Hall of Fame and Georgia 2022 Senate Republican nominee Herschel Walker. At first glance, he was a strong Republican candidate: a Georgia native, high name identification, a football hero, a Black conservative, and a friend of Donald Trump. But his Senate campaign to unseat incumbent Democratic senator Raphael Warnock uncovered a hornet's nest of political liabilities: a messy divorce, violent threats to his ex-wife, exaggerated claims of financial success, violent outbursts necessitating police intervention, and fathering children out of wedlock. Later in the campaign it was revealed he had paid for an ex-girlfriend's abortion, an act firmly at odds with his hard-line, "no exceptions" abortion position. Did these scandals matter? Hardly. An appearance on the Fox News network's *Sean Hannity Show* boosted his online fundraising. GOP leadership, including the minority whip and second highest ranking Republican in the Senate John Thune, rushed to campaign with him in Georgia.[66] Evangelicals who might object morally "care more about his policies than his behavior." Said one pastor, "the dilemma is, do you wait for a candidate who is perfect? Or do you take what's given to you and make the choice between the options?"[67]

Scholarship on both hypothetical and real-life cases indicates that partisans believe scandals involving in-party politicians are less serious or problematic than those committed by out-party politicians.[68] Even in the face of clear and undisputed charges, co-partisans backed a hypothetical scandal-plagued president despite evidence of illegal and "impeachable" activities.[69] When respondents were told about a scandal, then told it was fully fabricated, in-party politicians were still thought innocent and out-party politicians were still thought guilty.[70] Partisans weight scandalous information about out-party politicians more heavily than the same information about co-partisans.[71] Even when facing serious charges of sexual harassment, Republican partisans do not strongly penalize their own political candidates (although Democrats are more likely to penalize their own).[72]

While scandal-tainted politicians generally receive fewer votes and sometimes raise less money, when partisan politics emerges in elections, voters are less punitive of scandal-ridden politicians.[73] Shah et al. note that during the Lewinsky scandal the "mass approval of Clinton was sustained and encouraged by news content presenting the scandal in terms of attacks by conservatives and critical responses by liberals" in addition to positive frames about the president's performance.[74] President Trump's refrain that the legal allegations against him are a "witch hunt" is a defense against reality. And it works. Polling in Iowa before the critical Iowa 2024 caucuses found that 61 percent of likely Republican caucus goers said it would not matter to their support if former president Donald Trump were convicted of a crime before the general election.[75] More than 20 percent of those planning to vote for the Republican Trump in 2024 believed he had committed a serious federal crime.[76] Even if convicted, only 53 percent of voters in swing states would refuse to vote for him, and only 55 percent held that same opinion if he were sentenced to jail.[77]

Politicians today are also better at managing a scandal than in earlier periods—and partisanship lets them get away with it.[78] Voters are not blind to scandal-plagued candidates, but they do not always sanction them either. Remember the "scandal penalty" mentioned previously, in which the party responsible for a resignation and special election hurt that party; in fact, the party responsible for the resignation actually ran ahead of the previous election about a third of the time.[79] Morality matters to voters, just not as much as shared political views. Party loyalty is also affected by scandal, but in reverse: Republicans feel more positive toward their party after reading about the resignation of a hypocritical co-partisan politician (compared to mere hypocrisy of a politician).[80] Likewise, politicians caught in scandals who are portrayed as heroes actually win. Even disgraced politicians try to reframe their actions as heroic. After Democratic governor Andrew Cuomo resigned his office following allegations of sexually harassing several staff members, he tried to spend his way out of the political doghouse. To salvage his reputation in advance of a possible run again, he spend almost $400,000 on ads, not to apologize but to recast himself as the victim of politically motivated attacks.[81] Those portrayed as villains lose, especially those with whom the public had little familiarity.[82]

Excessive partisanship and perceived threats from opposition parties amplify this rigid, asymmetric effect.[83] This increased polarization leads to democratic norms being polarized, such as embracing policies restricting the other party's constitutional rights.[84] Rising polarization between the two parties increases the likelihood of a scandal, since both sides are looking for a political edge, while simultaneously decreasing the importance of that scandal to a partisan audience.[85] Voters are less punitive, and donors are often even more supportive of candidates facing scandals in the post-1994 period of nationalized elections.[86] These factors have been exacerbated since then. Ginsberg and Shefter conclude that partisanship increases scandals as the "perfect nonelectoral weapons" even while they fail to mobilize voters to vote violating politicians out of office.[87] Even presidential approval, normally sensitive to changes in the economy, now has an attenuated relationship in which presidential approval "appears to be a proxy for partisanship."[88]

This is true even on consequential matters of checks and balances. Support for norm-eroding policies increases when a person's party is out of power, and the norms-eroding effects are amplified by two indicators of polarization: strong excessive partisanship and perceived threat from the opposing party.[89] Some people have a "need for chaos," a novel psychological state in which individuals circulate hostile rumors to "burn down" the political order to gain political status. Members of both parties and marginalized groups do it to express frustration with the current political system and its leaders. The impeachment process for Donald Trump in 2019 is a good example. Support for acquittal was largely static over time, and scholars find "partisanship strongly influences whether the public accepts the veracity and importance of political information."[90] Even after exposure to information about the Trump-Russia scandal, Republicans still had a drastically more favorable opinion of the president than Democrats.[91]

Surviving scandal is intimately linked to an elected official's ability to stay in office, another feature where polarization helps. A predominant factor in predicting survival of scandal is the number of those within the politician's party providing "pillars of support"; this includes the likelihood of removal from office for crimes associated with the scandal.[92] For instance, the capacity to stay in office is directly related to the amount of support a chief executive might have, meaning that more partisans in a legislature would mean a greater chance of political survival.[93] Put another way, more partisans create a legislative shield for politicians.[94] For members of Congress, unified government decreases the likelihood of internal investigations by the House Ethics Committee, which can otherwise lead to negative electoral consequences.[95]

SCANDALS PRIME THE BASE

Partisans love it when political enemies take a political hit. Again, affective polarization is connected to this ideological divergence.[96] This is especially evident in the digital age where communication is cheap and direct to consumer: priming the base when your opponents are in political danger is a favorite pastime on social media. And protection among partisans is now the norm. In fact, affective polarization erodes support for democratic norms as these norms are politicized by elites and the political base responds to cue-taking from elites.[97] After the January 6, 2021 insurrection, although most Americans were appalled by Trump's actions (for which he was impeached a second time), he retained the support of nearly three quarters of Republicans.[98] During the Ukraine whistleblower scandal, Democrats were more likely than Republicans to sound off on social media, demonstrating a clear partisan effect.[99] A base is not just partisan. Scholars have found that co-ethnic respondents respond to co-minority cues in evaluating a scandalized politician: higher levels of perceived discrimination against one's in-group lead to higher levels of support for politicians in trouble.[100]

Even after the legal system gets involved, some politicians double down. Rick Perry, when as governor of Texas he was indicted on two felony counts of abuse of power for threatening to veto funds to a county unless a local official resigned, did not run from his felony indictment. Instead, the super PAC backing his 2016 presidential bid put his smiling mug shot on a T-shirt with the phrase "Wanted: for securing the border and defeating Democrats."[101] President Trump's first trial in 2024—a fraud case involving hush money payments to porn star Stormy Daniels—was a legal problem for the forty-fifth president but may have been *politically* beneficial. This is especially true with regard to fundraising: the best fundraising days of his early 2024 race for the White House were driven by his legal jeopardy as his joint fundraising committee worked to monetize the situation. Of the 150 fundraising appeals his campaign sent to supporters in the month the trial began, more than one third referenced his legal woes, alleging a witch hunt. "I JUST STORMED OUT OF BIDEN'S KANGAROO COURT! What I've been FORCED to endure would make any patriotic American SICK," said one email sent around the time that Trump left court. The day prosecutors threatened to seize the former president's assets if he failed to make bond, his Save America committee raised $2.6 million from nearly 48,000 donors, 21,500 of whom had never donated before.[102] The day he was convicted, donors channeled tens of millions of dollars to his campaign, erasing the massive fundraising advantage the Democrats held at that point.[103] The surge temporarily crashed the WinRed website used to bundle donations.[104]

When confronted with scandals, politicians have several options. They can stonewall or come clean. They can also engage in the "liar's dividend" by invoking informational uncertainty (claiming the scandal is "fake" or misinformation) or encouraging oppositional rallying of core supporters. Both strategies work. Claims of misinformation generate larger gains for politicians than simply ignoring the scandal or apologizing, making it a preferred strategy and more politically effective than a simple denial.[105] The classic response from politicians snared in scandals is "They aren't really coming for me. They're coming for you. I'm just in the way."[106] Such responses suppose a populist anger at unseen forces looking to limit the political reach of a partisan figure. Confronted by allegations he showed obscene pictures to colleagues on the House floor and embroiled in a federal sex trafficking investigation, Representative Matt Gaetz refused suggestions he resign. It has become a bit of a tradition for politicians from both parties to defy the traditional response to controversy (resignation): "rather than humbly step back from public life, they barrel ahead, insisting they did nothing wrong and betting that voters will forget alleged misdeeds once the news cycle eventually shifts."[107] This "never back down" mentality is a new chapter in the crisis response playbook.

WE LIVE IN OUR OWN (OFTEN PARTISAN) MEDIA ECOSYSTEMS

The rapidly evolving, all-encompassing information ecosystem we live in overwhelms people with information, often partisan information. Some of that information is "accurate, some of it is bogus, and much of it is intentionally misleading. The result is a polity that has increasingly given up on finding out the truth."[108] Partisan media polarize people and media distrust leads voters to discount certain kinds of information, especially when it is negative news about a co-partisan politician.[109] Media coverage of scandals is often partisan and shaped by ideological leanings of the media.[110] And it works. In a clever series of experiments, scholars teamed up with media organizations that performed their own investigations into state and local officials—and uncovered scandals. They produced four- to eight-page "newspapers" focused on these scandals and sent them to randomly selected households. Voters did punish politicians caught in scandals, but it was conditional on a politician not being a well-known partisan figure and learning about the events through the manufactured newspaper story. This means that the decline of quality journalism, the loss of local journalism, and rising partisanship and personal politics minimize the impact of scandal.[111]

Alternatively, media coverage of scandal may simply generate "white noise" that the public ignores.[112] The type of scandal the media are covering matters, with "competence qualities" more important as a factor in candidate evaluation.[113] Political elites—talking heads like Tucker Carlson or Rachel Maddow—also help frame the debate for partisan watchers. One study found "a jump in scandal-related tweets by one group affects the tweet volume of every other. But the groups wield unequal influence. Over the long-run, elites drive their supporters' attention to scandal more than vice-versa."[114] And what the media cover shapes attention to scandals, especially among partisans. Partisan media cover scandals involving the opposition party's politicians more intensely and scandals involving their own party's politicians more lightly.[115] Competition is an important element: in areas with more newspapers, bias in covering scandals decreases. But as the media contract and consolidate, especially local media, competition is now scare.

It is conservatives who have shifted the most in their media diets. Conservative trust in the mainstream media has cratered: trust in national news organizations among ideological conservatives has fallen by 14 percentage points since late 2019, compared to single-digit percentage point drops each year during the Trump era. As of 2021, only 35 percent of Republicans said they trusted national news organizations, compared to 70 percent in 2016.[116] That shift matters. Republican dislike and distrust of the mainstream media was so high that it did not influence their reaction to Trump-Russia scandal stories, in part because they did not even select them when offered the chance.[117] Partisans live in their own media silos, where they "believe different facts to be true" and are unlikely to see the political world from a different point of view.[118]

Partisan media funnel people to partisan opinions, through motivated reasoning, yet there are few options left for many voters. This has become increasingly troublesome at a time when local media are struggling. To quote the political scientist Danny Hayes, dramatic changes in the media environment in recent decades have "taken the teeth" out of local media's accountability function: "As each decade has gone by, newspapers have published fewer scandal stories. In the 1990s, a statewide scandal on average generated 228 stories. In the first decade of the 2000s, it was 112. But since 2010, that number is down to 88, which includes even the stratospheric Bridgegate coverage. Looking just at scandals since 2015, the average number of stories has fallen to 49."[119] Before 2010, an average House scandal generated seventy-seven stories in the district's largest newspaper; since then the average has plummeted to twenty-three. With smaller audiences, less revenue, and fewer reporters, newspapers simply cannot sustain coverage of what would otherwise be attractive and newsworthy stories. The result, as journalists write, is that politicians know they can "just wait us out—until our overstretched staff [leaves] to chase the next big story."[120]

Manufactured—or fake—scandals can also affect voters' perceptions of candidate, often asymmetrically. When the media conglomerate Sinclair (known to have a conservative bent) buys a local station, they cover more national and less local politics, feeding conservative talking points. Not surprisingly, watching Fox News translates into a significantly greater willingness to vote for Republican candidates.[121] Concern over Hillary Clinton's email scandal (what the liberal columnist Matthew Yglesias called "a bullshit email scandal") arguably helped elect Donald Trump.[122] It is not as though the parties, politicians, or big money backers are doing something new: weaponizing scandal has long been stitched into the fabric of U.S. politics. The problem is that the new media fragmentation means the race for the next big story—clicks, eyeballs, stimulating content—is susceptible to partisanizing scandals. When a scandal emerges, it is not hard for the opposition to generate more negative coverage by "feeding nonsense into the system."[123] The model of media coverage allows it, and partisan politics facilitates it.

ANGER SELLS

People, especially partisans, are primed for anger in modern politics. Political scientist Stephen Webster expresses a simple claim in his book *American Rage*: elites engage in rousing the anger in their electorate because it leads to voter loyalty. When voters are angry, they are more likely to support party objectives and candidates.[124] The electorate becomes angrier when they see angry displays from political elites. In fact, the public is more likely than not to vote for candidates who promise to pass policies that "disproportionately harm" supporters of the opposition political party.[125] Affect linkage—matching a display of emotions to witnessed emotions in others—is to blame. In experiments exposing respondents to anger, it primes angry emotions. Scandals find "exposure to an angry in-party politician significantly increases the amount of anger, disgust, and outrage expressed by co-rank-and-file partisans."[126] This is especially true when candidates on Facebook and other social media platforms use more toxic and emotional language to target donors (rather than voters).[127] Journalist Sean Illing wrote for *Vox*, "more people are comfortable siding with their political tribe. If everything's up for grabs, and it's hard to sift through the competing narratives to find the truth, then there's nothing left but culture war politics."[128]

PEOPLE FORGET—A LOT

People discount scandals over time. Voters relying on their fuzzy memories, filtered through partisan lenses, are often myopic when recalling information about a scandal that might otherwise damage a candidate. Scholarship on this question suggests that in processing information, both old and new, biased motivated reasoning shapes even the most knowledgeable. Partisans also seek out agreeable sources of information and discount challenging information.[129] This confirmation bias, affecting both parties, limits citizens' capacity to recall factual information. When merged with affective polarization and motivated reasoning, this forms a poisonous cocktail of ambivalence about past scandals.[130]

Stated bluntly by the *New York Times*, "in an era of hyper-partisanship, there's little agreed-upon collective memory, even about events that played out in public."[131] This environment—the frenetic pace of information, shrinking attention spans, and siloed media attention—creates an effect where people forget about controversies, crises, and even scandals. In a digital age, scandals are more personal and amplified by partisanship; they are "characterized by liveness wherein scandals are quick, explosive, and then dissipate."[132] The rapid pace of skullduggery from the Trump campaign and then the Trump administration was dizzying, even for an American public used to confronting scandals. The response from the president? "Constantly moving ahead," making it harder for the public to "linger on one issue for too long, even if that meant stirring up controversy on another topic."[133]

The 2017 Senate investigation into the Trump campaign's ties to Russia turned into a partisan free-for-all. In committee testimony, James Comey, the former FBI director, was hit with questions from Republicans about a separate investigation by the Department of Justice into errors by FBI agents involved in the surveillance of the former Trump aide Carter Page. Other issues emerged as well, such as criticism of the FBI for triggering the investigation in the first place based on a dossier compiled by a former British spy, Christopher Steele, which included salacious allegations that Trump had been compromised by Russia because of incriminating information the country had on the businessman candidate. The committee also discussed declassified material about an unverified and possibly fabricated analysis from Russian intelligence in 2016 that Hillary Clinton was attempting to tie Donald Trump to Russia to distract from the controversy over her private email server.[134] Confused? You are not alone. Of those polled who agreed that Russia interfered in the 2016 election, only 22 percent were "extremely" certain, compared to 32 percent who were "moderately" and 14 percent "a little" convinced.[135] What is real, and what is not real? Which information is the most credible? It is hard to tell, and in a scandal of this magnitude and complexity, we can forgive the public for being confused—or for tuning out altogether.

With information flooding our phones and inboxes, people have trouble separating fact from fiction. Years after President Trump left office, many of his fictions, misleading claims, and even outright lies were believed by more people than when he left office. On average, 28 percent of Americans believed his false claims four years after he left office. Even more significant, among Republicans, more viewed him as honest in 2024 than they did in 2018. For instance, in 2018, about one in four Republicans (26 percent) agreed that millions of fraudulent votes were cast in the 2016 election; in 2024, 38 percent of Republicans—including 47 percent of strong Trump supporters—believed this to be true. There are similar figures for Russia's interference in the 2016 election, unemployment being low, and the United States funding the majority of the NATO budget.[136] Some of these are mild exaggerations, but others, like election interference, go to the heart of accountability. According to one GOP senator, "I just don't think you can deal with allegations in the past as though they're facts."[137]

People forget in general but also in a partisan way. Table 0.1 displays results from a 2024 national survey on scandals past and present. The percentage of the sample answering the question correctly is listed for all respondents and by partisan affiliation. More Republicans than Democrats remembered it was the Democratic senator Ted Kennedy who drove his car off the Chappaquiddick bridge, the Democratic Speaker of the House Jim Wright resigned his office over an ethics investigation, and the Democratic president Bill Clinton lied in a statement to the American people about Monica Lewinsky. Republicans were less likely to recall the reason Donald Trump was impeached, which Trump cabinet member was charged in the Georgia racketeering case, and which Supreme Court case would decide the degree of presidential immunity for Donald Trump's action on January 6, 2021. Republicans were also less likely to remember that Oliver North was involved in the Iran-Contra affair; Democrats were more likely

TABLE 0.1 Successful recall of political scandals

SCANDAL	PERCENT CORRECT	PERCENT CORRECT: REPUBLICAN	PERCENT CORRECT: DEMOCRAT
PAST			
WHICH U.S. SENATOR IN 1969 DROVE HIS CAR OFF A BRIDGE IN MARTHA'S VINEYARD AND FLED THE SCENE OF THE ACCIDENT, WHICH RESULTED IN THE DROWNING DEATH OF MARY JO KOPECHNE, HIS TWENTY-EIGHT-YEAR-OLD COMPANION?	72	82	70
WHICH GOVERNMENT OFFICIAL WAS INVOLVED IN THE SCANDAL INVOLVING NICARAGUA CONTRAS RECEIVING PROFITS FROM THE SALE OF ARMS TO IRAN?	63	59	66
WHICH SPEAKER OF THE HOUSE RESIGNED HIS OFFICE DUE TO AN ETHICS INVESTIGATION?	23	22	18
CURRENT			
WHICH U.S. POLITICIAN FATEFULLY (AND FALSELY) DECLARED AT A PRESS CONFERENCE IN 1998: "I WANT YOU TO LISTEN TO ME. . . . I DID NOT HAVE SEXUAL RELATIONS WITH THAT WOMAN."	88	95	92
FOR WHICH OF THE FOLLOWING WAS PRESIDENT TRUMP IMPEACHED BY THE U.S. HOUSE?	37	31	42
WHICH FORMER MEMBER OF TRUMP'S PRESIDENTIAL ADMINISTRATION IS ALSO CHARGED WITH VIOLATING GEORGIA'S RACKETEERING ACT?	43	44	44
IN WHICH CASE WILL THE SUPREME COURT DECIDE IF PRESIDENTIAL IMMUNITY PROTECTS TRUMP FROM PROSECUTION?	36	38	35

Source: Cloud Research survey 2024, fielded by the author.

Note: Survey data weighted by party identification and race.

to recall that Ken Starr investigated the Clintons in Whitewater and Oliver North was involved in Iran-Contra.

PLAN OF THE BOOK

So where does that leave us? Do scandals still matter? Chapter 1 presents several case studies of how politicians have survived, and even thrived, following scandals. We also make use of a massive dataset of more than eight hundred scandals involving presidents, governors, and members of Congress between 1972 and 2021. These data include recent high-profile gubernatorial scandals (Governor Eric Greitens of Missouri, Governor Andrew Cuomo of New York) through the Trump administration. The findings are telling and give us long-term trends on how scandals function. Some governors and some presidents have a higher number of scandals than others, but in contrast to expectations about the scourge of scandals invading American politics, the overall rate of scandal is surprisingly low. The Trump administration, however, has taken the top spot for total presidential scandals, outpacing the Reagan administration by nine scandals in half the time. The number of congressional scandals has also increased in recent years, led by representatives such as Pat Meehan and George Santos. Fewer modern scandals for presidents, governors, or members of Congress end in resignation or indictment than earlier, previewing the results from chapter 2. Chapter 1 ends by charting cases of dozens of politicians who have left office following scandals but have run again (with mixed results).

In October 2022, the gossipy British tabloid the *Daily Star* started a livestream of a head of iceberg lettuce next to a framed photograph of Liz Truss, recently elected Conservative Party leader. Why? A near economic collapse that many blamed on Truss led the paper to start the livestream "Can Liz Truss outlast a lettuce?" She did, for a bit. Days before her resignation, the *Star* ran a headline "Lettuce Liz on Leaf Support." She resigned after forty-five days. Chapter 2 addresses which factors shorten or lengthen the survival of a scandal involving an elected official. Using duration analysis models, we investigated several institutional, political, and economic factors to determine what factors quicken a "negative" end to a scandal. We find that the negative consequences of scandals vary across time and institutions. Scandals in the Watergate era led to more resignations in Congress but fewer resignations of White House officials in the 1990s. During the first Trump administration, White House officials did not survive in office at rates greater than past eras, demonstrating modest support for the "Trump effect." However, politicians generally survived scandal more in the polarized era, hinting at the changing role of political scandals. Several case studies examining both past and more recent scandals illustrate the point.

Some elected officials survive scandals even when conventional wisdom suggests these scandals might be career-ending vulnerabilities. Indeed, politicians serving later generally survived in office longer than earlier politicians. Later politicians, especially beginning in the aftermath of the Lewinsky scandal and continuing through the Trump era, collectively confronted hardened partisan preferences, and this modestly inoculated them against the negative effects of scandal. But for some politicians, stronger opposition armed with ammunition to politically hurt incumbents minimizes the chances of survival. For instance, the political system appeared to "clean house" during the George W. Bush period, when White House officials (but not the president) resigned or were fired at higher rates following major scandals.

Using the results of three large, nationally representative public surveys from 2019 (Pew), 2022 (Qualtrics), and 2024 (Cloud Research), in chapter 3 I test how affective partisanship, polarized media trends, erosion of democratic norms, and fewer political friendships accelerate the impact of scandal. Specifically, using party loyalty, ideology, and various measures of affective partisanship (dislike of one party for another), this chapter examines how these factors affect public tolerance for scandals. A scale of "acceptable" political actions is created as a summary measure of how sensitive the public is to various types of scandals. Democrats are more sensitive to politicians' (hypothetical) negative or criminal acts while in office, but respondents from both parties are equally offended—although Republicans slightly more—by sexual misconduct. The scandal "breaking point" for the most partisan respondents is higher than for nonpartisan respondents, with the most partisan publics more tolerant of scandals involving their own party's politicians than less ideologically motivated publics. Higher scores on an affective partisan scale and greater tolerance for partisan bickering ("bare-knuckle politics") predict respondents' "enjoying" scandals more involving a political opponent. Attraction to scandals is strongly associated with dislike of the other party.

This chapter also probes the effect of scandals of the future: as technology and norms change and new perceived morality violations emerge, will the public be shocked by the political vulnerabilities of the next generation of politicians? To test this, we queried a representative sample of the public about their sensitivity to the next generation of "scandals," including inflammatory remarks on new social media sites, digital pictures of a candidate intoxicated, leaked nonconsensual nude pictures, and consensual sexual videos. We generally found similar patterns to more traditional scandals, suggesting that norms of morality are bendable but not breakable.

Outrage is everywhere in politics. If scandals can be manufactured on almost any issue, the role of scandal is changing from an accountability measure to a mobilization tactic. In chapter 4 we use an experimental design to "create" a scandal involving President Joe Biden's direction to the National Parks Service to reintroduce grizzly bears into federally managed lands to encourage procreation of the wild animals. As the outrage of the experimental treatment is increased, including real excerpts from Fox News and their *The Five* roundtable politics program, more (conservative) partisan-leaning respondents agree the operation constitutes a major scandal and lower their approval of Joe Biden—but only a little. The surprising results show there are small differences in these manufactured scandals but big differences in how partisans react to any information about out-partisans. The results suggest that manufacturing outrage is relatively simple but if almost any political action can be made into a scandal then scandals are politically less impactful.

How do scandals shape the legacy of an elected official? In chapter 5, using an elite survey of experts on the presidency, we investigate how some scandals affect presidential legacies while others do not. Scandals involving abuse of power tarnish presidential images, but scandals involving personal matters have little effect on perceived legacy. These findings are backed up by analysis of multiple survey findings on presidential legacy and the effect of scandals on assessments of presidential greatness. In addition, using a timely natural experiment involving the mayor of a large city, results from a scandal involving possible misuse of city funds show that voters are sensitive to scandals when assessing a politician's legacy in office. However, when controlling for key partisan and race variables, the effects are washed away, suggesting that legacy assessments are relatively immune from more recent scandals felling an incumbent politician.

Political scandals are frequently treated as a stain on the political system, resulting from poor personal judgment, lax rule enforcement, or bald political corruption. Media coverage treats these as unwelcome hiccups in an otherwise routine series of events. Yet just as a fire germinates and renews a field, political scandals may help the public and the media enhance accountability, renew trust in government, and focus on key issues of concern. In the book's concluding chapter, I review the findings and assess the legacy and impact of political scandals, underscoring the ways in which scandals have a potentially positive effect on institutional accountability and voter attentiveness. Scandals do still matter, and there are boundaries on behavior the public will not cross. However, the effects of scandals are changing as norms evolve and partisanship rises. Using various de-escalation tools, the system can make scandals matter again.

1

STUDYING SCANDAL

Empirical Evidence Since Watergate

Many politicians face scandals while in office. Conventional wisdom—or just asking your cynical friends—suggests that the number of scandals is on the rise. Marion concludes that "there have been an unprecedented number of scandals in national politics in recent years" and scandals "are now a constant occurrence."[1] Several of the last few presidents have undergone major investigations into their behavior and that of their advisers or associates, including two impeachments.[2] Eight governors or former governors were found guilty of criminal actions from 2000 to 2014, including four from Illinois alone.[3] For journalists who watch the parade of scandalous behavior by politicians, "barely a day pass[ed] in recent weeks without headlines from Washington to New York and beyond filled with word of scandal or allegations of wrongdoing."[4] The trend is particularly clear with respect to sex scandals. More than a hundred state legislators were publicly accused of sexual harassment between 2017 and 2020.[5] Apostolidis and Williams argue that there is a "deepening muck of scandal" and a "general sense among some politicians, commentators and the American public at large that at some point during the past fifteen years, a line was crossed."[6] Journalists have also noted that it is "getting a bit cliché" now as more politicians seem to be caught in such imbroglios.[7]

But are scandals commonplace? Political scandals can take a variety of forms, both in the institutions they affect and the kinds of scandals involved. Several definitions of scandals exist, but the definition remains elusive when any grievance can be labeled a "scandal," so we do not know whether official misbehavior is becoming more common, whether news coverage has become more scandal-focused, or whether the rules of the political game have changed (or all of the above). The news media and scholarly research often overemphasize a few scandals with major consequences, such as Watergate, Clinton's sex scandals, Trump's election meddling, and the extramarital affairs of Governors Sanford, McGreevey, and Spitzer. This narrow focus ensures that generalizations are unreliable. The term "scandal" may have become synonymous with lying, stonewalling, and obstructing justice, but not every scandal leads to a cover-up. Sometimes where there is smoke there is no fire. Clear data, separated by institution and type, can help tease out trends.

WHAT MAKES A SCANDAL?

The behavior of public officials in office is strongly connected to their capacity to govern and the trust citizens put in their actions. For that reason, several scholars have explored the issues of corruption and character of elected officials. For instance, Marion requires that a public figure has been "accused of unethical or immoral behavior," defined as offending behavior or an event "that is disgraceful, shameful or discredits someone" or that transgresses "societal norms, moral codes or values."[8] Thompson offers a detailed definition that requires that actions "transgress or contravene certain values, norms or moral codes" and that the actions' disclosure might damage responsible individuals' reputations, so that they attempt to conceal their actions.[9] Lowi argues that "scandal is corruption revealed" and "a breach of virtue exposed."[10] Williams argues that scandals are "events which provoke public concern, indignation or even outrage."[11]

Overly broad definitions impede scientific study because they allow the same label to be attached to a wide variety of acts that can create negative images or stimulate media coverage. These actions or events are not necessarily scandals. None of these definitions automatically excludes controversial policy decisions that garner negative publicity. For example, some might consider President Clinton's pardoning of Marc Rich in the final days of his presidency to be ethically inappropriate because Rich was the former spouse of a major donor. Many considered President George H. W. Bush's breaking his "Read my lips: No new taxes" pledge to be shameful, violating a moral imperative to keep one's word. Unwise and unpopular actions are not the same as scandals, however: "Controversial policies . . . don't constitute scandals. Nor does low performance in office. . . . A significant political scandal will typically involve identifiable transgressions with certain offenders—not simply abstract criticisms—and require some kind of institutional reaction."[12] Elected officials can change their minds about policies without triggering a scandal. Executive branch appointees and staff can likewise mismanage wars, crises, policies, and personnel, without their failings being scandals. A proper definition must be narrow enough to exclude mismanagement and issue-based controversy.

At the other extreme, some definitions of political scandals are too narrow. Indeed, Entman notes that discussions of scandal can become confusing when they fail to distinguish among the underlying unethical, careless, or illegal actions.[13] For example, Markovits and Silverstein define political scandal in terms of a "violation of due process."[14] This definition's focus is primarily on abuses of power and secondarily on financial corruption. Another overly narrow approach is that of Sabato, who examines media coverage of spectacular cases by identifying press-related "frenzies" that sprang from off-color remarks, revelation of embarrassing information that had been suppressed, exaggerations of accomplishments, accusations, and political corruption.[15] Likewise, Jamieson examines "dirty politics" in television campaign advertising that has the ability to "configure reality" by promoting deception and distraction.[16] These definitions, too, narrow the occurrence of scandals to a single source and instance of exaggerated behavior.

DEFINING SCANDAL

As noted, several general definitions of political scandals exist. Our definition requires that an individual scandal must involve allegations of illegal, unethical, or immoral wrongdoing. The definition includes adultery because of the unique place of inappropriate sexual relationships in the political world and follows my prior approach to measuring discrete scandals.[17] Including sex scandals ensures that we include "transgressions" of conventional morality, but we wish to exclude gossip, innuendo, and unsubstantiated rumors of private behavior.[18] An executive scandal requires that the misbehavior identified must involve the president, a member of Congress, a governor, the immediate families of these politicians, a senior administration official, or a federal nominee. The unit of observation is the individual involved in the scandal. Specifically, at the federal level, we include scandals involving the vice president, cabinet secretaries, officials with cabinet-level rank (the White House chief of staff or the director of the Office of Management and Budget), agency heads at the federal level, the elected officials' family, and senior campaign staff.[19] We also include nominees for national and state executive- or judicial-branch positions during the period when a nomination is under consideration. At the state level, we include scandals involving the governor, senior staff (including agency heads and high-level political appointees), the immediate family of the governor, and senior campaign staff. The scandal had to take place during the individual's time in office (not, for instance, after the principal or staff member has left office). For comparison, we have also included scandals involving members of Congress, using the same definition, while they are in office.[20]

To make the definition clearer, a few examples of what are *not* counted as scandals will be instructive. First, "corruption" or "graft," especially at lower levels of government, is excluded, such as when several employees of the U.S. Department of the Interior were accused of illegally using drugs and accepting gifts in 2008.[21] Second, rumors or unproven connections of wrongdoing are excluded, such as when Governor Richard Celeste of Ohio was linked (but not investigated, indicted, or charged) with a "political problem" of declaring a bank holiday for savings and loans entities in 1985, some of which were run by a campaign contributor who was being investigated for insider dealing.[22] Because neither the governor nor his administration was associated with these crimes, this amounted only to bad publicity in the speculative world of politics. Third, governmental mismanagement or waste does not count as a scandal, such as when state officials in the Department of Revenue in South Carolina were charged in 2007 with inadequately protecting the identity of four million tax filers and seven hundred thousand businesses in a computer hacking incident.[23] Cases like these, in which there is no personal or political gain for the actors involved, do not meet the criteria for scandal. Fourth, actions that were not illegal (apart from scandals related to personal affairs) are excluded. For instance, in a routine audit of state finances in Rhode Island in 2003, total charges on the 1,500 state credit cards amounted to $824,000. The Department of Administration director noted he had "no reason to believe a close look at credit-card spending today will unearth any more scandals, or produce huge savings."[24]

LOCATING SCANDALS

In order to collect the information pertaining to each individual scandal (including its beginning, the type of scandal, the allegations against the official, the veracity of the charges, and the reaction of the administration), several sources were examined. First, secondary texts were searched, following the lead of other scholars who have searched for a universe of political scandals.[25] Second, several media sources were searched. Using official sources to determine when scandals broke (and hence whether or not they existed) minimized the presence of false or malicious rumors in the data. A complex series of search terms were used to capture individual acts of wrongdoing, specific offices, and, in the case of governors, individual states.[26] Third, several excellent encyclopedic texts that catalog scandals, corruption, and ethics violations in government were searched. Finally, as a follow-up to these search strategies, the list of presidents and governors was searched individually with the term "scandal" in OneSearch, common library search software. Any additional scandals discovered were included in the list.[27]

This definition adds specificity to past definitions in three ways. First, regarding the class of actions that can generate a scandal, we include inappropriate sexual relationships because of the important and unique place they hold in the pantheon of political scandals, and we include instances of allegedly illegal and unethical behavior.[28] The "White House coffees" scandal fits our definition of scandal because the Clinton-Gore reelection campaign was investigated for legal violations, even though it was eventually uncovered that the coffees occurred in the residence.[29] The firing of seven federal prosecutors in December 2006 fits this definition, even though Justice Department officials chose not to press criminal charges, because if the allegations were true, it would have been a crime. Excluded, however, are activities that represent poor judgment or moderate abuse of authority, such as when Governor John Ashcroft's wife had the state library in Jefferson City, Missouri, opened on a Sunday (Mother's Day) so her son could work on a school project.[30] The definition also clarifies what events or actions are excluded, particularly instances of negative publicity. This definition excludes unpopular policy decisions and any instances of sheer incompetence, such as FEMA's response to Hurricane Katrina.[31] We also exclude any unsubstantiated allegations, rumors, innuendo, and gossip.[32] These limits allow us to avoid (as much as possible) so-called scandals that are partisanship-based charges with little or no merit.[33]

Second, the definition is specific in terms of the class of actors whose misbehavior can generate a scandal. Actors must be part of the legislative branch or the executive branch, or executive nominees, but must also be placed high enough that the scandal is relevant to the institution's image or efficient administration. Even a "lightning rod," who absorbs political damage on the president's behalf, can cause some damage to the administration.[34] Third, the definition is specific about when misbehavior occurred and when it was revealed to limit the dataset to those scandals that had an impact on the current executive occupant. Misbehavior by persons who have left an administration and revelations of a past executive's misbehavior (e.g., Warren Harding's or John Kennedy's affairs) would not directly affect the current occupant, unless the current occupant were somehow allegedly involved. Misbehavior by presidential, vice presidential, congressional, or gubernatorial candidates, especially those who withdrew or lost the election (e.g., Gary Hart), might also be scandalous, but would not count as a scandal unless the scandal affected the public official while in office.

THE SCANDALS

Using the definition defended above, we identified 156 individual presidential-level scandals (involving 198 individuals), 338 gubernatorial-level scandals (involving 385 individuals), and 327 scandals involving members of Congress that occurred between 1972 and January 2021 (the end of Donald Trump's first term).[35] Using secondary texts follows the lead of other scholars who have searched for a universe of political scandals.[36] If the principal focus of the scandal was the elected official, we recorded this as well and included it in the model to control for the fact that the duration of the scandal will be different for elected officials than for others (such as the president versus an agency head). This also allows comparable evaluation of political figures, at both the state and national level, who have unique institutional settings.

PRESIDENTIAL SCANDALS

How frequently do presidential scandals occur? Between 1972 and 2021, we observed 156 presidential scandals (involving 198 individuals), averaging just a little over three per year, or one every four months. Notably, some years saw no scandals while others experienced peaks, such as 2018 with twenty-two scandals and 2017 with sixteen. Although most were minor, typically involving financial misconduct by lower-ranking officials and not always the president, their frequency remains significant. Figure 1.1 illustrates the total number of scandals, distinguishing between serious and minor ones, across various presidential administrations. Surprisingly, despite Nixon and Clinton dominating scandal discussions in the past, Trump's administration recorded the highest number of scandals, with fifty-five (35 percent of the total) occurring during his tenure, followed by Reagan with forty-five (29 percent). Clinton's administration comes next with thirty-one scandals (20 percent), split between his two terms, then George W. Bush with twenty (13 percent). Nixon had only fifteen scandals from 1972 on, while Obama had twelve in his first term and five in his second term. Ford, Carter, and George H. W. Bush each had between three and six scandals during their presidencies.

Presidential scandals can also be categorized by the individuals involved and the alleged misconduct. Only 25 out of 156 scandals (16 percent) directly involved the president, encompassing notable cases like Watergate, the Iranian arms-for-hostages exchange, Whitewater, Clinton's Lewinsky affair, and Bush's National Guard service controversy. Alternatively, looking at individual involvement, presidents accounted for only 25 out of 198 implicated persons (13 percent). Seven of these were Donald Trump. Bill Clinton was also personally embroiled in seven identified scandals, including sexual, political, and financial infractions. Despite overseeing numerous scandals, Reagan was directly implicated in only one, as were Gerald Ford and George H. W. Bush. Jimmy Carter and George W. Bush each faced direct involvement in two scandals.

Journalists and scholars suggest that second presidential terms tend to be more scandal-prone because of heightened opposition, declining party

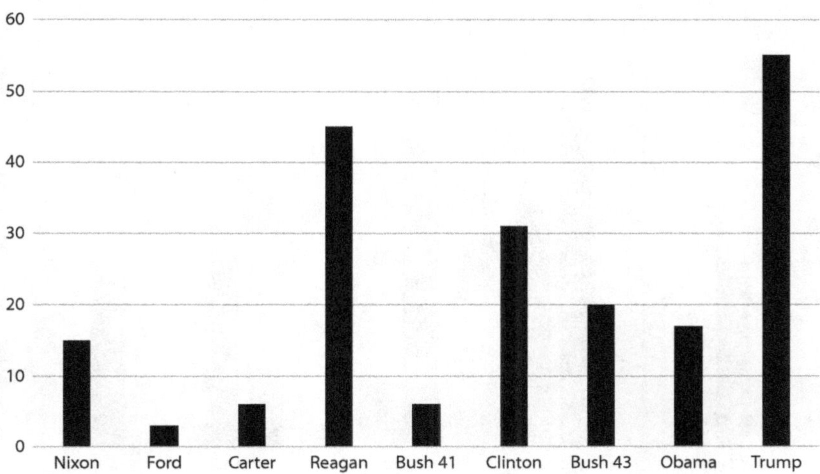

FIGURE 1.1 Presidential scandals since Watergate. Trump's administration recorded the highest number of scandals (35 percent of the total), followed by Reagan (29 percent) and Clinton (20 percent).

Source: Data collected by the author.

support, and the introduction of new government actors who may lack loyalty to the administration. Empirical evidence also suggests that second-term presidents often face more scandals than those in their first terms. Figure 1.2 illustrates and tests this trend, examining both total and serious scandals across presidential terms for those who secured reelection. Except for the Bush (43) administration, presidents generally experienced fewer total scandals in their second terms compared to their first. Specifically, Nixon, Reagan, and Clinton had fewer scandals in their second terms. However, with the exception of Nixon, most serious scandals occurred during second terms, including fourteen for Reagan, two for Clinton, and two for Bush (43). Notably, while Watergate originated in Nixon's first term, its climax unfolded in the second term. In summary, presidential second terms witness fewer total scandals but a higher frequency of serious ones.[37]

Are Watergate, Iran-Contra, and the Monica Lewinsky scandals representative of modern presidential scandals? Watergate revolved around political corruption, Iran-Contra dealt with congressional statute violations,

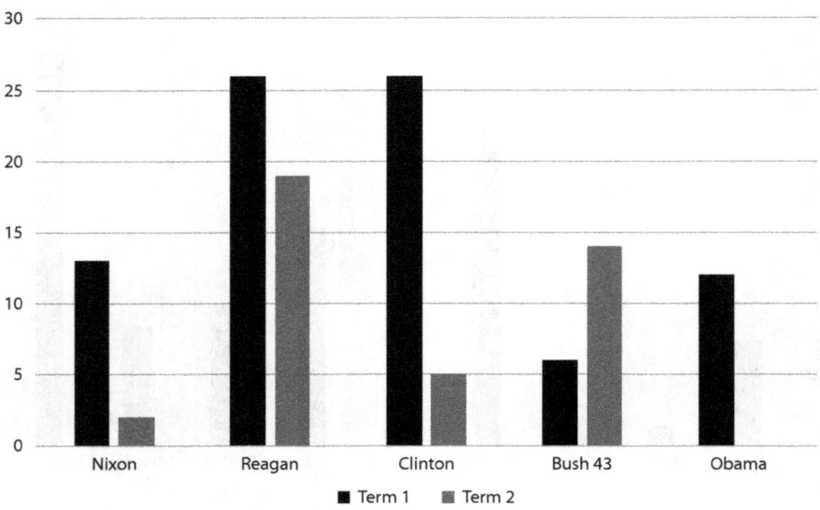

FIGURE 1.2 Presidents have fewer scandals in second terms, but more serious ones. Except for the Bush (43) administration, presidents generally experienced fewer total scandals in their second terms compared to their first—but more important ones.

Source: Data collected by the author.

and Clinton's impeachment centered on lying under oath to conceal an inappropriate relationship. Surprisingly, these behaviors are more common but not dominant in the pattern. Figure 1.3 delineates scandals into three types: financial, political corruption, and personal. Financial scandals, constituting 29 percent of the total, involve individuals illicitly profiting from their actions. This category encompasses a wide spectrum of misconduct. Minor instances include FBI director Clarence Kelley's government-funded curtains and National Security Adviser Richard Allen accepting one thousand dollars for arranging an interview. More serious cases include Vice President Spiro Agnew taking cash bribes and officials like John Sununu and Robert Nimmo misusing government transportation. At the extreme end are examples like Webb Hubbell's billing fraud and Commerce Secretary Ron Brown's sale of trade mission seats, potentially yielding millions.

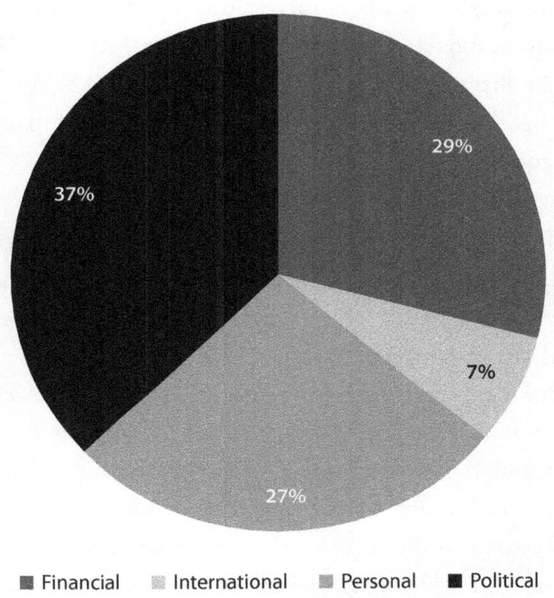

FIGURE 1.3 Presidential scandals by type. Financial scandals constitute 29 percent of the total, political scandals account for 37 percent, and personal moral scandals constitute only 27 percent.

Source: Data collected by the author.

Political scandals account for 37 percent of all scandals in the present span of data—for instance, Watergate, involving nine individuals including President Nixon; "Chinagate," implicating four individuals including President Clinton; and the NSA's warrantless surveillance involving four individuals, including President George W. Bush. This category also includes campaign fundraising violations, lying to Congress or federal prosecutors, and using political influence to obtain FBI files and passport records from the State Department. Contrary to popular belief, personal moral scandals constitute only 27 percent of all scandals, although this number is higher than in prior eras.[38] These typically involve sex scandals, instances of employing undocumented workers, and illicit drug use. For example, during the Carter administration, the president's "drug czar" was accused of writing false prescriptions (he resigned immediately). The number of personal scandals is increasing because many of the Trump administration scandals were personal in nature, such as Housing and Urban Development secretary Ben Carson spending $31,000 on a dining room set for his office, triggering an internal investigation. He was cleared of any wrongdoing.[39]

International scandals make up 7 percent of all scandals, including the Iranian arms-for-hostages trade and illegal aid to Nicaraguan Contra rebels. These incidents involve alleged lawbreaking rather than mere policy disagreements. The Trump-Ukraine scandal is the most damaging international scandal because of the connection to election tampering, leading to President Trump's first impeachment trial. The scandal stems from allegations that in July 2019 the president improperly sought help from the Ukrainian president to dig up dirt on Joe Biden and his family, especially his son Hunter Biden, who worked with a Ukrainian energy company. Because it is illegal to involve foreign entities in U.S. elections, an anonymous whistleblower flagged the call, triggering an investigation. The call occurred days after President Trump blocked $391 million in military aid to Ukraine, which critics accused him of using as a bargaining chip (the White House denied this).[40] In December 2019, Democratic leaders in the U.S. House unveiled two impeachment charges—abuse of power and obstruction of Congress—voting a week before Christmas to impeach the president, making him the third president to face a Senate trial. The Senate trial, over two weeks in January and February, required a two-thirds majority to convict. On mostly party line votes, the president was acquitted on both counts (52–48 on one and 53–47 on the other).

CONGRESSIONAL SCANDALS

Congressional scandals (figure 1.4) are often individualistic, driven by greed or morality issues. Some of these are errors in judgment. Democratic representative Cynthia McKinney of Georgia struck a Capitol police officer in the chest after he stopped her from moving through a metal detector at a security checkpoint. She was not wearing her special pin that designated her as a member but remarked that the police responsible for

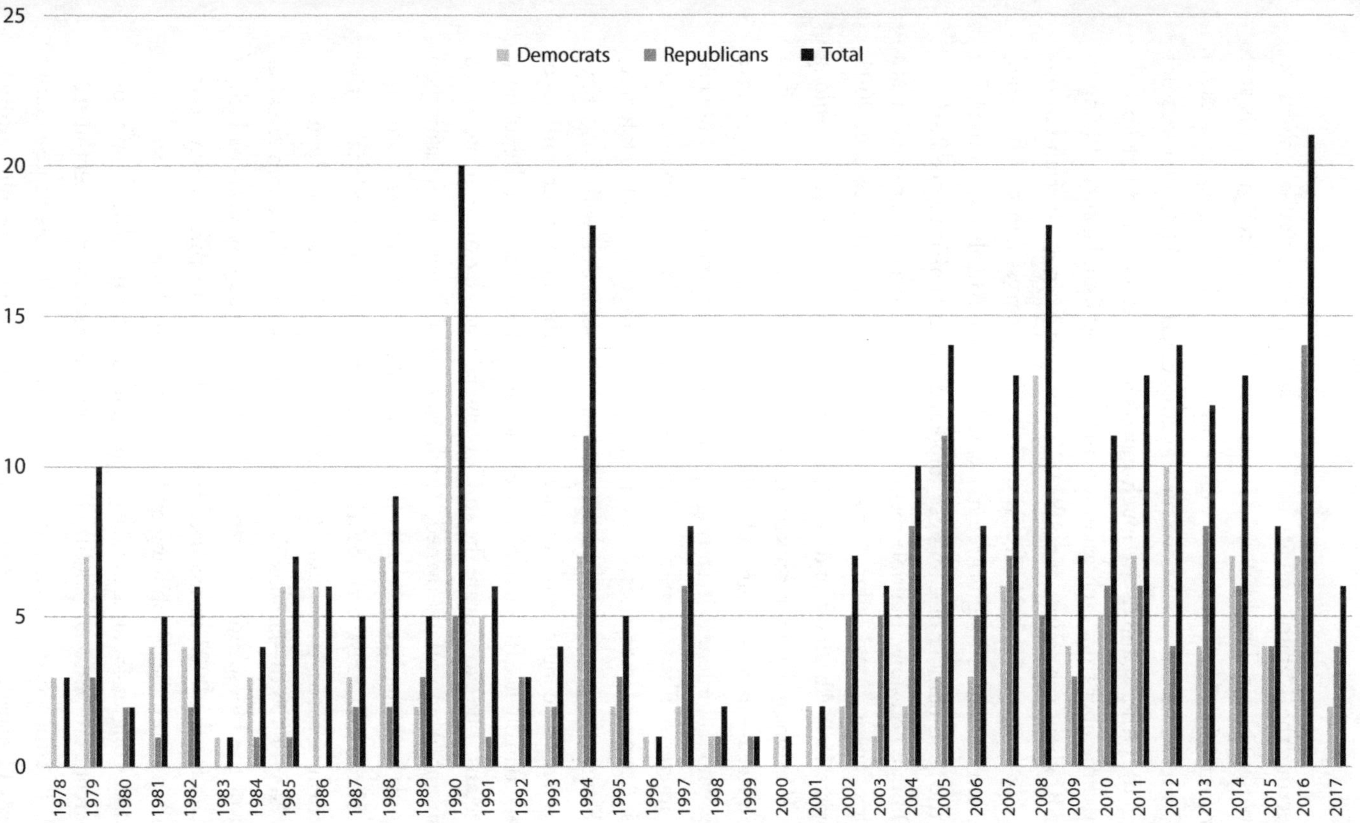

FIGURE 1.4 Congressional scandals since Watergate. Congressional scandals spiked during the congressional banking scandal and during the Abramoff scandal.

Source: Data collected by the author.

protecting the Capitol and its buildings should recognize members on sight. Republican Thaddeus McCotter from Michigan resigned his seat after four of his staff members were convicted of falsifying signatures on McCotter's reelection petitions for the 2012 elections (McCotter was not charged). Other scandals are much more serious. Republican Jeff Fortenberry, a member from Nebraska, was indicted and found guilty of lying to the FBI about the source of a $189,000 donation from a Nigerian billionaire. He resigned in 2021 after the trial. The congressman had funneled the contributions through three strawmen at a Los Angeles fundraiser. He was the first member of Congress convicted while in office since 2016.

On rare occasions, multiple members get snared in a similar scandal as a result of institutional failures or sometimes old-fashioned greed. In 2005, lobbyists Jack Abramoff and Michael Scanlon hatched a scheme—along with Washington power brokers Grover Norquist and Christian activist Ralph Reed—to coordinate and bamboozle several clients, including native tribes who had interests in setting up casinos, by lobbying against those clients' interests. The fees were exorbitant—more than $85 million over three years. Abramoff (recognizable for his large black overcoat and black fedora) and Scanlon pled guilty to corrupt practices in connection with this lobbying caper. The congressional connection is that Abramoff spent millions of dollars to influence (through campaign donations) and entertain Republican politicians. The excesses are the stuff of scandal legend: expensive meals at a restaurant Abramoff co-owned, fundraisers at skyboxes to Washington Wizards basketball games, and millions of dollars in donations. Some, like Republican J. D. Hayworth of Arizona, cochair of the Congressional Native American Caucus, gave most of the money back. Others, like Republican Bob Ney of Ohio—famous for renaming French fries "freedom fries" as chair of the House Administration Committee because of France's lack of support for the 2003 invasion of Iraq—pled guilty to three felony counts stemming from illegal lobbying on behalf of Native American tribes.

Most congressional scandals (51 percent) are financial in origin; only 25 percent are personal (slightly lower than the rate for presidential scandals). But the personal scandals are often doozies. Illinois representative Dennis Hastert, a former Republican Speaker of the House, pled guilty to charges he lied to the FBI in a scheme to pay $3.5 million in hush money to conceal sexual misconduct with an underage boy from his days as a high school wrestling coach before he entered Congress. Democrat David Wu from Oregon resigned in 2011 after a sexual harassment report from a staff member accused him of an "unwanted sexual encounter." Wu's "worrisome antics," which included "loud and angry behavior," saying "kooky things to staffers," and lambasting his opponent as being "stingy with tips," led Wu's staff to keep him away from the public for three days before the election. The congressman also sent a series of "strange middle-of-the-night e-mails, including a 'bizarre' one in which the congressman posed in a tiger suit."[41]

GUBERNATORIAL SCANDALS

State-level scandals (figure 1.5) involving governors or their staff often mirrored national patterns, involving individual wrongdoing or moral lapses rather than reflecting on the overall competency or efficiency of a gubernatorial administration. Instances of scandals ranged from bribery and illegal workplace behavior to minor indiscretions, such as Democratic governor Corzine of New Jersey being ticketed for not wearing a seat belt or a controversial "booze cruise" that led to the termination of the Massport director.[42] Even when only one person was implicated, several governors oversaw administrations with multiple scandals. In Arkansas, for example, despite only five total scandals during the period, attention often centered around Governor (later President) Bill Clinton. These included scandals related to his brother's drug use in 1984, his affair with Gennifer Flowers during the 1992 presidential campaign, and his association with Democratic governor Jim "Guy" Tucker, who resigned amid the Whitewater scandal in 1995.

Out of 338 state scandals (involving a total of 385 individuals), only 24 (8 percent) involved two individuals; occurrences involving three or more individuals—what we might consider a conspiracy—were rare. Only six scandals had three or more participants. For instance, Republican Kentucky governor Ernie Fletcher faced accusations of violating civil service laws by favoring politically aligned applicants for state jobs, resulting in

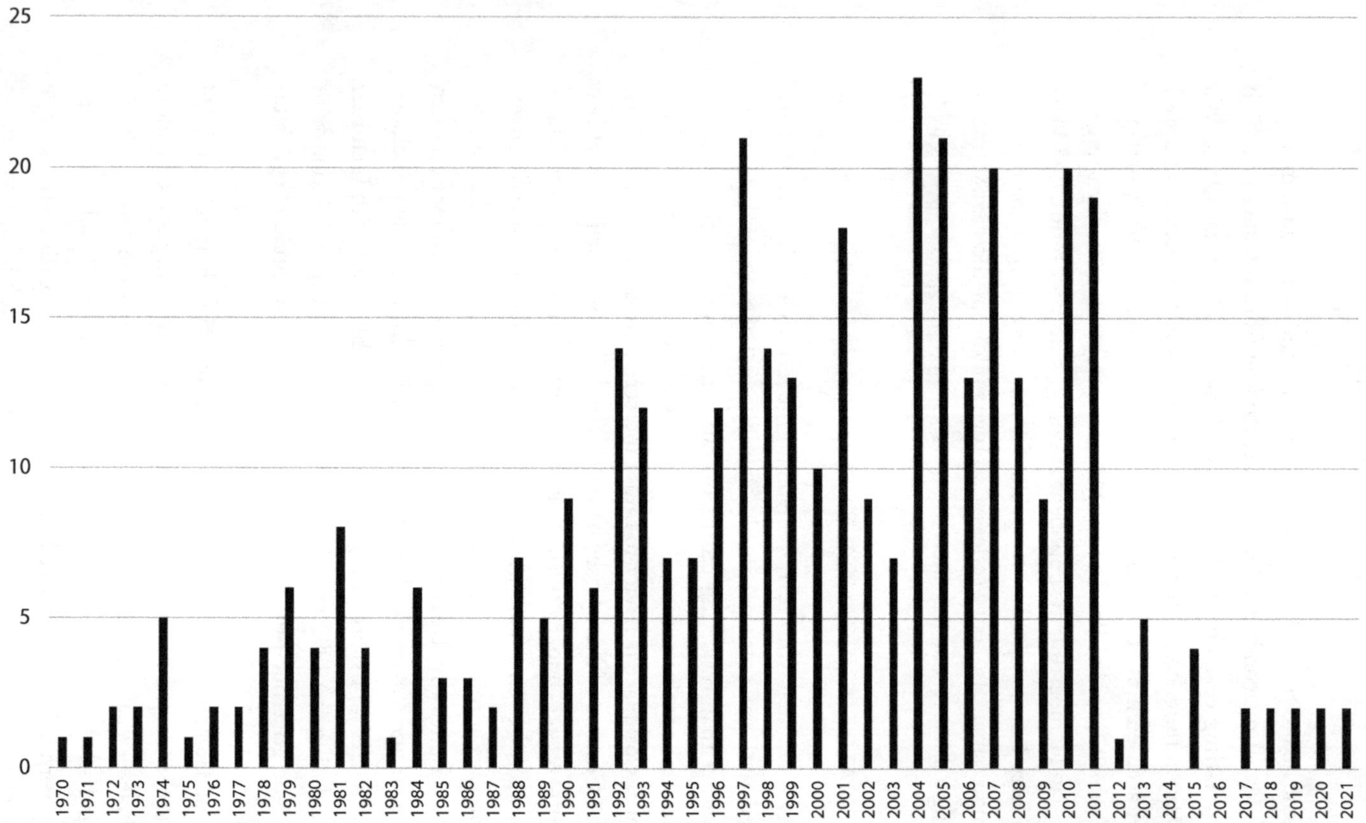

FIGURE 1.5 Gubernatorial scandals over time. Gubernatorial scandals spiked in the late 1990s and the early 2000s, led by New Jersey, New York, and Illinois. The number has been decreasing since then because of more unified party control.

Source: Data collected by the author.

indictments for him and his associates, including his deputy chief of staff, Richard Murgatroyd, and a senior adviser, Daniel Groves.[43] Governor Fletcher eventually pardoned these individuals, citing a desire to avoid "gotcha" politics, although he himself was indicted after leaving office.[44]

Other governors faced multiple scandals. Democratic governor Ryan of Illinois, for instance, grappled with six scandals during his tenure, primarily centered on allegations that officials in his administration accepted bribes for driver's licenses and subsequently covered up these actions. The investigation stemmed from a tragic car accident that claimed the lives of six children, revealing widespread corruption across various state departments, including transportation and vehicle licensing.[45] Several of the governor's aides, including his chief of staff, were implicated and indicted.[46] Governor Ryan himself was indicted, found guilty, and sentenced to seventy-eight months in prison for racketeering and fraud.[47] However, not all gubernatorial scandals are government-related. Republican governor Jim Gibbons of Nevada faced five scandals, three of which were linked to his messy divorce, misuse of state funds to communicate with his mistress, and accepting gifts from a CEO seeking state business opportunities, although he was later cleared of this last charge.[48]

State scandals involving chief executives or their staff varied widely across states during the period, with some states experiencing numerous scandals while others remained unscathed. Collins suggests that states with a strong political culture tend to have fewer scandals, while others foster environments ripe for corruption or illicit activity among elected or appointed officials.[49] Scandals that get the most attention tend to be those that are more salacious, such as Republican governor Sanford of South Carolina's famous "hiking the Appalachian Trail" lie that covered up his affair with a news reporter in Argentina or Democratic governor Blagojevich of Illinois using his position to gain politically (and perhaps financially) from bartering for an appointed position to the U.S. Senate. These types of scandals are also rare. Scandals that involve governors, although the most numerous, rarely involve allegations of serious criminal wrongdoing.

The number of gubernatorial scandals has been decreasing since 2011, the total number falling to under five in most years between then and

2021. Why? It is possible that, consistent with the overarching story about polarization minimizing scandals, increasing polarization in state legislatures has provided a protective shield for co-partisan governors in this period. The *Washington Post*'s Phillip Bump writes, "Over the past 15 years, the number of state legislative bodies dominated by one party or the other has increased dramatically." According to MultiState, before the 2022 elections, thirteen states had "divided governments," in which a single political party did not control the governorship and both chambers of the legislature. After the election, that number dropped to eleven states, with the remaining thirty-nine states under single-party control.[50] The consequences? "There's less need to reach across the aisle."[51] Another consequence: allowing co-partisan public officials to survive while in office.

Serious scandals are less common than typical scandals, and the states experiencing more serious scandals differ from those with higher overall scandal counts. When asked by a federal prosecutor if New Jersey was the most corrupt state, Democratic governor Chris Christie jokingly replied, "Thank God for Illinois and Louisiana."[52] Florida tops the list of scandals at the state level with twenty-five. New Jersey, New York, and Illinois are tied for second with twenty-one each. All states have at least one scandal, but Colorado, Hawaii, Idaho, and Wyoming are the only states to have only one scandal over this forty-year period. Illinois leads in serious scandals with seven, with four out of its seven governors imprisoned between 1980 and 2010. Following closely are New York and New Mexico with six and seven serious scandals, respectively, fueled by the administrations of Republican governor George Pataki and Democratic governor Andrew Cuomo (see next chapter) in New York and the Democratic Bill Richardson administration in New Mexico. These scandals typically involve "pay to play" schemes, with officials accused of accepting bribes in exchange for political favors such as state contracts or parole. On the other hand, Utah, Missouri, Nevada, and North Carolina are the only states with more than five scandals but no serious ones.

Interestingly, when state-level scandals are categorized (see figure 1.6), the percentages closely resemble those at the national level. Financial misconduct, in which individuals personally benefit from illicit actions,

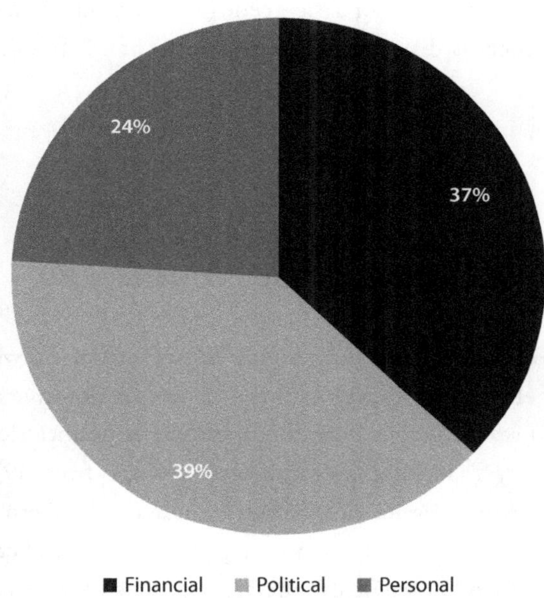

FIGURE 1.6 Gubernatorial scandals by type. Most scandals are not personal. Political scandals make up 39 percent and financial scandals 37 percent of cases; personal scandals account for only 24 percent. These percentages mirror national trends.

Source: Data collected by the author.

constitutes 39 percent of cases. For instance, an appointed emergency financial manager in Michigan, under Democratic governor Jennifer Granholm, was compelled by a jury trial initiated by the state's attorney general to repay $264,000 he misappropriated for himself.[53] Political scandals make up 37 percent of cases, often involving abuse of power by officials, such as Republican governor Carcieri of Rhode Island using government resources for campaigning or Texas Republican governor Rick Perry indicted on charges of abuse of power for threatening to veto funds earmarked for an ethics unit run by the Travis County district attorney, who was caught drunk driving. These cases frequently entail violations of campaign finance laws, circumventing donation limits.

Personal scandals account for 24 percent (91 cases), involving individual indiscretions such as drug or alcohol abuse, marital infidelity, or sexual harassment.

DO SCANDALS CAUSE GUBERNATORIAL TURNOVER?

A clear way to test whether or not scandals matter is to look at whether scandals have an effect on turnover in the party of the governors involved—essentially, do scandals contribute to gubernatorial political losses for the incumbent party? Tracking political party change from 1972 to 2012, the analysis shown in figure 1.7 investigates individual gubernatorial scandals. The dependent variable is party change, so the question here is whether scandals (and the other variables) affected elections of governors in these time windows. Additional covariates include the number of years a governor has served, the number of years left in a governor's term, whether the governor is male or female, whether the governor is a Republican or a Democrat, and how many years it has been since the other party was in power.

Since the primary argument here is that scandals have less impact in the modern partisan era, we estimate two models: one from 1970 to 1994 and a second from 1994 to 2012. Consistent with expectations, scandals have a small effect before polarization took root but not after. Specifically, in the earlier era, scandals have a small positive and statistically significant effect. In the partisan era, by contrast, scandals have less of an impact: the coefficient for scandal is negative and not statistically significant, suggesting no effect of scandals on partisan turnover in this era. Years served by the governor and years since the other party was in power are negative and significant in this estimation, as they were in the pre-partisan era. In addition, in the pre-polarized era, the number of years left in a governor's term was positively related to partisan turnover while the total number of years in office and the number of years since the other party was in power are both negative negatively related to partisan turnover.

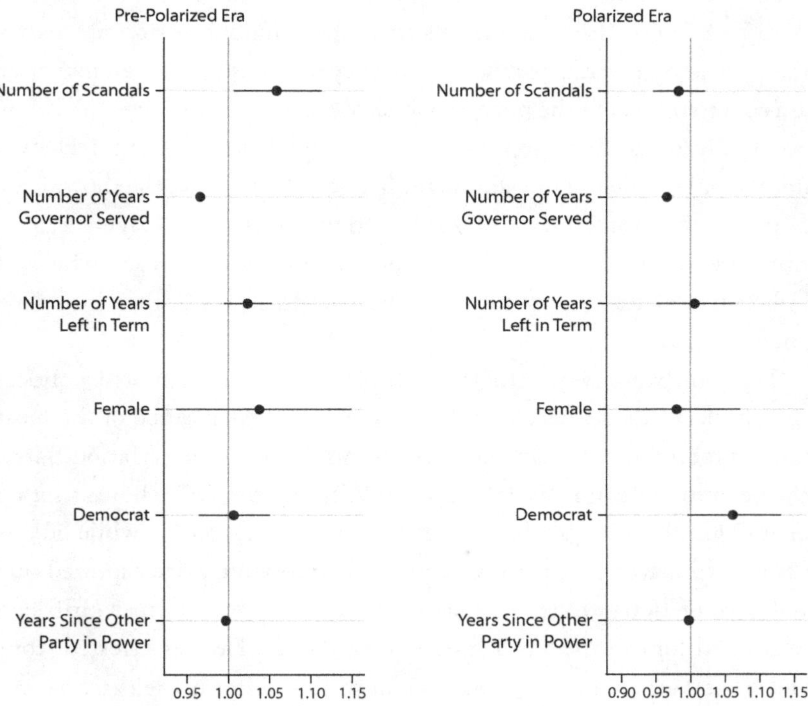

FIGURE 1.7 Gubernatorial scandals have a small effect in the pre-polarized era (left) but not in the polarized era (right). In the earlier era, scandals have a small positive, statistically significant effect; in the partisan era, they have less impact.

POLITICAL COMEBACKS

One of the great ironies of American politics is that scandals are not uniformly debilitating. Tom DeLay resigned from Congress in 2006 while awaiting trial on charges of campaign finance laws; he was eventually convicted and sentenced to three years in prison, but the conviction was overturned. His redemption? A turn on *Dancing with the Stars*, where celebrities partner with professional dancers and compete every week against other duos. During the time he was appealing his conviction, he tried to change the narrative and move on from his scandal. From the *New York Times*: "Elected officials trade their dignity, performers barter their privacy—it's transparency as currency. Famous people can monetize almost anything, but the price of publicity keeps getting steeper."[54] DeLay eventually lost to 1970s pop star Donny Osmond and his partner. He was not the only former politician caught in a scandal to be on the show: Jerry Springer, the former mayor of Cincinnati who was caught paying a prostitute by check, and Rick Perry, former governor of Texas who was indicted on abuse-of-power charges, were on the show in the year before and after DeLay.

Do comebacks work? Table 1.1 displays a list of attempted political comebacks of former elected officials since the 1990s. Some of the most famous (or infamous) politicians are on this list, including Marion Barry, the beloved but controversial mayor of Washington, DC who was set up on a 1990 drug sting by the Federal Bureau of Investigation while he was the elected mayor of the city. Grainy black-and-white video captured surveillance of Berry smoking crack cocaine, set up by a former girlfriend who lured him to the Vista International Hotel. He was arrested, convicted, and sentenced to six months in prison. After his release, he was again elected to the DC City Council and, in 1994, elected again as mayor—a comeback that gave him the nickname Mayor for Life. Other politicians were not so lucky. Eliot Spitzer, the Democratic governor of New York who resigned amid a prostitution scandal in 2008, tried to make a comeback running for comptroller of the City of New York in 2013. "I failed, big time," a direct-to-camera ad noted, stating the obvious. "I hurt a lot of people," Spitzer says in a one-minute spot attempting to persuade New Yorkers to give him "a fair shot."[55] He ended up with a respectable 48 percent of the vote but lost to New York City borough president Scott Stringer.

Are comebacks successful? Generally no, but the changing nature of scandals, especially sex scandals, leaves room for some politicians to mount comebacks. Overall, the politicians in table 1.1 were mostly unsuccessful in making comebacks after they left office in disgrace. About 75 percent of the time, a comeback effort was unsuccessful whether the comeback

TABLE 1.1 Attempted political comebacks

YEAR	POLITICIAN	STATE	POSITION	TYPE OF SCANDAL	WHAT HAPPENED	COMEBACK?
1988	Evan Mecham	Arizona	Governor	Campaign finance, fraud	Removed from governorship in 1986	Lost 1992 bid for Senate
1990	Marion Barry	District of Columbia	Mayor	Drugs	Resigned	Won reelection 2024
1992	Carroll Hubbard	Kentucky	Representative	Campaign finance	Lost reelection	Lost 2006 and 2008 bids for state senate
1992	Mary Rose Oakar	Ohio	Representative	Campaign finance, ethics	Lost reelection	Won 2000 bid for state legislature; lost 2001 bid for Cleveland mayor; won 2012 bid for state board of education
1994	Judith Moriarty	Missouri	Secretary of state	Ethics	Removed	Lost 2002 bid for state legislature
1994	Mel Reynolds	Illinois	Representative	Sex	Won reelection, then resigned	Lost 2004 and 2013 bids for old seat
1996	Barbara-Rose Collins	Michigan	Representative	Campaign finance, ethics	Lost reelection	Won 2001 bid for Detroit City Council; reelected in 2005
1997	Jay Kim	California	Representative	Campaign finance	Lost reelection	Lost 2000 bid for old seat
1997	Fife Symington	Arizona	Governor	Fraud	Resigned	Lost 2006 bid for local GOP chairmanship
1997	Newt Gingrich	Georgia	Representative	Ethics and sex	Won reelection, then resigned	Ran for president in 2012

(*continued*)

TABLE 1.1 Continued

YEAR	POLITICIAN	STATE	POSITION	TYPE OF SCANDAL	WHAT HAPPENED	COMEBACK?
2001	Albert Cianci	Rhode Island	Mayor	Racketeering	Removed	Lost 2014 mayoral election
2002	Jim Traficant	Ohio	Representative	Corruption	Removed	Lost 2002 and 2010 bids for old seat
2002	Edwin Edwards	Louisiana	Governor	Racketeering	Removed in 2002	Lost 2014 congressional election
2003	Roy Moore	Alabama	Supreme court justice	Insubordination	Removed	Lost 2010 bid for governor; won 2013 bid to return to supreme court
2004	Jim McGreevey	New Jersey	Governor	Sex	Resigned	Running for mayor in 2025
2008	Eliot Spitzer	New York	Governor	Sex	Resigned	Lost 2013 bid for New York City comptroller
2009	Mark Sanford	South Carolina	Governor	Sex	Was term-limited out	Won 2013 bid for Congress
2011	Anthony Weiner	New York	Representative	Sex	Resigned	Lost 2013 bid for New York City mayor
2014	Rick Perry	Texas	Governor	Abuse of power	Retired, then lost bid for president	Appointed Secretary of Energy in 2017
2015	Paul LePage	Maine	Governor	Abuse of power	Was term-limited out	Lost 2022 bid for governor
2015	James Comer	Kentucky	Agriculture commissioner	Abuse	Lost bid for governor	Won 2016 bid for Congress
2016	Roy Moore	Alabama	Supreme court justice	Insubordination	Removed	Won 2017 Republican nomination but lost general election for Senate
2016	Alan Grayson	Florida	Representative	Ethics, abuse	Lost bid for Senate	Lost 2018 bid for Congress

2016	Terry McAuliffe	Virginia	Governor	Campaign finance	Was term-limited out	Lost 2021 bid for governor
2018	Megan Barry	Tennessee	Mayor	Affair, fraud	Resigned	Lost 2024 House election
2018	Scott Taylor	Virginia	Representative	Election fraud	Lost reelection	Lost 2020 bid for Congress
2018	Kris Kobach	Kansas	Secretary of state	Contempt of court	Lost bid for governor	Lost 2020 bid for Senate, won 2022 bid for attorney general
2018	Eric Greitens	Missouri	Governor	Sexual assault, campaign finance	Resigned	Lost 2022 bid for Senate
2018	John Hickenlooper	Colorado	Governor	Illegal gifts	Was term-limited out	Won 2020 bid for Senate

Source: Data collected by the author.

Note: About 75 percent of the time, a comeback effort was unsuccessful; in 25 percent of the cases, a political comeback was successful.

attempt was soon after the initial scandal jolted the politician from office or years later. But, looking at it from another perspective, in 25 percent of the cases a political comeback *was* successful. Comeback attempts were most successful when the initial scandal that drove the politician from office was of a personal nature (sexual harassment, an extramarital affair, or accepting illegal gifts). Politicians made successful comebacks in 38 percent of those cases, compared to 24 percent when the scandal involved campaign finance or other abuse-of-power issues.

Why? There may be legal impediments, even if shame alone does not dissuade. Ask former Illinois governor Rod Blagojevich about the challenging path back—he triumphantly declared "I'm back," like Michael Jordan returning to basketball from baseball in 1995, after spending almost a decade in federal prison. President Trump freed the former Illinois governor in February 2020 after he served time for trying to sell an appointment to Barack Obama's Senate for campaign cash. The former governor sued his home state for stripping him of his right to run for elective office again in Illinois. In a whimsical legal smackdown, a federal judge dismissed the suit, debunking the claims issue by issue and closing with a quote from a Dr. Seuss book, *Marvin K. Mooney Will You Please Go Now!* to suggest what Blagojevich should do: "The time has come. The time has come. The time is now. Just Go. Go. GO! I don't care how. You can go by foot. You can go by cow. Marvin K. Mooney, will you please go now!"[56]

Parties may object as well. As candidates, scandal-ridden former politicians might hurt their party or lose a seat. In 2018 former Republican governor Eric Greitens—who resigned amid sexual assault allegations from a woman with whom he had had an affair that he took "her to his basement, blindfolded her, bound her hands and coerced her into performing oral sex"—entered the race for an open U.S. Senate seat in Missouri. "Greitens is a clear and present danger to botching the race for the GOP," said one political strategist.[57] But his rebranded status as a partisan warrior, along with a solid base, a right-wing savvy media strategy, and a billionaire backer, gave the scandal-plagued Greitens another chance.[58] It didn't work, but the attempt itself, and that the scandal did not deter him from running, speaks volumes about the changing nature of scandal in a partisan world.

RESIGN OR RETURN?

The crux of the argument of this book is that scandals today do not have the same political impact they used to have—that the liability of scandals is smaller now than before partisanship, news silos, the decline of local news, and low trust in political institutions set in. One way to test this is to look at resignation rates across time and institutions.

Do different eras independently affect survival of scandal? Figure 1.8 graphs the rate at which scandals end badly for each office across five decades (lower percentages mean *higher* survival rates)—basically, what percent of officials resigned following a scandal. The results show that politicians generally survived most frequently in the 1990s. For most of the major scandals during that time period, White House officials (including President Clinton himself), governors (George Ryan of Illinois and Edwin Edwards of Louisiana), and members of Congress faced political scrutiny, but revelations of scandal did not always lead to resignations or removal from office (or the effect was considerably delayed).

Survival percentages for the other eras were mixed across office type. Survival of state executive scandals was consistent across time, although slightly higher in the 1970s. Resignation rates for those embroiled in scandal have generally been dropping over time. Resignation rates are generally lower in the modern period (2016–2021) than in earlier periods. The largest drop was for members of Congress, who were more likely to hang on politically in the later period than earlier. In presidential administrations of the 1980s and 2000s, more officials left office due to scandal than in other periods. The 2010s had higher than average rates of survival across all institutions. Some have labeled this the "Trump effect," pointing to him as changing the nature of political scandals ("the ringleader of

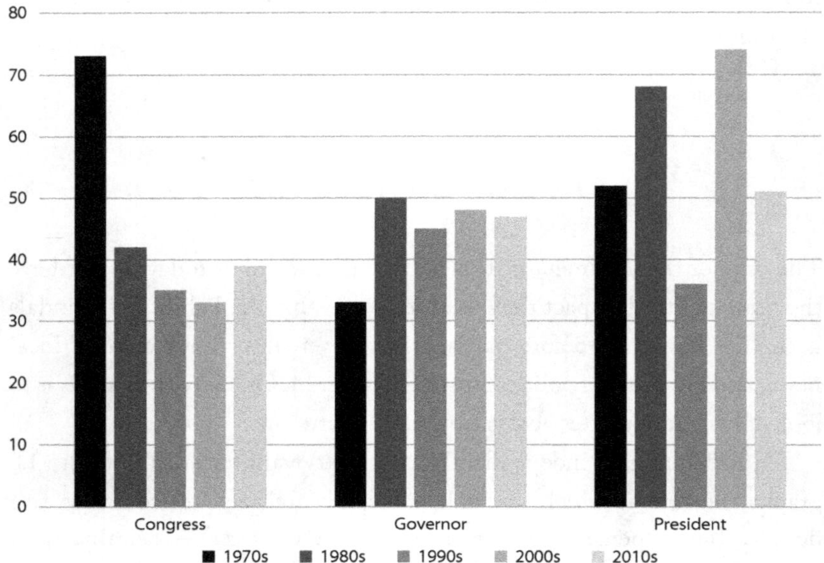

FIGURE 1.8 Scandal "end-in-disgrace" rates by era and office. Bars indicate the percent of scandals that ended badly (removal from office, resignation, firing) for each office across five decades. Lower percentages mean *higher* survival rates.

looser standards").[59] Earlier periods of scandal history (the 1970s, the Watergate era) had "bad ending" rates significantly higher than in later decades, especially for members of the House, implying that politicians of earlier eras faced more scrutiny and pressure to leave office than politicians in more contemporary times. Scholars find scandals in the modern era generally face similar outcomes of scandals on their political careers. This may be because of saturated coverage of scandal during that era and fewer media sources to dilute coverage.[60]

Organized by scandal era, the results show that politicians survive in office longer in more recent times. In order to explore whether the negative effects of scandals are worsening or improving, we divided the span of the full data into five periods corresponding to the major scandals of that era: Watergate and post-Watergate (1972–1980, n = 65); Keating Five, Abscam, and Iran-Contra scandals (1981–1993, n = 208); the Monica

Lewinsky scandal (1994–2001, n = 162); George W. Bush and lobbyist Jack Abramoff scandals (2002–2015, n = 360); Donald Trump scandals (2016–2021, n = 115). These are imperfect time divisions and eras that encompass multiple unrelated scandals but allow for a rough estimate of the impact of scandals in each era. As expected, there are variations across time in survival rates of politicians: Watergate and post-Watergate, 47 percent resigned or were removed from office; Keating Five, Abscam, and Iran-Contra, 50 percent; Lewinsky, 40 percent; Bush and Abramoff, 43 percent; Trump, 45 percent.

CONCLUSION

The impact of scandals is changing. The congressman turned governor turned congressman again Mark Sanford is a good example. The South Carolina governor was a darling of the right wing and a putative presidential candidate in 2012. Then one day he disappeared—for days. The official story was that he was hiking the Appalachian Trail, a two-thousand-mile rugged hike through several states. Rumors of international travel and an extramarital affair were exposed when a political enemy tipped the media that he had traveled to Argentina to meet his lover. When the governor was accosted at the airport by reporters, he came clean, admitting to the affair. Investigations showed he did nothing wrong—other than breaking a core moral code by breaking his marriage vows—and impeachment efforts fizzled in Republican-run South Carolina. He served out his second and final term in relative obscurity. But he was not done. In 2013 he was back in electoral politics, winning election to his old seat in Congress and serving for two terms.

Writing for *Politico*, John Harris observed that "in some ways, the muscles of public accountability have grown much stronger and more demanding. Sexual and racial misconduct, which in an earlier time was more likely to fester undisturbed in the shadows, is now finally being brought into the light. At the same time, other muscles of accountability have atrophied in alarming ways. As a general rule, as long as a politician can maintain a base of support—usually animated by people who dislike his or her accusers more than the alleged transgression—it is easier than ever to escape serious consequences."[61] The evidence from this chapter makes clear that any study about scandals must have a wide latitude and look at different institutions. But the evidence also supports Harris's core point that partisanship shapes scandal survival.

2
WEATHERING THE STORM

How to Survive a Scandal

Many politicians face scandals while in office. The themes in these scandals are as old as the republic itself. One senator caught in a scandal was an active financial speculator who hatched a get rich quick scheme to get himself out of some nasty financial difficulties while in office. The plan was to get residents of an area to create a ruckus, increasing the value of the land the senator held, allowing him and a new economic group to swoop in, take over, and reap the profits. The scheme was so bold that the drama made its way to the president, who passed the details to the Senate, leading to the senator's expulsion from the chamber. Although politicians using their offices to advance their own economic interests happens fairly frequently, this scandal is quite old. It took place in 1796 and involved Senator William Blount, a Continental congressman and signatory of the Constitution.

The episode led to an ignominious honor: Blount was the first politician to be expelled from the U.S. Senate for his plan to aid the British in seizing Spanish-held territory in what is now Louisiana and Florida. The bizarre plan called for frontiersmen (Blount was from Tennessee) and Cherokee Indians to rise up against the Spanish and drive them off the

Gulf Coast. After the chaos, the British would move in, opening it to settlers and land speculators like Blount, who owned huge tracts of western land and would "make a killing on his investments."[1] A letter outlining this caper made it to President John Adams, who saw evidence of a crime and promptly turned it over to leaders in the Senate, who suspended Blount from his seat. But his Washington difficulties did not have a negative effect on his popularity in Tennessee. Shortly after his return home, Blount won a seat in the state senate, later became speaker of the body, and served there until his death in 1800.[2]

The survival of scandal has serious implications for governance. In this chapter, the life cycle of scandals is examined to determine which factors hasten an ignominious end for individuals facing scandal. If scandal is "politics by other means," then the fate of politicians' scandals should be tied to the environmental factors each faces.[3] This chapter argues that political strength is the key to surviving scandal: the stronger a politician is with respect to public approval or partisan legislative support, the more likely he or she is to weather the effects of (or "survive") a scandal. This effect should be exacerbated in the modern era as polarization strengthens politicians' resolve to stay put. Using the points outlined in chapter 1, we chart the duration of each scandal faced by elected officials, staff, or nominees. The relevant political and economic factors are then connected to investigate what factors quicken the "end" of the scandal, defined as when the scandal ends in a negative outcome for the individual or the administration. These results help clarify the conventional wisdom of how politicians manage crises, the role of the political environment in affecting and influencing the scope of accusations, and the role of scandal in politics.

The emergence of scandals presents strategic choices for elected officials and staff to resign or not and political choices for legislators to sanction or impeach an elected executive. These strategic decisions relate to the political environment, most prominently the amount of political strength a politician possesses.[4] One factor often referenced in the survival of a scandal is the amount of political support for a politician in the legislature, with greater numbers of "willing defenders" within the politician's political party providing "pillars of support."[5] The state of the economy is also pointed to as a factor in surviving scandal. For instance, it has been suggested that President Clinton survived the Monica Lewinsky scandal and subsequent impeachment because he presided over a robust economy.[6] Public approval may also play a role, with greater political strength flowing from higher poll numbers.[7] The "entertainment" value of a scandal, often directly related to salacious charges of infidelity or personal indiscretions, may also factor into the end for politicians embroiled in scandal.[8] These political disruptions, both short and long, may have consequences for the durability of elected officials.

Type of Scandal. For purposes of analysis, we focus on two categories: financial scandals (*Financial Scandal*) and personal scandal (*Personal Scandal*), drawing on the findings from chapter 1. Financial scandals are scandals in which an individual personally profited financially from his or her actions, such as embezzlement of funds, acceptance of bribes or political payoffs, or nonpayment of state or federal taxes.[9] For instance, in 2019 Republican representative Chris Collins was arrested by the FBI, charged, and pled guilty to wire and securities fraud for tipping off his son with insider financial information. Personal scandals involve immoral or unethical personal behavior, especially adulterous behavior (Lewinsky affair during the Clinton Administration) but also the use of illegal drugs (Supreme Court nominee Douglas Ginsberg), illegal household staff (Secretary of Labor nominee Linda Chavez), or theft.[10] The third group (not included) are political scandals. Many of the Trump administration scandals, such as efforts to overturn the 2020 election, fall under this category.

Institutional Variables. To examine the effect of institutional variables, we examine the relationship between the executive and legislative branches—which may lead to an official's removal from office—through two variables. First, we include a dichotomous measure of divided government, with any amount of divided government (in either or both chambers at the federal or state level) treated as divided government (*Divided*). Second, we include variables for the percent of co-partisans of the president or governor in the upper chamber (*Partisans Senate*).[11] As a corollary measure for Congress, we include a variable to capture if the member caught in scandal is of the party that controls Congress (*Same Party*). The key to each variable is that fellow partisans provide a political shield from removal. National-level data were taken from *Vital Statistics on American Politics* (2022).[12] State data are updated from Klarner (2003).[13]

Polarization and Scandal Era. Since polarization is a contentious but continuous process, we use a dummy variable to indicate the pre- and post-polarized era, cut in 1993 with the inauguration of Bill Clinton, a period of rising elite political polarization and "weaponization" of scandal.[14] Although scandals have beset politicians since the beginning, scandals moved to "institutional combat" in the 1990s as polarization grew.[15] In addition, to explore whether the negative effects of scandals were worsening or improving over this time period, we divide the full span of the data into decades, which roughly correspond to the major scandals of that era described in chapter 1: the 1970s (Watergate and post-Watergate, n = 48); the 1980s (Iran-Contra, House banking scandal, and Abscam, n = 146); the 1990s (the Monica Lewinsky scandal, n = 215); the 2000s (Abramoff scandal, n = 250); and the 2010s (multiple governors and Donald Trump scandals, n = 249). These time divisions encompass multiple unrelated scandals but allow for a rough estimate of the impact of scandals in each era.

Control Variables. To examine any temporal aspects of the survival of scandal, we include two key control variables in the models. First, the effects of scandals is gendered when women politicians involved in scandals activate traditional gender norms and provoke hostile respondents to punish women more severely than men.[16] To capture this dynamic, we include a control variable (coded "1") for the individual's gender (*Female*). Second, to measure executive approval at both the national and state level, we recorded the approval measure of the president or governor taken as close as possible before (but not after) the date the scandal story broke (*Approval*). The question asked was "Do you approve or disapprove of the way [President or Governor (name)] is handling his job as [(president) or (governor)]?" Responses are collapsed into positive and negative values, excluding those who responded "don't know." National-level data were taken from iPoll's report of Gallup Poll data for the appropriate time period. The state-level data were taken from the U.S. Officials' Job Approval Ratings (JARs), a cooperative project of the University of Rochester, the University of North Carolina at Chapel Hill, and George Washington University.[17] In instances where more accurate state-level data could be located at SurveyUSA, those data were used.[18] We also included a variable (*House*) to distinguish between House members and senators only in the congressional models. Finally, we captured party by coding whether a politician was a Republican or not (*Republican*).

Model. Because we are interested in the factors that contribute to a politician's "survival" of a scandal, we use a series of duration models.[19] A Cox proportional hazard model is a semiparametric model that allows the hazard model to be unestimated—especially useful when the shape of the baseline hazard model is unknown.[20] This model also assumes that the shape of the hazard is the same for all the subjects, a reasonable assumption considering that the effect of scandal in the modern era (especially post-Watergate) should be theoretically similar. The Cox model asserts that a hazard rate for the *j*th subject in the data is $h(t|_{xj}) = h_0(t)\ \exp(x_j\beta_x)$, where the regression coefficients, β_x, are estimated from the data.[21] This also allows us to control for duration dependence.[22] The parameterized effects of each variable are measured, using categorical and continuous variables. We also cluster by scandal because the effects of each scandal (including the severity and personnel involved) are likely to be similar within each scandal, providing within-subject correlation.[23] This provides a valid representation of the "sample-to-sample variability" of the coefficients.[24] Although selection effects are problematic for some duration models, the nature of the data collection for these data resolves these possible issues.[25]

Scandal Length and "Failure." In establishing a span of time as required for duration models, the scandal begins (t_{1x}) when the charges are made public for the first time and is considered ended (t_{nx}) when the accused individual is exonerated, formally leaves his or her position, or the presidential or gubernatorial administration ends. The origin of the scandal can involve a news story in a major daily newspaper (searched in Lexis-Nexis), a report to Congress, an internal investigation, or other secondary sources. This variable spans the life cycle of the scandal from the first break of the story to the end of the scandal, whether that end be politically or legally favorable for the individual charged in the scandal. Each scandal has a definite temporal beginning and end, allowing for completion of the duration models.

To be more specific in predicting the end to the span of the sequence, "failure" in the duration models (or the right censored variable) is when the scandal ends in a negative outcome for the individual or the administration. This includes the following scenarios: an individual being fired from their position, resigning (or being forced to resign), being indicted at any level, or being removed from their position or office in some other way. Failure excludes losing an election, being charged with a crime after leaving office, or being indicted but remaining in office until their term runs out. Nonfailure, such as evidence of an extramarital affair that lasts the duration of the incumbent's time in office, does not have an official end, so the time length spans the rest of the incumbent's time in office.[26] If a politician is exonerated, including evidence of innocence, a favorable court ruling, a committee report with evidence of innocence, the guilt of another associate, or restitution (a fine paid), the scandal is considered ended.

Politicians with less support in the legislature to begin with are less likely to be able to govern effectively after news of a scandal breaks. For example, if chief executives are unable to govern in the aftermath of a scandal, because of blocked initiatives, delayed votes, or lengthy and distracting investigatory hearings, they may be more likely to step aside quickly after a scandal breaks.[27] Indeed, Meinke and Anderson found that scandals have significant negative effects on presidential support on key legislation, suggesting a negative relationship between effective governing and scandal-ridden presidential administrations.[28] Raizada found there were more verified scandals when government was divided, suggesting that institutional friction and accusations of scandal are related.[29] It has been argued that political insiders play a more important role in removing presidents from office than either the public or the media.[30] This is certainly true for chief executives. Upper-level administration officials may be fired to minimize political damage or resign to save the chief executive or the administration an embarrassing scandal so as not to exacerbate already discordant legislative relations. In either case, the ability to govern (and govern effectively) with greater partisan support should be positively related to survival.

It is also argued that public approval plays an important role in enhancing the political strength of a public official. If the public backs a politician who is linked to a scandal, the politician should have a reservoir of support to preclude removing that associate from his or her position. A move toward impeachment or expulsion would be unpopular for legislators, and it would similarly be unnecessary for a chief executive to step down if he or she enjoyed strong popular backing. Presidents under fire from scandal may maintain positive public support by being linked to popular initiatives or by successful public relations.[31] Approval and legislative strength may be connected, as Hinojosa and Perez-Linan note for presidents: "popular presidents are more capable of enduring accusations, while declining presidential approval typically provides a strong signal for legislators to defect from the president's camp."[32]

INTERPRETING THE FINDINGS

The analysis in table 2.1 presents the results of the models run with a Cox proportional hazard model as specified above.[33] In general, the data fit the models well. Plotting Cox-Snell residuals against Nelson-Aalen cumulative hazard function demonstrates substantial similarity, suggesting that the model fits the data.[34] In addition, the Harrell's C concordance statistic and the Somers' D statistic, which measures the agreement of predictions with observed failure, demonstrate high levels of correctly identified order of the survival times.[35] The coefficients in each table are exponentiated coefficients of the hazard ratio, meaning that these coefficients are an interpretation of the ratio of the hazard for a one-unit change in the corresponding covariate.[36] In essence, the models substantively explain the amount of time to "failure" based on the conditions outlined above: coefficients above 1.0 show a quicker negative end to a scandal; coefficients below 1.0 show a longer negative end to a scandal (akin to "surviving" scandal).

WHAT INCREASES THE RISK OF A SCANDAL'S ENDING BADLY?

The focus in this section is on explaining the factors that contribute to an elected official's survival of a scandal. Table 2.1 identifies five models of scandals, involving members of Congress, governors, presidents, and two reduced form ("combined") merged models with all three office types together. In none of models in table 2.1 are the political support variables statistically significant for cases involving state-level scandals.[37] There is a positive effect for the percentage of the governor's partisans in the Senate, but the hazard ratio is 1, meaning no positive or negative effect on survival. This suggests that governors' and their staffs' survival during scandal is not related to their institutional support or opposition.[38] Moreover, gubernatorial approval at the time the scandal breaks is not statistically significant (the period is truncated to 1993 to 2011 because of the availability of accurate polling data). The nature of the scandal seems to be of greater importance than the ability of the governor or the staff to count on loyal partisans for survival assistance. Since most of the cases of state-level executive scandals involve the governor him- or herself, and the governor is less likely to have a scandal end a political career, institutional and political issues may not play a major role in affecting the chance for survival.

In the models for governor and president, if the scandal affected the elected chief executive (governor or president), the individual was much more likely to survive the scandal. This is not surprising since administrations confronted with scandals frequently rally around their elected leader to protect their greatest political assets.[39] Party organizations and partisans often back their elected officials during scandal to insulate them from removal from office. House members (signaled by the "House" dummy

TABLE 2.1 Scandals duration models

	CONGRESS	GOVERNOR	PRESIDENT	COMBINED	COMBINED (POLARIZED)
ELECTED OFFICIAL	—	.088 ***(.034)	.246 ***(.094)	—	—
HOUSE MEMBER	4.19 ***(1.82)	—	—	—	—
DIVIDED	.825(.216)	.797(.158)	1.41(.415)	.793 **(.087)	.770 **(.009)
FINANCIAL SCANDAL	1.08(.260)	.889(.186)	1.56 *(.445)	1.04(.116)	1.03(.115)
PERSONAL SCANDAL	4.32 ***(1.01)	.913(.269)	—	1.31 **(.172)	1.29 **(.167)
REPUBLICAN	.813(.172)	.727 *(.146)	.389(.134)	.904(.098)	.944(.099)
APPROVAL	—	.989 (.007)	1.00 (.009)	—	—
FEMALE	1.85 *(.765)	1.41(.330)	.554(.207)	1.14(.186)	1.15(.183)
SENATE CO-PARTISANS	—	1.00 (.006)	.927 ** (.033)	—	—
SAME PARTY	1.17(.335)	—	—	—	—
1970S	5.83 ***(3.67)	—	.833(.393)	.798(.203)	—
1990S	1.21(.467)	.970(.399)	.316 **(.151)	.652 ***(.107)	—
2000S	.788(.259)	1.11(.433)	2.42 **(1.03)	.814(.125)	—
2010S	.805(.275)	1.54(.704)	2.10 *(1.00)	.743 *(.122)	—
POLARIZED ERA (1993–)	—	—	—	—	.770 **(.091)
N / FAILURES	232 / 94	255 / 190	190 / 103	855 / 390	855 / 390
LOG PSEUDO LIKELIHOOD	404.8	-481.3	-438.8	-2314	-2314
WALD X^2	350.5 ***	62.3 ***	48.5 **	16.1 **	14.0 **
HARRELL'S C	.729	.714	.692	.578	.560
SOMERS' D	.459	.429	.385	.157	.121

Note: Coefficients are exponentiated coefficients of the hazard ratio, clustered by scandal. Dependent variable: total time (in days) from when the scandal broke to when the scandal ended. Failure means the scandal ended in resignation, firing, or removal from office. The standard errors are robust standard errors, clustered by each scandal.

*** indicates statistical significance at $p < .01$.

** $p < .05$.

* $p < .10$. Robust standard errors in parentheses.

variable) are significantly more likely to have a scandal end badly than senators (400 percent more likely). Female incumbents are less likely (185 percent) to face risk of a scandal ending a political career than males; however, this is true only for members of Congress, not federal or state executive officials. This finding confirms what others have found about the double standard for women involved in political scandals, primarily in Congress.[40] The relatively few women involved in scandal in executive offices may partially explain these modest findings. In addition, select scandals, such as sex scandals, hurt women more, and these tend to be somewhat rare.

Turning to national chief executive scandals, table 2.1 identifies the results of specifications involving the president, the cabinet, the White House staff, or executive nominees. Similar to governors, presidents are substantially less likely to end a scandal with removal from office, resignation, indictment, or conviction than their staff or executive nominees. Clearly the White House seeks to protect the president, even at the expense of public accountability. The formal structure of the White House encourages those individuals who are damaging the administration to step aside. Such staff can be thought of as political "lightning rods," erected to draw the heat of blame away from more highly ranked administration members.[41] Indeed, embattled political advisers have historically been the first to depart from office in the aftermath of a scandal.[42]

The type of scandal also affects survival. Personal scandals are more likely (432 percent) to bring an end to a political career for the combined models and significantly for members of Congress. Financial scandals end careers for presidential officials but not necessarily for other institutions. The results show that both personal and financial scandals are likely to end to a political career, but personal scandals tend to do so more quickly. The hazard of the scandal's ending in "failure" is between one and a half and two and a half times greater for personal scandals. Although personal scandals (especially those involving personal indiscretions) may not be "career killers" as they once were, the results in table 2.1 demonstrate that scandals involving personal indiscretions shorten political careers.[43] The public clearly does distinguish among types of scandals.[44]

Partisanship matters too. Although there are no significant differences between Republicans and Democrats across the models, we do find a small statistical effect suggesting Republican governors survive more than Democratic governors (about 28 percent more likely). Surprisingly, the number of co-partisans in upper chambers (the institutional responsible for putative impeachment) and the presence of divided government have inconsistent effects. The presence of more co-partisans in a position to save officials has strong statistical effects on scandal survival only in the presidential models (about 8 percent).

When government control of the executive and legislative branches is split between the parties, federal executives hit with scandals are less likely to head for the political exits. Divided government has an unexpected positive effect on survival in the two merged models for related reasons: without clear consensus on a political course of action, as often occurs during divided government, attempts to impeach may fail. With divided government comes greater popularity of elected officials, able to blame the opposition party.[45] In divided government, everybody retreats to their corners and the messaging becomes "us versus them." That can lead to a political stalemate.

Investigations, hearings, and old-fashioned partisan barbs all intensify when executive officials face an opposition Congress.[46] The greater the partisan divide, the easier it is to survive scandal. The closer the partisan ties, the more likely an official will survive a political scandal.

With regard to the political and institutional mechanisms for surviving scandal, polled approval has no effect, but institutional factors have a larger effect.[47] The president's approval at the time before the scandal breaks, like that of governors in table 2.1, has no effect on the duration of a scandal. But when presidents have more co-partisan members of the House or Senate, they are 9 and 10 percent, respectively, less likely to have a scandal culminate in removal from office, resignation, indictment, or conviction. Conversely, putative opposition to the president has a positive effect on scandals ending in a politically challenging manner. When presidents face a greater percentage of opposition party members in Congress, a scandal is 10 percent more likely to end in removal from office, resignation, indictment, or conviction, and when government is divided, presidents are twice as likely to have scandals end in removal from office, resignation, indictment, or conviction. In short, political strength in the form of more partisan supporters leads to a greater probability of survival, while more opposition leads to a quick and negative end, consistent with expectations. This finding mirrors what scholars find in other presidential democracies.[48]

Executive officials were more likely to survive in earlier than later eras, confirming the findings from chapter 1. The findings in table 2.1 show that survival of federal executive officials was longer in the 1994–2001 period than in the later 2002–2015 period (there was no statistically significant effect for the period 1972–1980). Why the differences? First, scandals in the Obama White House were treated with medical efficiency: get the cancer out. Observers called his term in office "no drama Obama" for their desire to move quickly away from political scandals. Second, the frequency of scandals does not mean they all survived. Although a shocking number, a half dozen of President Trump's cabinet members did end up resigning under scrutiny. However, members of Congress in earlier years (1972–1980) were more at risk in the survival models in table 2.1 than members from later periods. The results all point in the same direction: members of Congress are more likely to survive scandals longer in the later periods than in the earlier periods.

Because of the growing partisan nature of modern politics, later era scandals should less frequently end political careers, as explained above. For the combined models, the 1990s and 2010s produced significant survival rates, confirming expectations that they would be more likely to survive in this polarized era. Figure 2.1 displays predicted survival (Kaplan-Meier) estimates for the pre-polarized (1972–1993) and post-polarized era (1993–2021) (results from the combined model in table 2.1). The graph shows that survival rates in the polarized era are slightly higher than those of the prior era (about 23 percent), providing support for the expectation of polarized politics leading to scandal survival.[49] For individual offices, the expectation is not uniformly supported across political positions, although there is a

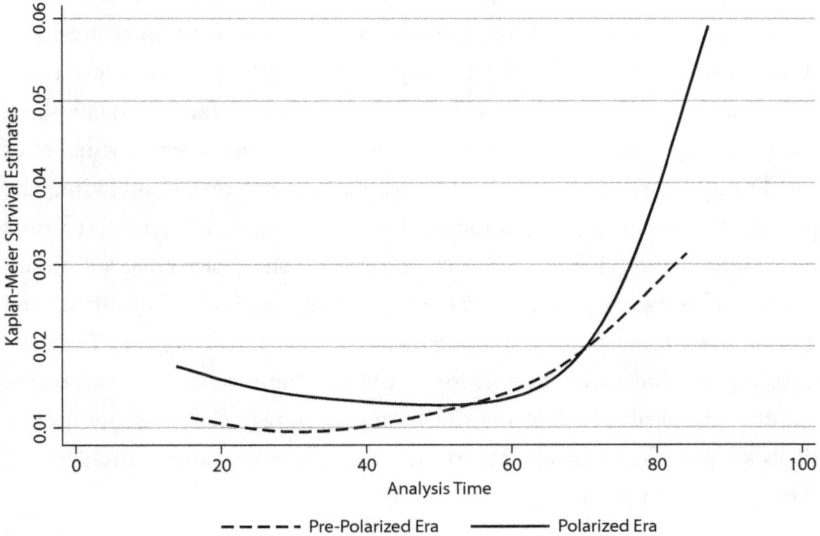

FIGURE 2.1 Predicted smoothed hazard estimates by era. Politicians survive scandals more in the polarized era.

Note: Kernel smoothed survival estimates, truncated at 100 days for clarity of presentation.

significant survival rate for federal executives, cabinet, and staff during the time around the Lewinsky scandal. In contrast, scandals in the Watergate era for members of Congress led to significant and large hazard rates, more than five times the rates of later eras (more than 500 percent).

In Table 2.1 there is no consistent statistically significant survival effect for time periods across individual office types. In particular, presidential scandals were more likely to be survived in the 1990s than in the 2000s and 2010s (technically compared to the 1980s as the comparison category). The Clinton administration weathered several scandals, most prominently the Monica Lewinsky affair that led to his impeachment but also including fallout from the Whitewater land deal, illegal foreign fundraising, the White House travel office controversy, and other allegations of sexual assault by multiple women. However, in the later period, President Trump,

Trump White House officials, and their staffs did not survive in office at rates greater than other White Houses past (although Trump as president did survive, as expected). This finding for the 2010s era contradicts assertions that scandals matter less than in prior eras. In fact, scandals seem more damaging to politicians. For instance, although several members of the Trump administration caught in scandal did not resign, including the president, others like Environmental Protection Agency head Scott Pruitt and Health and Human Services secretary Tom Price resigned rather quickly. However, collectively there is a strong survival effect during the Trump era, although not as strong as during the Lewinsky era. That the normally heighted survival rates for past White Houses (such as the Lewinsky era) was diminished during the Trump administration does not definitively support the assertion that the negative effects of scandals disappeared during the Trump era.

DISCUSSION

Not all politicians survive scandal; every year scandals fell politicians of every stripe. Indeed, "the mere whiff of a scandal once unraveled political careers with stunning speed. Not anymore."[50] But that conclusion is too harsh for the findings here. Some elected officials survive scandals even when conventional wisdom suggests these scandals might be career-ending. Indeed, demonstrating modest support for expectations, modern politicians generally survived scandals in office longer than earlier politicians. Later politicians, beginning in the aftermath of the Lewinsky scandal and continuing through the Trump era, collectively confronted hardened partisan preferences, and this modestly inoculated them against the negative effects of scandal. But for some politicians, stronger opposition armed with ammunition to hurt incumbents in more ways minimized the chances of survival. For instance, the political system appeared to "clean house" during the George W. Bush terms when White House officials (but not the president) resigned or were fired at higher rates following major scandals.

The findings here also demonstrate institutional differences in survival of scandal. Senators (as opposed to House members), governors, and presidents are all individually likely to survive scandals. Shorter electoral cycles and the emergence of strong candidates at the local level to run for the U.S. House amplify the negative effects of scandals on members of Congress. Senators, governors, and presidents face longer electoral horizons, possibly enabling the negative effects of scandals to deteriorate with time. Statewide and nationwide officials may also have substantial significant political support and a more sizable financial cushion to absorb political blows from opponents following scandals. Not surprisingly, the elected officials themselves (especially when the principals are governors or presidents) are the most likely to survive these scandals because of the protection provided by their political organizations and allies. This is especially true for incumbents in polarized times, who reason that the likelihood the truth will emerge (and be believed) is lower because partisan media attention shapes perception, so politicians may be more likely to prevaricate or stonewall.[51]

When controlling for time eras, neither divided government nor the number of co-partisans in the upper legislative chamber significantly affects the prospects of a political career post-scandal. For members of Congress, divided government could lead to more investigations into wrongdoing related to scandal, which often leads to more resignations.[52] For governors and presidents (and their administrations), divided government may be a signal of opposition party desire to use scandals as a weapon against out-partisan incumbents. Yet polarized politics seems to have generally changed these expected dynamics. Decisions about resignations (or terminations for staff) are somewhat independent of the structural, institutional elements of the system. Over time, partisanship has hardened the resolve of politicians to stay in office because of the near impossibility of removal as a political outcome or a political boost from fighting charges with partisan return fire.

CASE STUDIES

The case studies presented here investigate three sets of political institutions and individuals caught in scandals to illustrate how recent partisan trends shape the survival of politicians snared in career-altering controversies. The core claim is that modern politicians are hurt less by scandals than were politicians of earlier ears. These cases show that earlier copartisan politicians broke rank and made scandals matter by holding elected officials accountable for questionable behavior, or the elected official resigned because of the controversy. Later politicians, in the partisan era, hold on for longer, getting support from fellow partisans to survive, using tricks and tactics to keep their positions longer. These case studies illustrate these dynamics.

CONGRESS: HOUSE BANKING SCANDAL

The most embarrassing scandal to engulf the U.S. House involved a little-known perk of House members: the House Bank. The scandal, which touched more members—one in four—than any ethics controversy in history, involved the 150-year-old institution that had, in the past, seen rapscallions make off with huge sums of money. In 1889 one cashier bolted with his mistress to Canada after cramming more than fifty thousand dollars into a satchel, never to be heard from again. The whole enterprise was a scandal waiting to happen.[53] The House Bank was not like an ordinary bank. It operated under loose rules, using a pencil-and-ledger system, and the bank manager did not provide regular statements to House members who used the bank. Between 1988 and 1992, dozens of House members abused the perk by taking advantage of generous overdraft policies totaling about twenty thousand bad checks, some in the six-figure range. Some members blamed the bank for not posting deposits in a timely manner, sometimes weeks after withdrawals or deposits. Others took advances on their salaries they would pay back later (or not). The scandal, sometimes called Rubbergate because of "how high the checks bounced," is misleading—the real scandal was that the House Bank provided overdraft protection to the members, so there were technically no bounced checks, figuratively or otherwise.

Twelve-term Democratic Speaker of the House Tom Foley, with a statesmanlike demeanor fitting his twenty-four years of legislative experience, found out about the bank's difficulties in late 1989. The General Accounting Office (GAO) discovered that the House sergeant-at-arms, Jack Russ, was bouncing personal checks at the bank—$104,825 worth over several years. Further investigation found that several House members were doing the same: 257 individuals wrote more than six hundred bad checks totaling $462,000 between February 1988 and November 1989. GAO found that in one twelve-day period, an average of thirty checks totaled almost twenty thousand dollars in insufficient funds.[54]

The scandal blew up quickly after the GAO disclosed on September 18, 1991, that there had been a total of 8,331 bad checks passed. Foley worked to defuse the situation and contain the political damage. He said he was "gravely disappointed" that Russ had not corrected the bank's shortcomings and was "very unhappy" with Russ, "but again, my focus was less on firing people than on finding a way to correct the situation."[55] Internally the members debated whether to reveal the names, considering the banking practices had been sloppy. Under a complex standard, the panel planned to publicly single out members who had been substantially overdrawn in at least 20 percent of the months in which they had an account and whose shortfall exceeded the member's net monthly salary. Dissenting members of the committee argued the standard was too lenient because it overlooked some egregious abuses. The standard was arbitrary, the members admitted. "Reasonable people can differ," said Democratic House member Matthew McHugh, who was acting chair of the committee investigating the overdrafts, "and we cannot say that they're wrong and we're right." The Speaker urged support for the panel's disclosure.[56]

Then all hell broke loose. Republican minority whip Newt Gingrich, along with seven freshmen Republicans referred to as the Gang of Seven, publicized the scandal, hoping it would hurt Democrats politically. One member, Republican Jim Nussle, found national fame when he made a speech from the well of the House with a paper bag with holes cut for eyes and mouth over his head to protest the "shameful" ethical behavior of members. Taking the bag off his head, Nussle said it was time to take the "mask" off the institution. "It's time to bring honor back to this institution," he added.[57] But high-ranking Democrats also agreed, including two top deputies to the Speaker, majority leader Richard A. Gephardt of Missouri and whip David E. Bonior of Michigan.

The leadership acceded to their demands, moving toward disclosure despite the damage to their party and members. The House passed two resolutions on March 12, 1992 to publish the names of the worst abusers. That same day, the House ethics committee announced that 355 current and former House members had written at least one overdraft at a bank during a thirty-nine-month period. Same "abusers" had chronic overdrafts amounting to thousands of dollars. Most of the worst violators were Democrats, but of the twenty-four top offenders, four were Republicans. Some, like Robert Mrazek of New York, used House Bank checks in business deals. Another, like Harold Ford of Tennessee, financed his reelection effort, lending his campaign a total of forty thousand dollars, with one check leading to an overdraft.[58] Republicans worked with nonaffected Democrats to vote to fully disclose the names of all of those involved and to allow a special counsel appointed by Attorney General William P. Barr to subpoena House Bank records.[59] The House sergeant-at-arms, after a renewed public uproar, resigned. The politics would play out in the 1992 and 1994 elections.

The House voted October 3, 1992 to close the bank, but retribution was swift for most of those involved. In the midst of stalemates in government, soaring deficits, and an economic recession, the public was pissed. Seventy-seven House members resigned or were ousted in the 1992 elections. Only six of the seventeen sitting members accused by the ethics committee of having "abused their banking privileges" were reelected.[60] Scholars found that the more overdrafts a member had, the more likely they were to be defeated or retire; the scandal reduced the vote for House incumbents by about 5 percent across the board.[61] Four ex-members and one delegate were convicted of illegal wrongdoing. Republican Buz

Lukens was convicted on bribery and conspiracy charges; Democrat Carl C. Perkins pled guilty to multiple charges, including a check kiting scheme. Former Democratic member Carroll Hubbard pled guilty to three felonies. Democratic representative Matthew McHugh, who steered the Ethics Committee investigation through the most difficult period, stunned his colleagues by announcing he would retire from Congress. He had entered Congress in 1974 with seventy-four other Democrats with a public mandate for reform in the aftermath of Watergate. "The banshees and monkeys are staying, and the sequoias are falling," said Democratic Wisconsin representative David Obey.[62]

Conclusions: In the House banking affair, the scandal had an impact on the longevity of those involved, signaling how in the pre-partisan era, scandals had serious electoral consequences.

CONGRESS: MATT GAETZ

Matt Gaetz was a scion of Florida politics and a political disruptor. His father was the former president of the Florida state senate. He had the backing of former Florida governor Jeb Bush in his early political career. Elected to Congress in 2016, he quickly became one of Donald Trump's most outspoken advocates. To the political left, he "embraced the role of villain," increasing his national profile and serving as one of President Trump's enablers, often with theatrical flair: according to the *New York Times*, "he wore a gas mask on the House floor last year in the early days of the [Covid-19] pandemic, insisting he was demonstrating concern for public safety amid accusations he was mocking the seriousness of the spread of the coronavirus."[63] He invited a right-wing Holocaust denier to the State of the Union in 2018 and attended an event in 2020 where members of the Proud Boys (a white supremacist group) provided security. He was also an organizer among lawmakers to challenge President-elect Biden's victory during the certification of the Electoral College votes on January 6. According to *Politico*, the "smart money was that he was angling for a job in the Trump administration or a permanent gig on Fox News."[64]

The federal investigation into Matt Gaetz began—like many scandals—by accident. In late January 2020, U.S. Secret Service agents received a tip that Representative Gaetz had accompanied a Florida county tax official (whom they were already investigating for identity theft and stalking) on an unusual nighttime visit to a local branch of a tax collection agency. Joel Greenberg was a tax collector in Seminole County. Grainy surveillance footage captured Greenberg with another man making IDs that night. Greenberg forgot to set the alarm when he left, triggering an investigation that led them to Gaetz.[65] Greenberg was already under a thirty-three-count federal indictment with a diverse list of crimes ranging from wire fraud to making fake IDs to sex trafficking. He pled guilty in 2020 and was sent to jail for violating the terms of his bail.

Greenberg and Gaetz were close. Both were rising stars in Florida's Republican Party in 2016—but the association did not end there. The Justice Department's investigators believe Greenberg met women online and enticed them to go on dates in exchange for gifts, dining, and travel.[66] The DOJ investigation in the closing months of the Trump administration into Congressman Gaetz examined whether he had sex with a seventeen-year-old girl and whether she received anything of value in exchange. One sex trafficking count against Greenberg involved the same girl. A variety of federal statutes make it illegal to lure someone under the age of eighteen to travel across state lines to engage in sex for something of value. Gaetz allegedly also asked other women to find friends who might be interested in having sex with him and his friends, offering to pay for hotels and meals, according to the *New York Times*.[67] Reports indicated that receipts from Apple Pay and a mobile cash app revealed payments from Gaetz to Greenberg and then to a woman who said this payment was for sex with Gaetz and Greenberg.[68]

Gaetz played offense, claiming he and his father were the targets of a bizarre extortion plot by two men—including a former Department of Justice official—trying to secure funding for a separate venture: "I have a suspicion that someone is trying to recategorize my generosity to ex-girlfriends as something more untoward."[69] Days later, the bipartisan House Ethics Committee announced it was opening a similar probe about

Gaetz's travel to the Bahamas with women and allegations he showed other House members nude photos of young women and used illegal drugs.[70] He again called the allegations a "smear" in fundraising appeals sent out after the allegations became public. "I may be a canceled man in some corners, I may even be a wanted man by the deep state. But I hear the millions of Americans who feel forgotten, canceled, marginalized and targeted," Gaetz told a crowd at Trump Doral resort: "They're not really coming for me, they're coming for you. I'm just in the way."[71]

Gaetz initially considered retirement, telling close friends he was not running for reelection and would take a job at the conservative news outlet Newsmax.[72] But he quickly pivoted to attack, saying in an op-ed that he "absolutely" would not step down from Congress and blamed the allegations on the "deep state" and "fake news" media. Republican leadership in Congress was coy about yanking Gaetz's committee assignments or any other rebuke. Few Republicans called on him to resign, but even fewer rushed to his defense. Even Congresswoman Liz Cheney, a Gaetz target who saw the Florida congressman fly into her Wyoming district to troll her at a campaign rally, was mum. The highest-ranking Republican woman called the allegations "sickening" but refused to comment beyond that.[73] Moderates in the party came under increasing pressure to distance themselves from Gaetz, and at least two members returning donations they had received from the Florida Republican.[74] In the wake of the lengthening scandal, he brought in more than a million dollars, a reflection of how controversy pays for inflammatory lawmakers. "Outrage equals visibility," in a way that it would not have before social media.[75] The allegations did not stop voters either—he won an overwhelming victory in the 2022 elections even though his GOP primary opponents ran ads about the allegations.[76]

He survived. In February 2023 the federal prosecutors announced they would not be filing charges against Congressman Gaetz in the long-running sex trafficking probe, clearing a dark cloud that had been hanging over his career. His stock actually rose in Congress. He kept his high-profile spot on the Judiciary Committee and scored a spot on a subcommittee, led by conservative Republican Jim Jordan, that investigated some of the GOP's favorite targets: the FBI, the Justice Department, and the intelligence community. He was also the ringleader of an insurgent group of Republicans that brought down his party's Speaker, Kevin McCarthy in 2023, sewing chaos in the Republican Party's new majority. Even his exit from Congress in 2024 was fortuitous: he was nominated by president-elect Donald Trump to be attorney general in the second Trump administration. Many of the controversies described here caught the intense spotlight and he withdrew his nomination, but it had come at a welcome moment. The House Ethics Committee's full report about separate allegations of sexual misconduct, illicit drug use, accepting improper gifts, and doling out favors was quashed because he was no longer a member of the body, and a forty-two-page report was released indicating that Gaetz "violated House Rules and other standards of conduct prohibiting prostitution, statutory rape, illicit drug use, impermissible gifts, special favors or privileges, and obstruction of Congress."[77] In his defense, he denied all charges, tweeted that the investigators "hated him," and responded that "my 30's were an era of working very hard—and playing hard too. It's embarrassing, though not criminal, that I probably partied, womanized, drank and smoked more than I should have earlier in life. I live a different life now." He had dodged a bullet. In 2025 he started a new job as the host of his own political talk show on One America Network and hinted at a run for Senate or governor in Florida in 2026.

Conclusions: Gaetz survived his scandals. Although the scandal crippled his ability to continue to serve in Congress, he survived longer than expected and maintained a prominent position alongside the elite voices of the Republican Party (joining the right-leaning One America News as a pundit in 2025).

GOVERNORS: EVAN MECHAM

Evan Mecham was no stranger to controversy. He was elected governor in 1986 and started his term in January 1987. By the time his brief term as Arizona's chief executive ended in April 1988, he was the first and only U.S. governor to simultaneously face removal from office through impeachment (the first and only governor of Arizona to be impeached), a scheduled recall election, and a felony indictment—all within nine months of his election to office.[78] The new Republican governor charged that his political enemies caused his downfall, but they had a lot of fodder. Mecham was popular among conservative groups in Arizona. A World War II hero, he was shot down over Europe in March 1945 and spent twenty-two days as a prisoner of war.[79] But he made enemies; some called him "a veritable faux pas factory sporting a constant smirk and a vindictive manner."[80] Although he had run for governor four times previously, the influx of new voters to Arizona meant that most voters did not know his history—many new him only from his Pontiac dealership's TV commercials. He was elected with only 40 percent of the vote in a three-way race. Controversy erupted almost immediately.

He began feuding with other elected officials and the media from the start. Republicans held the statehouse for the first time in twelve years, but Mecham would not play ball. He wrote letters to Republican precinct committee chairs asking them to ignore their Republican representatives and to follow his lead on budget negotiations. A statewide business coalition joined moderate Republicans in opposing the governor's cuts to public education. In July 1987 eleven House Republicans, in the first major break in the GOP, held a press conferences denouncing the governor's actions.[81]

He rescinded an executive order by his predecessor declaring Dr. Martin Luther King Jr.'s birthday a state holiday, arguing the creation of the holiday had been illegal. He separately suggested that working women were the leading cause of divorce and referred to an African American child as a "pickaninny," a term most took as a racial slur. The episode landed him as a reoccurring stylized character in the political comic strip *Doonesbury:* "'It's ludicrous! I'm a Mormon! Tolerance is a basic tenet of my faith,' the strip shows Mecham as saying. The next panel has Mecham proclaiming the charges are 'lies spread by queers and pickaninnies.'"[82] The governor threated to sue any newspaper that ran the comic. He asked for a list of state employees who were gay and accused a political enemy (he suspected the state's attorney general) of using a laser to spy on him—an effort the governor thwarted with a Coke can transistor radio. After Mecham returned from a trade mission to Asia, he told a luncheon meeting that when his Asian hosts heard about all the golf courses in Arizona "their eyes got big and round."[83] The collective effect was a boycott of Arizona by tourists, business (led by Coretta Scott King), and prominent musicians. At the height of their popularity, the band U2 announced they would donate funds from their recent shows in Arizona to the Mecham impeachment fund.[84] The National Basketball Association moved their winter meetings out of Phoenix in protest. Republican state representative Jane Hull put it directly: "This state has had enough. It's just getting too damaging."[85]

The reaction from Arizona's political establishment was swift. Weeks after the boycott, more than three hundred thousand signatures were certified on a petition for an election to recall him from office (set for May 17)—an effort the governor said would fail because the organizer, Ed Buck, was gay. Mecham (the real one, not the Doonesbury character) doubled down, arguing that his enemies were led by a "band of homosexuals and dissident Democrats."[86] A former Republican congressman agreed to run against Mecham in the recall.[87] Polling indicated that more than 50 percent thought Mecham should be recalled.[88]

The legislature was even quicker. A group of thirteen Republican state legislators, dubbed the "Dirty Dozen" by local media, met and issued a joint statement critical of the governor. The Speaker of the Arizona House of Representatives appointed a special counsel to investigate three charges: that he had failed to report a $350,000 loan to his election campaign from a local real estate developer, that he had loaned himself $80,000 in public funds to help his auto dealership, and that he had instructed the head of the Arizona Department of Public Safety not to provide information on an incident alleging that one of his appointees made a death threat to a government official.[89] Calls for the governor to resign came from prominent Republicans, including former U.S. senator Barry Goldwater, Congressman Jon Kyl, and U.S. Senator John McCain—to no avail. The investigation coincided with a grand jury investigating Mecham and his brother (and campaign finance manager). On January 8, 1988, the governor was indicted by a state grand jury on six felony charges of fraud, perjury, and filing false documents connected to his charged concealment of a $350,000 campaign loan. The prim and polished governor shot back that these were funds from his inaugural ball and insisted that "it was his to spend as he saw fit" aside from political purposes.[90] On January 15, 1988, the special counsel report concluded that the charges against the governor merited impeachment. On February 5, an emotional house of representatives voted forty-six to fourteen to proceed on impeachment charges.

A rift formed early between Arizona Republicans and the governor, spreading then to questionable political appointments and cronyism. The senate trial started on February 29, just as the governor was running out of allies. The governor again refused to resign, saying he had done nothing wrong and was "the victim of a conspiracy by the attorney general, the media, selected members of the House, and the Department of Public Safety." His defense was filled with contradicting testimony from him about key details and focused on the personal lives and sexual habits of the prosecution witnesses.[91] The governor vowed that if he was returned to office, he would fire the director of public safety and others who were witnesses against him. State senator Jan Brewer, a Republican from Mecham's hometown of Glendale, said she was deeply troubled by the actions of his administration, which she called "shameful, embarrassing and disappointing." The Republicans worried about reprisals from voters, but "they did muster the courage to venture into the street at Arizona's 'high noon.'"[92]

After a quick twenty-five-day trial and an hour and a half of deliberation, the senate decisively ousted him from office on April 4. The impeachment vote found him guilty of two charges, obstruction of justice and trying to conceal a campaign loan, making him the first U.S. governor to be convicted in an impeachment trial in almost sixty years.[93] Mecham's attorney, who was fired from his Washington law firm after he took the case, said "the defense put on a hell of a case, a convincing case. I think it was a political decision. Let's face it, he's a plurality governor. That's the seed for political disaster."[94] In a self-published 1988 book, *Impeachment: The Arizona Conspiracy* (and a follow-up book, *Wrongful Impeachment*, in 1999), the governor fumed that the real reason he was impeached and convicted was "pure and simple raw political power exercised by those groups who wanted to remain in control" and that he was a victim of a widespread conspiracy.[95] Although the scandal removed him from office, in a later criminal trial, he was acquitted of all charges.

Conclusions: With behavior so outrageous that even his fellow partisans abandoned him, Governor Mecham's scandals ended his political career. Seventy days after scandalous allegations were revealed in the special counsel's report, the governor was history. In this pre-partisan moment, the scandals the governor confronted contributed to an end to his political career.

GOVERNORS: ANDREW CUOMO

Andrew Cuomo almost broke the curse. Governors of New York rarely got third terms, but it was looking as though the fifty-sixth governor of the Empire State would cruise to a third term in Albany. And why not? After all he was the son of a famous warhorse governor (Mario Cuomo), flush with campaign cash, and besting every other opponent in the polls. But a Covid scandal and multiple sexual harassment allegations derailed that hope for the hardball politician many considered a bully. No amount of favor-pulling or threats could save his political life. "A lot of people in New York state have received those phone calls," remembered the New York City Mayor Bill de Blasio. "The bullying is nothing new."[96] For a governor who had won reelection three times, was a prodigious fundraiser, and was heir to a New York political dynasty, surviving multiple controversies at once became a challenge. Hailed as "America's Governor" for his transparent and fact-based handling of the Covid crisis, Andrew Cuomo ended up fighting for his political life.[97]

Twin controversies pinned the Cuomo administration starting in the spring of 2021. In February of that year, he faced allegations that his staff had covered up the scope of Covid death tolls in New York's nursing homes. Top aides admitted they withheld data because the Democratic administration feared an investigation by the Republican-led Trump Justice Department.[98] The irony was that the governor was positioned as a national leader on the state's Covid response, appearing daily on television with a carefully cultivated public image as a competent chief executive.

The governor even published a memoir about his handling of the pandemic, offering "leadership lessons" to other leaders (the memoir was also eventually investigated over alleged illegal use of state resources such as staff assistance). The state's attorney general, Leticia James, published a damning report documenting the scale and scope of the misreporting.

The governor and top aides pushed back. They tried to blame President Trump and political partisanship, saying they were committed to facts and suggesting, after additional data were released, that the statistics were beside the point. "We're below the national average in number of deaths in nursing homes, but who cares?" Governor Cuomo said after the story broke, arguing that the percentages were unimportant. "Died in a hospital, died in a nursing home? They died." But even allies were worried. The revelations were a "betrayal of the public trust," according to Democratic state senator Andrew Gounardes, who called for full accountability for what happened and a trimming of emergency powers given to the governor. The FBI and federal prosecutors in Brooklyn opened an investigation.[99] The report forced the administration to add 3,800 previously unreported deaths of residents who had died outside of a facility (like in a hospital) to the official tally, which was already large. His polling numbers dropped from 56 percent approval to 51 percent—not fatal, but falling. However, the misreporting of nursing home deaths was just the start of Cuomo's downfall.

Then the bombshell: a former aide to the governor accused him of kissing her without her consent and making inappropriate remarks while she worked in his office. The woman, Lindsey Boylan, claimed Cuomo suggested the two of them "play strip poker" on a flight in October 2017. Cuomo, Boylan alleged, "would go out of his way to touch me on my lower back, arms and legs," with the final straw coming in 2018 when she allegedly he kissed her.[100] The governor and his office, including the adviser, press secretary, deputy press secretary, and Empire State Development CEO who were on the flight, denied the charges. Then another allegation: a second aide, Charlotte Bennett, accused him of sexual harassment, saying Cuomo had asked her uncomfortable questions about her sex life, whether she was monogamous in her relationships, and if she ever had sex with older men. Again the governor denied the charges, saying he had "never made advances toward Ms. Bennett, nor did I ever intend to act in any way that was inappropriate." The governor requested an independent review of the matter and asked that "New Yorkers await the findings before making any judgments."[101]

Following these two blockbuster allegations, many more emerged: between February 24, 2021, and March 8, 2021, five women, including four former aides, accused Cuomo of sexual harassment, uncomfortable romantic overtures, or inappropriate questions about their sex lives. Eventually eleven women would make similar complaints against the governor. The governor apologized on March 3 for "making the women feel uncomfortable," claiming it was unintentional.[102]

Calls for resignation came quickly, but Cuomo, insisting he would stay put and run for reelection in 2022, was unphased. Only ten state legislators (out of forty-seven) called for his resignation, and important New York politicians such as Democratic senators Chuck Schumer and Kirsten Gillibrand did not immediately follow suit (they eventually did after the charges continued to mount). Most New Yorkers actually did not want him to go anyway. According to a Quinnipiac University poll from March 2–3, although 40 percent of voters thought Cuomo should resign, 55 percent of registered voters did not. In another poll that generally favored resignation, 23 percent were not sure. The public pressure for him to resign was not overwhelming.[103] "I'm not going to resign, I was not elected by the politicians, I was elected by the people," said Cuomo at a news conference on March 12.[104]

The governor had allies, and his record, especially on Democratic core issues, was strong. Even his detractors conceded that the governor's "heavy-handed approach has often been effective in delivering concrete liberal accomplishments, including legalizing same-sex marriage, raising the minimum wage and enacting criminal justice reforms."[105] The governor's commanding wins, defenders said, made his policy successes well known. Even if they did not like his management style, they liked the results. He faced primary challengers—about one third of New Your Democrats were "solidly anti-Cuomo"—but he had won more than 60 percent in his past two races thanks to his strength among nonwhite voters.[106] In polling after the scandals emerged, 62 percent of New York voters said "a COVID-19 vaccination plan is more important than an investigation into either one of the scandals," and voters still approved, 56 to 41 percent, of Cuomo's handling of the pandemic.[107] One veteran New York consultant noted that the nature of New York politics is tough. "Has he raised his voice on calls with me? I'm sure he has," Mr. Sunshine said. "Have I done it sometimes? Sure. And by the way, we're from a place called New York. It's not for the timid."[108]

Cuomo refused to resign. In July he sat for thirteen hours in a Manhattan office building for a monthlong investigation including interviews with 179 people and more than 74,000 documents. The governor questioned the accuracy of the report: "the facts are much different than what has been portrayed."[109] "The attorney general's report was designed to be a political firecracker on an explosive topic, and it worked," Cuomo said. "There was a political and media stampede. But the truth will out in time—of that, I am confident."[110] In a video recorded in the governor's mansion, he was adamant he would not resign from his post, despite a damning independent investigation from the attorney general that found he had sexually harassed multiple women in violation of federal and state law, personally engaging in "unwelcome and nonconsensual touching, and making numerous offensive comments of a suggestive and sexual nature that created a hostile work environment for women." Following the charges being made public, Cuomo and his staff retaliated against at least one former employee for coming forward and fostered a "toxic" workplace environment.[111]

But the report changed the game. Cuomo reversed course and said he would formally step down from his office. What happened? Public opinion turned against him: between 60 and 70 percent of New Yorkers thought he should resign—no backroom deal to stay through his term but not seek reelection.[112] Important donors began to withhold funds. Other donors went into "wait-and-see" mode as they anticipated further retribution.[113] ActBlue, the Democratic small-dollar fundraising platform, removed Cuomo from its donation page.[114] New York politicians began to rebel against the governor. Mayor Bill De Blasio, one of the most vocal politicians calling for Cuomo's ouster in late April, traded online shots with the governor about Covid restrictions. The feud was over the mayor's announcement that he hoped to loosen most if not all Covid-19 restrictions by July 1. The governor implied that the mayor was wrong, to which City Hall press secretary Bill Neidhardt responded: "Serial sexual assaulter says what?"[115] The governor was increasingly politically lonely, isolated with just a few defenders and his lawyers. Lawmakers began impeachment proceedings against him, eyeing a September hearing. Nearly two thirds of the lower chamber (responsible for impeachment) said they favored impeachment if the governor did not resign.

He resigned on August 24, two hundred days after the nursing home scandal broke. The governor "well, just doesn't get it," wrote CNN's Chris Cillizza. "Cuomo is not the victim here. Nothing is being done *to* him. Instead, his actions as outlined in the James report are having consequences—pure and simple."[116] Most of what the governor was doing was buying time. His best chance for political survival was to drag out the process for as long as possible, hoping it would be overtaken by another scandal or he could mount an increasing defense. Cuomo's "Trump" strategy was fitting for a new breed of politician surviving scandal. John Harris wrote in *Politico*: "In that generation, the choice was to either resign or throw oneself on the mercy of the court of public opinion. In this generation, Trump and other politicians have shown there is another choice: Contemptuously challenge the legitimacy of any court that would presume to judge you, and take advantage of the reality that there is no elite consensus that transcends partisan and ideological divides on any subject."[117]

Conclusions: Consistent with the findings of this book, Governor Cuomo's scandals still mattered in the partisan era, but the partisan support he received from his base and his use of a deflection playbook to attempt to wiggle out of controversy allowed him to survive longer, even if eventually the scandals shortened his career. He came in second in the Democratic primary to be elected mayor of New York City in 2025.

PRESIDENTS: JIMMY CARTER AND BERT LANCE

In the shadow of Watergate, Jimmy Carter from humble Plains, Georgia promised a fresh approach. His tone was direct, colloquial, and engaging, if sometimes flat. A government as good as its people, he promised.[118] Other promises were even harder to keep: "There are a lot of things I would not do to be elected. I wouldn't tell a lie. I wouldn't make a misleading statement. I wouldn't betray a trust," said the Georgia governor.[119] In post-Watergate America, as president he signed and implemented the Ethics in Government Act, which instituted financial disclosure rules and lobbying restrictions on government officials. He famously put his family's peanut farm—significantly in debt at the time—into a blind trust while in office.

But scandals catch up to all presidents. In 1977 President Carter's longtime confidant and tennis-playing ally Bert Lance, serving as the director of the president's Office of Management and Budget, was accused of several financial infractions stemming from his tenure as the director of two banks in Georgia, alleged improprieties in Carter's campaign for governor in 1974, and problems with his government financial disclosures. Lance ran his Calhoun Bank like a personal piggy bank. He offered below market loans and overdraft privileges to friends and relatives—a common practice in rural America but hard to explain in the context of a presidential administration that was supposed to be clean as a whistle. Many of these "cozy Georgia relationships looked sketchy under the microscope of federal regulation," according to a Carter biographer.[120] He made friends on Capitol Hill and maintained his close relationship with the president, but his old banking practices caught up with him.

These were past failures of judgment, thought the president, and the White House did not fear that any significant harm would come to them politically if they were truthful. President Carter immediately asked for an investigation by the comptroller's office in the White House, which determined that Bert Lance had not broken the law but had engaged in some questionable practices. The president publicly vindicated his OMB director despite bowing to the initial pressure to fire him. Given his perception that the comptroller's report vindicated Lance, the president released it and publicly stood by his friend. The administration's reading of the report as vindicating Lance—although it had not totally—led the president to remark "Bert, I'm proud of you" on August 18. But the maelstrom did not stop. Carter estimated that two thirds of the questions at his news conference a week later were "still devoted to the Bert Lance affair."[121]

The president did not lie or stonewall—he told the truth by ordering an investigation and releasing the results. In fact, he took much of the blame, telling reporters he was the one who forced Lance to promise to stay and fight. Throughout the affair, President Carter emphasized openness with the media, Congress, and the public and withheld firing Lance until he could testify in front of the Senate Government Affairs Committee, noting that "an honest man could explain his own position."[122] It did not go well. Lance testified for twenty-four hours over two days, asking the committee at one point "is it part of our American system that a man can be drummed out of government by a series of false charges, half truths, and misrepresentations, innuendos, and the like?"[123] Many senators, including Tom Eagleton, spoke in favor of his party's administration, saying the scandal mixed rumor and facts to "create guilt by accumulation." But more hearings ahead meant continued political trouble for the young administration.

On September 21, 1977, Carter finally (reluctantly) accepted Lance's resignation less than a year after the scandal broke. The two had talked it over during a tennis match the day before, and Carter's advice was to resign while "his name had been cleared."[124] The president's actions resulted in modest political damage to his administration—his approval ratings remained high but eroded quickly—but they had set the ethical bar too high. Vice President Mondale noted that the media were gunning for a president who "seemed so inordinately pure that people were waiting for a way to take the luster off." Indeed, the media pounced. William Safire, a former Nixon speechwriter, led the charge, sniffing out problems with a "sweetheart loan" of $3.4 million from the First National Bank of Chicago and reversals at a second bank Lance controlled, the Atlanta-based

National Bank of Georgia. Safire would win the Pulitzer Prize for his coverage.

The White House learned its lesson—the scrutiny was too much to bear in an administration with a squeaky-clean image. Senior staff lamented they had not cut ties to Lance earlier when it was clear he was "dead" politically. The media, including William Safire, conceded that "Lancegate was no Watergate," but the allegations led to three months of bad headlines, displayed a dithering management style, and jeopardized the impeccable ethics the president hoped to promote.[125] The next year, Peter Bourne, President Carter's "drug czar," resigned within forty-eight hours when he was caught writing a prescription for Quaaludes to a staffer (under the guise of giving the prescription to a White House colleague). Lance would eventually face eight federal investigations into his banking practices, going to trial in Georgia in 1980. He was acquitted on all charges. Lance even became friendly with Safire, his chief protagonist.

Conclusions: Indicative of earlier political scandals, the Lance affair demonstrated the White House's willingness to work within the political system to decipher any wrongdoing. That process took a while—and did not work in the accused's favor—but the system worked in a frictionless manner to address the issue and return to normal away from the White House's crisis footing. In short, the scandal mattered.

PRESIDENTS: DONALD TRUMP AND SCANDAL CABINET

Donald Trump entered the presidential race at a different period in American political history than Jimmy Carter. A reality TV star for decades, and in frequent legal trouble after leaving the White House—the first president with criminal indictments post-presidency—"Trump is turning his court cases into a political reality show."[126] He had an auspicious start to his 2016 campaign, declaring the American Dream dead and directing his wrath at the nation's southern neighbor Mexico, which he accused of "bringing their worst people to America, including criminals and rapists" and promising to make them pay for a wall along the southern border.

After a video emerged in the final weeks of the campaign of him boasting of grabbing women by the genitals, Trump apologized "if anyone was offended" and chalked the episode up to "locker room talk." He refused calls by fellow Republicans to leave the presidential ticket.[127]

Ryan Zinke—a former Navy SEAL and the first Montanan in a presidential cabinet role—was sworn in on January 31, 2017 by Vice President Mike Pence and rode a U.S. Park Police horse named Tonto the few blocks from the Capitol to the Department of the Interior's main building for his official welcoming ceremony. Controversy erupted months later as Zinke was accused of using his position for personal gain. In total there would be fifteen investigations or inquiries into "a real estate deal involving a company that Interior regulates; whether he bent government rules to allow his wife to ride in government vehicles; and allowing a security detail to travel with him on a vacation to Turkey at considerable taxpayer cost."[128] Zinke boasted in public he would fight the charges and continued to attack his critics.

The trouble started in the fall of 2017. On September 28 it was reported that in June Zinke had chartered several private jets or military aircraft for himself and aides to fly to a speech in Las Vegas and to events in his hometown, as well as private flights to two Caribbean islands, at a total cost of more than $12,000.[129] Later military flights flew Zinke and his wife to Norway.[130] The secretary also booked more than $14,000 in government helicopter flights to events around Washington, DC.[131] The office of inspector general opened investigations into these flights, specifically probing if the meeting in Las Vegas for a tête-à-tête with the NHL Vegas Golden Knights owners was a violation of the Hatch Act. Zinke also came under fire for the department's spending too much to upgrade three sets of double doors. The Interior Department later opened a probe into whether a land deal the director struck with the chairman of oil services giant Halliburton in Zinke's hometown in Montana constituted a conflict of interest. The documentation was clear—the inspector general had receipts.

Zinke resigned on December 15, 2018, more than a year and four months after the scandals first broke. In a private resignation letter, Zinke blamed "vicious and politically motivated attacks"; he wrote that he was resigning because he could not "justify spending thousands of dollars defending myself and my family against false allegations" but was proud of his record and achievements.[132] President Trump suggested that he was too, tweeting "Ryan has accomplished much during his tenure. I want to thank him for his service to our nation." But privately the White House had been trying to push him to resign for weeks, indicating he had until the end of the year to leave or be fired. Yet Zinke held on for months longer. With an average of one federal investigation per month and aggressive efforts to advance oil and gas drilling on and near public land, Zinke made few friends. The Natural Resources Defense Council quipped in a press release that Zinke should not "let the $139,000 door hit [him] on the way out." Gene Karpinski, president of the League of Conservation Voters, called Zinke "the most scandal-plagued interior secretary in recent memory."[133]

After he left the Interior Department, the agency's inspector general found he and his chief of staff knowingly made false statements to investigators while in office.[134] The false statements came in an agency decision to block a request by two Native American tribes to open a casino in Connecticut. True to form, scandals matter less in the modern era. Zinke won his old House seat back in 2022. In the end, Zinke was the fourth member of Trump's cabinet to resign under an ethics cloud in the Trump administration's first two years. Health and Human Services secretary Tom Price, Veterans Affairs secretary David Shulkin, and Environmental Protection Agency administrator Scott Pruitt also relinquished their posts amid scrutiny on subjects including how they spent taxpayer money on travel.[135]

Conclusions: Partisan politics changed the impact of scandals, and none more so than for the Trump administration. The playbook has changed for modern politicians caught in scandals, and more recent politicians have used it to extend their time in office while fighting scandals. The cabinet members discussed here illustrate how rigid partisan support, evasion tactics, and the ability to hide behind multiple controversies allow more recent political figures to exploit these political changes. While some of these officials had their careers sidetracked or ended, the net result is that they were able to survive longer in office.

CONCLUSION

The case studies tell us that politicians are more able to wiggle out of scandal, either by delaying or denying the inevitable loss of office, and are able to do so in a much brasher and more partisan fashion. Politicians are better able to use the collective playbook of scandal, avoidance, and sidestepping responsibilities than earlier. Even if they last less time in office, the manner of their survival, especially the brazen way they do it, is instructive. This could be because hanging on puts them in a slightly better political or legal position. The partisan media also allow them to hide. It could be that a new breed of politician is less affected by shame than past generations. Modern politicians may fear fewer legal restrictions or may reside in a state where ethical standards are not strictly enforced. Or it could be because partisanship—especially partisan voters but often co-partisan politicians—are less likely to hold these politicians accountable for their misdeeds.

3

HOW POLARIZATION MINIMIZES SCANDALS

The previous chapter showed that politicians survive scandals for longer in the more modern (partisan) period. The effects varied across time and institutions, but the message is clear: politicians caught in scandals are able to stay in office longer or delay leaving office, often bypassing grave negative effects altogether, in a more partisan period. Without question, partisanship has long been a buffer for scandals. Partisan loyalties make supporters impervious to news that portrays party members in a negative light.[1] Dimock and Jacobson found that in the House banking scandal discussed in the previous chapter, voters backed scandalized incumbents of their own party more than those from the opposition party.[2] Moral foundations (care, fairness, loyalty) "seem malleable when partisan actors are involved": in experiments that vary a politician's transgression on these foundations, partisanship drives responses.[3] In experimental studies, even after respondents were told that a made-up story involving harassment was fake, partisans of both parties were more likely to say an in-party politician was innocent and an out-party politician was guilty.[4]

Why? What are the precise mechanisms for how individual people, especially voters, give politicians a pass on illicit or illegal behavior? Certainly partisanship is a primary culprit, but what other dynamics create an environment that is favorable to political scandals?

SURVEYS ON SCANDALS

We draw on three large, national surveys to explore how sensitive voters are to scandals of different types and how much partisanship shapes this receptivity. First, an American Trends Panel created by the Pew Research Center fielded a national sample of randomly selected U.S. adults (n = 10,107) who were surveyed from April 29 to May 13, 2019 (1.48% margin of error). We use one wave of this for analysis. Second, a Qualtrics panel of nationally representative adults (n = 7,897), which used some of the same questions, was in the field from February 23 to March 3, 2022. Third, we created a survey using a sample from Cloud Research (n = 1,700). This survey was in the field from June 20 to June 22, 2024.

A simple way to frame the impact of scandals on the public is to ask respondents directly about their preferences for political scandals involving elected officials of their party and the opposition party (see table 3.1). Scandals produce *schadenfreude*—a German term for reveling in another's misfortune—among partisans. Simply put, an individual partisan may be more excited about an opponent caught in scandal than a co-partisan. The question at issue asks respondents to choose which of the following two statements comes closest to their opinion: "I enjoy it when elected officials I dislike get caught up in personal setbacks" or "Even when it comes to elected officials I dislike, I don't enjoy seeing them get caught up in scandals or facing personal setbacks." The question is generic on purpose; it allows us to test—without party labels, type of scandals, personalities, or policy issues—the sensitivity of the respondent to political scandals in the system in general.

TABLE 3.1 Enjoy when political opponents caught in scandal

	REPUBLICANS 2019 / 2022 (PERCENT)	DEMOCRATS 2019 / 2022 (PERCENT)	NEITHER 2019 / 2022 (PERCENT)
I ENJOY IT WHEN ELECTED OFFICIALS I DISLIKE GET CAUGHT UP IN PERSONAL SETBACKS.	25 / 28	34 / 36	15 / 32
EVEN WHEN IT COMES TO ELECTED OFFICIALS I DISLIKE, I DON'T ENJOY SEEING THEM GET CAUGHT UP IN SCANDALS OR FACING PERSONAL SETBACKS.	73 / 72	65 / 64	69 / 68

Source: Data from Pew Research Center survey, 2019, and Qualtrics survey, 2022.

The results are telling. First partisanship: more Democrats than Republicans claimed they enjoyed scandal when opposition politicians were caught in personal setbacks (see figure 3.1). Because the 2019 survey was fielded during the tumultuous Trump presidency and the 2022 survey in a period with similarly raw emotions, Democrats were out for blood, primed to look for scandals in the opposition. We also know from separate studies that liberal users of social media responded to and shared more toxic content than conservatives, by 56 percent, in this period.[5] In addition, there was growth in how much people enjoyed scandals in both parties between 2019 and 2022: Republicans' embrace of scandals befalling opposition candidates rose by 3 percent and Democrats' by 2 percent in the three years between surveys. The "blood sport" of scandal politics escalates quickly, and especially in trying political times, we see the public more accepting of political scandals. Finally, even nonpartisans (those without parties or refusing to say to which party they belong) spiked by 17 percent in the "enjoy" scandals category.

The finding that even putative nonpartisans have grown more covetous (or accepting) of scandals is important. Nonpartisans are often collateral

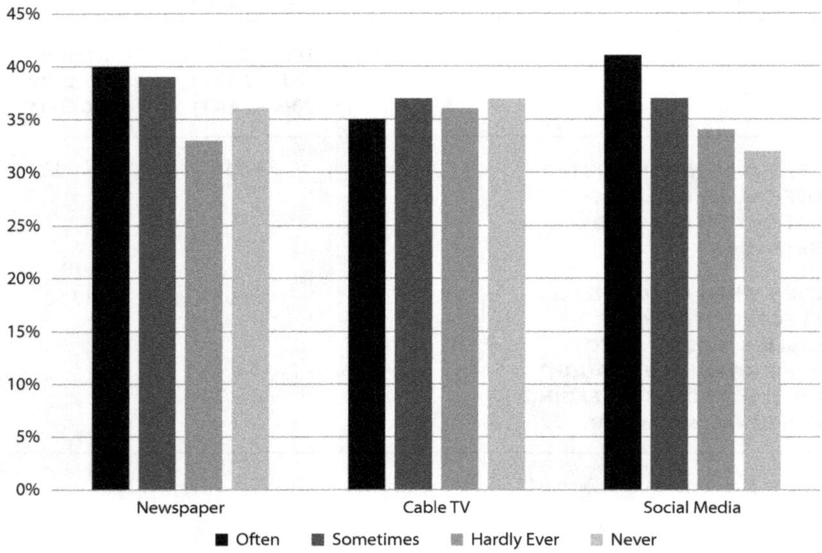

FIGURE 3.1 Enjoy scandals by media consumption. Media "junkies" are more likely to embrace scandal, especially heavy newspaper readers or consumers of social media.

Source: Qualtrics survey 2022.

damage in the partisan wars waged by hardcore partisans. That they are willing to accept—and even embrace—scandals as part of political reality as much as or more than partisan players signals a growing belief that scandals are "business as usual." It may also be that these nonpartisans enjoy the accusations back and forth as sport, like watching football on Sunday. Following the salacious allegations and charges of wrongdoing may be a political voyeur's dream, especially if witnessed from the sidelines instead of in the game. Unattached partisans like watching the mud being thrown even if they have no desire to pick a side—all because someone might get splattered. The danger here is that acceptance of these scandals is now more commonplace. Seeing politicians in trouble is no longer novel or shocking; it is considered part of the process.

Who is more likely to enjoy politicians getting caught in scandals? While we explore this question more below, a simple crosstabulation of

TABLE 3.2 Enjoy opponents caught in scandal, by conversation type

	DO NOT ENJOY SCANDAL(PERCENT)	ENJOY SCANDAL(PERCENT)
(1) I ENJOY CHALLENGING THE OPINIONS OF OTHERS.	82	18
(2)	85	15
(3)	86	14
(4) I DON'T ENJOY CHALLENGING OTHERS, EVEN WHEN THEY ARE WRONG.	89	11

Source: Pew Research Center survey, 2019.

this question with a question about how forceful people are in political conversations is instructive. Table 3.2 shows the results of this interaction with a question that asks respondents about their approach to political conversations. The question asks people to respond on a scale from "enjoy challenging the opinions of others" to "don't enjoy challenging others, even when they are wrong." This is an imperfect but clear measure of how people communicate their political ideas to others, ranging from pushy and opinionated to meek and willing to listen quietly. Not surprisingly, people who are more willing to challenge the opinions of others are more likely to enjoy scandal (18 percent, compared to 11 percent who do not enjoy scandal). On the flip side, 89 percent of people who prefer quiet compromise to challenging others do not enjoy scandals.

Media choice is a culprit too. Media echo chambers—partisan outlets covering scandals of allied parties or politicians less than those of the opposition—might enhance a lust for partisan scandal.[6] Figure 3.1 displays the results of a series of crosstabs with media consumption and respondents' reports about enjoying opposition scandals. Heavy users of both newspapers and social media (using these resources "often") are more likely to want to see their partisan opponents involved in scandals. This is especially true for heavy social media users. The partisan blood lust driving social media users is well documented. The most extreme partisans post the most: studies show the top 10 percent of tweeters produce

80 percent of the tweets.[7] Cable news use seems to have less effect for the heaviest watchers, compared to those consuming more news through traditional newspapers or social media, although lighter watchers of cable TV are more likely to embrace scandals befalling their opponents than lighter consumers of newspapers or social media. This suggests a continued strong role for cable news in promoting scandals, but the strongest effect is among heavier social media users.

SCANDAL SENSITIVITY

Another way to assess the depth of the impact of scandal is to test how willing respondents are to accept certain "bad" behaviors, often connected to scandal. Table 3.3 tracks a series of these negative behaviors from a hypothetical politician and asks respondents if it is sometimes, always, or never acceptable for a politician to engage in these behaviors, separated by party preferences. Scholars argue that Republicans are more likely to see politics in black and white—ideology matters more to them than to Democrats, and this "bright line" shapes political acceptance of behavior that make those lines clear. Put differently, Republicans see the world as "us versus them," and their willingness to accept certain behaviors reflects that. For instance, Republicans are 16 percent more likely than Democrats to claim that saying an opponents' policy positions are evil is sometimes or always acceptable. Republicans are also 13 percent more likely to argue that politicians can sometimes or always say their opponent is "stupid" and 34 percent more likely to claim their opponents are "anti-American." This is not to argue that Democrats do not sometimes condone those actions in their own partisans—they clearly do—but Republican respondents are more willing to find it acceptable to let their politicians off the leash.

However, there are limits to the political combat the public is willing to accept from their politicians. For instance, Republicans, Democrats, and Independents are uniformly unlikely to claim it is permissible for a politician to say something negative about an opponent's physical appearance

TABLE 3.3 "Sometimes" or "always" acceptable for a candidate to . . .

	REPUBLICAN (PERCENT)	DEMOCRAT (PERCENT)	INDEPENDENT (PERCENT)
SAY AN OPPONENT'S POLICY POSITIONS ARE EVIL	39	23	2
SAY SOMETHING NEGATIVE ABOUT AN OPPONENT'S PHYSICAL APPEARANCE	4	4	3
SAY AN OPPONENT IS STUPID	20	7	12
SHOUT OVER AN OPPONENT IN A DEBATE	21	12	13
SAY AN OPPONENT IS ANTI-AMERICAN	46	12	25
DELIBERATELY MISLEAD PEOPLE ABOUT AN OPPONENT'S RECORD	3	4	4

Source: Pew Research Center survey, 2019.

(around 4 percent claim this is sometimes or always acceptable). Donald Trump's modus operandi has been name-calling, using labels like "Sleepy Joe" Biden or "Lying Ted" Cruz for opponents inside and outside of the political sphere.[8] This type of name-calling is among the least acceptable of behaviors for all parties. This incivility effect has long roots. Throwing "red meat" to the base was a tradition long before partisanship took hold in American politics and uncivil attacks have become more common. But scholars have also found that most voters "dislike it when politicians go nasty."[9] Even diehard partisan supporters of a candidate who responds with civility to a personal attack evaluate that politician more favorably, suggesting an appetite for civility.[10] Political leaders are also held to a higher standard than fellow rank-and-file partisans.[11]

The public across the political spectrum is also likely to claim that deliberately misleading the public about an opponent's record is not acceptable (around 3 to 4 percent claim this is sometimes or always acceptable). It seems that intentionality is key here—the public does not condone lying about an opponent on purpose. This language is often used when targeting donors, who are more ideologically motivated than voters.[12] But this does not mean that partisan voters are not attuned to this rhetoric. Thomas Zeitzoff argues in his book *Nasty Politics* that although the public is sincere in its dislike of politicians who insult, accuse, and threaten violence against opponents, voters do like "tough and strong" leaders, especially when voters perceive their group is under threat. Out-partisans, of course, see this language as a threat. Insulting statements or half-truths can be a way for outsider politicians to grab attention, so it is often employed by outsider candidates or incumbents losing power. How voters perceive this language from candidates matters: if it is done to preserve in-group status, partisan voters will approve; if not, it risks turning off voters or worse, leading to political violence.[13]

But what's good for the goose isn't always good for the gander. Partisans, not surprisingly, have a different opinion on what is acceptable for their own party rather than the other party. Tables 3.4 and 3.5 display results from the same set of characteristically "bad" behaviors described above. Across both parties and most of the rude politician actions, partisans of each party are more likely to believe that it is more acceptable for politicians in their own party to engage in bad behavior than it is for the other party's politicians. For Democrats (table 3.4), the data show that they are much more likely than Republicans (table 3.5) to say it is acceptable for their party's politicians to say a Republican's policy positions are evil (25 percent to 8 percent), call Republicans "stupid" (15 percent to 8 precent), shout over a Republican opponent in a debate (23 percent to 9 percent), and say a Republican opponent is anti-American (23 percent to 10 percent). This is consistent with past findings in which Democrats have shown stronger negative responses to moral violations than Republicans.[14] Again, however, limits apply. Democrats are not any more willing to embrace their own politicians saying something negative about an opponent's appearance or deliberately misleading people about Republicans' record.

Republicans, as seen in Table 3.3 above, are more willing than Democrats to tolerate certain behaviors from their candidates in some, but not all, categories of bad behavior. The pattern in table 3.5, isolating the trends

TABLE 3.4 "Sometimes" or "always" acceptable for Democratic elected official to . . .

	REPUBLICAN (PERCENT)	DEMOCRAT (PERCENT)	INDEPENDENT (PERCENT)
SAY THEIR [OPPOSITE PARTY] OPPONENT'S POLICY POSITIONS ARE EVIL	8	25	15
SAY SOMETHING NEGATIVE ABOUT THEIR OPPONENT'S PHYSICAL APPEARANCE	5	6	5
SAY THEIR OPPONENT IS STUPID	8	15	10
SHOUT OVER THEIR OPPONENT IN A DEBATE	9	23	14
SAY THEIR OPPONENT IS ANTI-AMERICAN	10	23	15
DELIBERATELY MISLEAD PEOPLE ABOUT THEIR OPPONENT'S RECORD	3	5	3

Source: Pew Research Center survey, 2019.

among Republicans (similar to table 3.4 for Democrats), is similar: Republican are more likely to accept bad behavior from their own party's politicians. In fact, as discovered above, Republicans are slightly more ruthless when it comes to accepting their politicians' use of harsh campaign tactics in electoral politics. Two features come to life in table 3.5. Republicans are much more likely than Democrats to say it is acceptable for Republican politicians to say a Democrat's policy positions are evil (35 percent to 6 percent), call Democrats "stupid" (22 percent to 6 percent), shout over a Democratic opponent in a debate (23 percent to 9 percent), and say a Democratic opponent is anti-American (23 percent to 10 percent). In addition, while Democrats draw a line on negatively commenting on Republicans' appearance or misleading voters about a Republican's record, Republican respondents have no such limits. Republicans are significantly more likely to agree it is acceptable to say something negative about an opponent's physical appearance (10 percent to 4 percent) or to deliberately mislead people about

TABLE 3.5 "Sometimes" or "always" acceptable for Republican elected official to . . .

	REPUBLICAN (PERCENT)	DEMOCRAT (PERCENT)	INDEPENDENT (PERCENT)
SAY THEIR [OPPOSITE PARTY] OPPONENT'S POLICY POSITIONS ARE EVIL	35	6	15
SAY SOMETHING NEGATIVE ABOUT THEIR OPPONENT'S PHYSICAL APPEARANCE	10	4	5
SAY THEIR OPPONENT IS STUPID	22	6	9
SHOUT OVER THEIR OPPONENT IN A DEBATE	23	9	14
SAY THEIR OPPONENT IS ANTI-AMERICAN	44	7	19%
DELIBERATELY MISLEAD PEOPLE ABOUT THEIR OPPONENT'S RECORD	8	4	4%

Source: Pew Research Center survey, 2019.

an opponent's record (8 percent to 4 percent). This asymmetry is a consistent finding in the literature. Stark and Collignon find that while Democrats are significantly less likely to support a candidate who faces sexual assault charges, Republicans do not generally penalize candidates facing these charges, especially if the candidate in question is a Republican.[15]

Acceptable behavior is one thing; ending support for a candidate is another. To broaden the analysis, table 3.6 poses a battery of hypothetical actions taken by a candidate of the respondent's party and displays the resulting likelihood of declining support for that candidate by party identification. A few trends are interesting. First, Democrats are more sensitive than Republicans or Independents to negative campaign ads or nasty social media posts. Second, Independents are much more likely to stop supporting candidates who trade favors for financial gain (60 percent compared to 53 percent for Republicans and 51 percent for Democrat), have committed major criminal acts in the past (52 percent compared to 49 percent for Republicans and 48 percent for Democrats) or while in

TABLE 3.6 Conditions in which a person would stop supporting a candidate

	REPUBLICAN (PERCENT)	DEMOCRAT (PERCENT)	INDEPENDENT (PERCENT)
CANDIDATE RUNS A NEGATIVE COMMERCIAL AGAINST OPPONENT	22	17	25
CANDIDATE RAISES VOICE IN POLITICAL DEBATE	11	10	10
CANDIDATE MAKES NASTY COMMENTS ABOUT OPPONENT ON SOCIAL MEDIA	33	21	33
MARRIED CANDIDATE HAD SEXUAL AFFAIR IN THE PAST SIX MONTHS	29	28	31
MARRIED CANDIDATE HAD SEXUAL AFFAIR IN THE PAST SIX YEARS	24	24	24
CANDIDATE TRADES POLITICAL FAVORS FOR FINANCIAL GAIN	53	51	60
CANDIDATE COMMITTED MINOR CRIMINAL ACTS IN THE PAST (MISDEMEANOR SUCH AS SPEEDING)	14	13	11
CANDIDATE COMMITS MINOR CRIMINAL ACTS WHILE IN OFFICE (MISDEMEANOR SUCH AS SPEEDING)	17	13	16
CANDIDATE COMMITTED MAJOR CRIMINAL ACT IN THE PAST (FELONY SUCH AS AGGRAVATED ASSAULT)	49	48	52
CANDIDATE COMMITS MAJOR CRIMINAL ACT WHILE IN OFFICE (FELONY SUCH AS AGGRAVATED ASSAULT)	58	54	63
CANDIDATE COMMITS FINANCIAL FRAUD AT THEIR WORKPLACE OR BUSINESS	55	51	61
CANDIDATE HAS CHILD OUT OF WEDLOCK	11	11	11

Source: Qualtrics survey 2022, fielded by the author.

office (63 percent compared to 54 percent for Republicans and 58 percent for Democrats), or commit financial fraud at their workplace (61 percent compared to 51 percent for Republicans and 55 percent for Democrats). Third, Republicans are slightly more likely than Democrats to stop supporting a candidate who has committed minor criminal acts in either the past or the present. Democrats are slightly more offended by recent minor and major criminal acts than Republicans.

Although these differences are important, the similarities are even more telling. Republicans, Democrats, and Independents are equally likely to drop their support for candidates who are married and have had an affair in the past six months (29, 28, and 31 percent, respectively) or six years (24 percent for all three groups) or if a candidate has a child out of wedlock (11 percent across the board). Sexual peccadilloes may no longer be as detrimental to candidates as when Colorado senator and political wunderkind Gary Hart, running for the Democratic nomination for president in 1988, chided reporters into following him around to check whether or not he was having an affair. In fact, polling suggests that divorce is less a social sanction than it was years ago.[16] But partisanship still colors negative evaluations of the personal lives of politicians. Voters punish other-party politicians more harshly than same-party voters.[17]

A slightly different tack was taken in another series of survey questions. We asked respondents to identify a candidate—any candidate—they "most strongly support." We then asked a series of question about more modern scandals—episodes that might compromise current or future candidates in the digital age. The survey was fielded in the summer of 2024 (Cloud Research) with the presidential primaries in full swing. We examine extreme ideology instead of party for comparison in table 3.7. Marijuana use was not acceptable to conservatives whether or not it was legal in the state where consumed. Sex is also still taboo for conservatives—even in circumstances where an explicit video was leaked, conservatives were 13 percent more likely to stop supporting a candidate in that scenario. For mental health, although there is not a wide gap in the percentage of the party faithful terminating their support for a candidate, the ideological span is clearer: 10 percent of those identifying as "very liberal" were likely

TABLE 3.7 Stop supporting candidate, by ideology

	VERY LIBERAL (PERCENT)	VERY CONSERVATIVE (PERCENT)	UNDER 54 / 55+ (PERCENT)
PICTURES OF CANDIDATE DRUNK AT A PARTY	14	15	24 / 21
CANDIDATE CAUGHT SENDING NAKED PICTURES OF SELF	36	40	50 / 57
CANDIDATE SMOKING MARIJUANA IN A STATE WHERE IT IS NOT LEGAL	16	30	34 / 39
CANDIDATE SMOKING MARIJUANA IN A STATE WHERE IT IS LEGAL	8	21	19 / 23
CANDIDATE HAS A TINDER ACCOUNT	18	18	27 / 25
CANDIDATE HAS AN ONLYFANS ACCOUNT	15	19	41 / 25
CANDIDATE APPEARS IN A LEAKED CONSENSUAL SEX VIDEO	19	32	44 / 43
CANDIDATE HAS SOUGHT TREATMENT FOR MENTAL HEALTH ISSUES	10	21	20 / 24

Source: Cloud Research survey 2024, fielded by the author.

Note: Results weighted by party identification and race.

to stop supporting the candidate, compared to 21 percent for those identifying as "very conservative."

DYNAMIC MODELS

The preceding findings make clear that some level of scandal is acceptable—even preferable—for some partisans, and party supporters are uniquely concerned with certain types of scandals. The results also show similarities across scandals. Some politicians' actions are uniformly disliked by the public across all ideologies and parties. The key question is what factors predict scandal attraction—the belief that seeing opposition party candidates felled by scandal is enjoyable (or not). Using statistical techniques, we can carefully measure an individual's receptivity to scandals and compare this to additional variables of interest such as party, ideology, gender, education, and news consumption.

Several covariates are included in our dichotomous empirical models to explore the nuances of political scandal acceptance, controlling for the political environment:

- *Party.* A respondent's political party, coded here as Republican, collapses party affiliates and those who "lean" toward one party or another.
- *Attention to government and media.* Two measures of attentiveness to politics are included. First, a general question asks "Would you say you follow what's going on in government and public affairs?" Second, a media question asks respondents how often they watch cable television news.
- *Capacity for political disagreement.* Two variables capture generally how much people believe that individuals can express themselves and whether or not they should attempt not to offend people. One question asks if the respondent has felt "unfairly judged by others because of language used to express yourself." A second question asks "how comfortable" the respondent thinks liberals in their community are to "freely and openly" express their political views.
- *Education.* Coded into three categories (high school or below, college, and post-college), this measure captures educational attainment.
- *Feeling thermometer.* A consolidated preference measure includes low warmth for every type of political persuasion, merging how a respondent feels about Republicans, Democrats, liberals, or conservatives on a scale of 0 to 5. Respondents who registered low feelings toward zero, one, or two of those four political groups were coded as 1.
- *Extreme ideology.* This variable captures an individual who is to the very left or very right on the ideological spectrum. Individuals who self-identify as "very liberal" or "very conservative" are coded as 1.
- *Affective polarization.* Dislike of one party for nonpolicy reasons is affective polarization. One standard way to measure this is the limits an individual puts on proper political discourse or interactions. Respondents

who stated that the following actions are "always acceptable" were coded 1: saying an opponent's policy positions are incorrect, saying something negative about an opponent's physical appearance, calling an opponent "stupid" or "anti-American," raising an opponent's vote in a debate, and misleading people about an opponent's record. In effect, this variable measures how sensitive respondents are to bare-knuckle politics.

The dependent variable—the variable being changed by the other variables—is the same question asked in table 3.1: whether or not a respondent enjoys seeing political opponents embroiled in scandals. The main independent variable is how acceptable a range of negative actions by a politician are, essentially a collective measure of the variables from table 3.3. In order to summarize the sensitivity of respondents to various scandals, we created an "index of acceptability" of several negative political scenarios: saying an opponent's policy positions are evil, making negative comments about an opponent's spouse, saying an opponent is uninformed about the issues, shouting over opponent in debate, or saying they love America more than their opponent. These variables represent the core of acceptance of various campaign tactics. Each element in the scale is treated as equally important. The scale is additive and uses factor analysis to determine the variability and correlation between the variables and the underlying factor.[18] Each item is positively correlated with the scale, and the item-test correlation is high for each, implying that the measures are highly correlated with the scale.[19]

Figure 3.2 displays the marginal effects—the size of the predicted change in the dependent variable—of tested conditions on whether a respondent "enjoys scandal" (the dependent variable). The results show that people who generally prefer conflict to consensus in political conversations are no more likely to approve of scandals. But, as expected, if a respondent approves of one or more negative actions taken by a candidate, they are significantly more likely to embrace political scandals. We know this because the estimate (coefficient) for the summary measure of "acceptable candidate behaviors" (people more likely to say that bad candidate behaviors are not acceptable) has a large and statistically significant on an

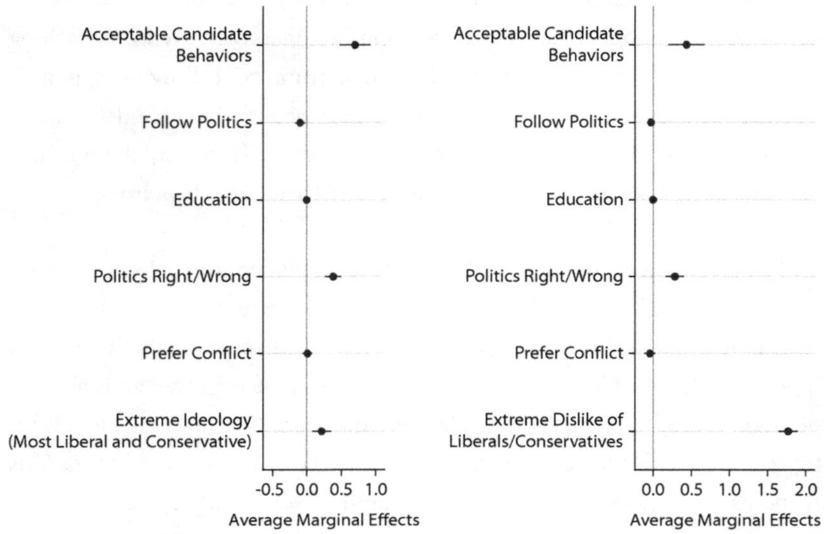

FIGURE 3.2 Enjoy scandal predictions.

Source: Pew survey 2019.

Note: Marginal effects estimated from OLS regression ("enjoy when opponent caught in scandal" is dependent variable).

individual's embrace of scandals. In table 3.2 we saw that individuals who preferred expressing their political opinions regardless of the consequences were more likely to embrace scandal in political opponents. Similarly, respondents who believe politics are a matter of "right or wrong"—a bright line of partisan conflict—are much more likely to enjoy when political opponents are hit with scandals.

Ideology plays a big role too. Those with extreme ideologies are more likely to revel in opponents' political misdeeds. The strongest effects of enjoying seeing political enemies mired in scandal were from those respondents who were most extreme in their ideology (those responding they were "very liberal" or "very conservative" to the question about their ideological fit on a five-point scale, represented in the left portion of the figure). Figure 3.2 (left side) demonstrates that extreme partisans are 1.3

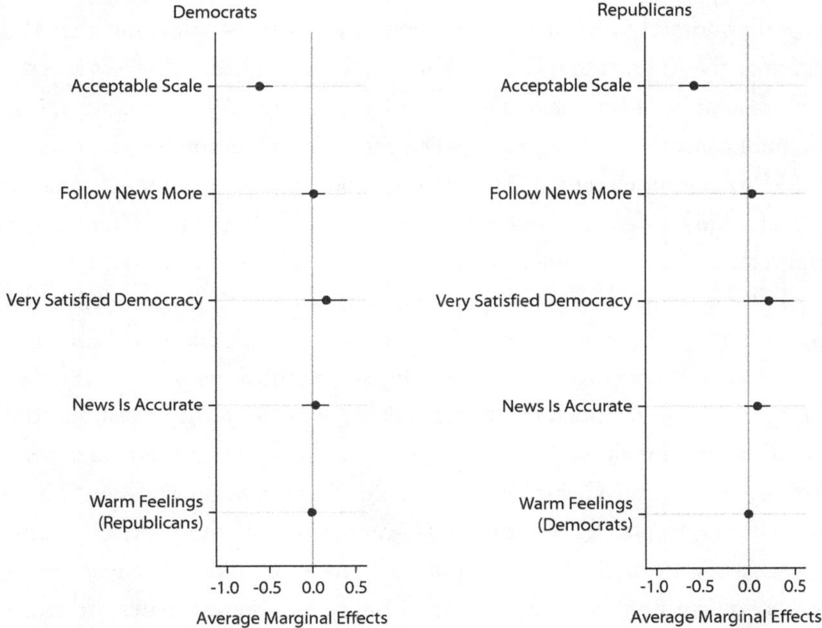

FIGURE 3.3 Partisans enjoy scandal.

Source: Qualtrics survey 2022, fielded by the author.

Note: Marginal effects estimated from OLS regression ("enjoy when opponent caught in scandal" is dependent variable).

times more likely than less partisan respondents to embrace the joy in scandals hitting political opponents.

A common way to estimate sympathy or a positive relationship with political opponents is to use a feeling "thermometer." Respondents are asked to rate their feelings about various groups or figures. In this case, we asked respondents about their feelings toward their own party and the opposition party (see figure 3.3). We should expect that people with "warmer" feelings toward their political opposition (the "loyal opposition") would be less likely to enjoy seeing a member of the opposite party embroiled in a scandal. Limiting the data to just Democrats' feelings about Republicans (not displayed), the simple correlation between a feeling thermometer of warmth for Republicans is –.34, meaning that the warmer the feelings that Democrats have for Republicans, the less acceptable is a range of actions by Democratic politicians. When looking at just Republicans, the correlation between the index of acceptable actions and a feeling thermometer for Democrats is –.009, suggesting a much smaller effect. This is an asymmetric partisan effect: Republicans are more aggressive in their embrace of scandals, as found by other scholars.[20]

Putting these conditions together in a dynamic logit model—using the same feeling thermometer as a key explanatory variable—confirms the asymmetry of how much partisans enjoy seeing the other party in scandal. In figure 3.2 (right side), those respondents who are in the lowest quintile of "affection" for either party are significantly more likely to embrace politicians in scandal. Clearly partisan dislike (affective polarization) has a sizable role to play in the impact of scandal: those who have less warm feelings toward their political opponents are more likely to enjoy seeing them squirm politically. Similarly, in figure 3.3, the estimates are truncated to just Democrats (left) and Republicans (right). Each model also includes a feeling thermometer for the opposite party (Democrats' feelings toward Republicans and Republicans' feelings toward Democrats). For Democrats, there is a very small (less than 1 on a scale of 100) statistically significant negative effect for warmer feelings for Republicans, meaning that Democrats with more positive feelings toward their opposition are less likely to want to see them in scandal. However, there is no statistically significant effect for Republican feelings toward Democrats, suggesting that no matter how positive Republicans feel about Democrats, they are still likely to approve of Democrats getting caught in scandals.

While it is clear that personal peccadilloes do not have as much impact on a politician's future as they did in the past, the timing of the events matters. The graph in figure 3.4 depicts the marginal effects of whether a respondent would stop supporting a candidate who had had an affair in the past six months (left) or in the past six years (right). The dependent variable is the same as in table 3.3: would a person stop supporting a candidate in a scandal involving those circumstances? There are substantive

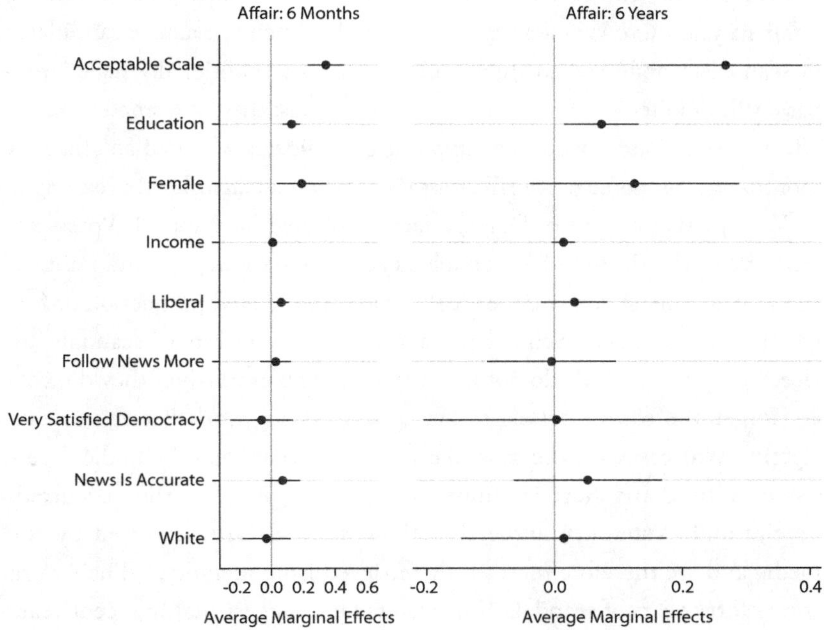

FIGURE 3.4 Scandals in the past matter less than recent scandals.

Source: Qualtrics survey 2022, fielded by the author.

Note: Marginal effects estimated from logistic regression ("enjoy when opponent caught in scandal" is dependent variable).

differences for voters in the timing of certain scandalous activity. For instance, Republican respondents who were less willing to accept certain behaviors (the summary measure of sensitivity to scandal) are more likely to stop supporting a candidate if they had an affair six years ago versus six months ago. This makes sense: voters who are generally less willing to support rambunctious politicians are less likely to embrace them if they had an affair more recently. Education has a small effect too. People with more education are more likely to stop supporting candidates who have had affairs in the past or the recent present.

There are important gender differences too. Female respondents are more likely to stop supporting a candidate who had an affair six months ago, but there is no similar effect among women and candidates who had an affair six years ago. Women are more likely than men to evaluate candidates in scandal favorably when the scandal involved a traditionally male "trespass" (like adultery).[21] The same is true for liberals: there is a small negative effect among liberals who stop supporting candidates who had an affair six months ago but no negative effect for those who had an affair six years ago.

Voters either forgive or forget, a factor explored in chapter 1. Voters are sensitive to the timing of a scandalous activity: six years ago is a political lifetime, and most voters either see that as an unrelated past action or forget that it took place. Scholarship shows that the effects of scandals are fleeting. Most scandals do not last very long, and even when they do, voters forget the sordid details rather quickly. Prior work has found that election-year cases are the most damaging but that "moral scandals" persist over time and hurt incumbents regardless of when they occurred. Pereira and Waterbury argue that these scandals are amplified by the media and are therefore more easily retrieved from memory.[22] Their work covers forty years of scandals. The results here suggest that in recent years the public is less sensitive to older scandals than newer ones, regardless of the type.

Another way to examine the impact of scandals is to isolate the effect to one set of partisan respondents. Let's use Republicans. As found in the survey described above, Republicans are generally less likely than Democrats or Independents to approve of scandals, making them a good test case for exploring some granular trends. In the models in Figure 3.4, Republicans are more likely to express greater negativity toward politicians of the other party when they violate a moral foundation.[23] The evidence generally confirms these trends.

Although party loyalty has compartmentalized ideology into the two political parties, a polarization process we have seen in slow motion for more than a decade, we do see some ideological variation within the parties, enough that we can probe how ideology might mute the desire to see opponents in scandal. We might expect that those party loyalists who are less polarized—that is, more moderate—are less likely to want to see opponents swept up in scandals. Party identifiers who are more partisan in their ideology are more likely to want to see opponents squirm, expressing the belief that they enjoy seeing opponents caught in scandal. In general, this expectation is correct. Republican respondents who are more moderate than their fellow conservatives are less likely to say they enjoy a juicy scandal for the opponents. The effect is small but statistically significant, as seen in figure 3.5. Respondents with more education and those who follow politics more closely are also less likely to enjoy when opponents get caught in scandal. Seeing the negative impact of scandal on policymaking and the resulting friction, those paying close attention to politics register scandal as a bad thing for the system, their putative political opponents included. Education has the same effect—in fact, education minimizes the tolerance for negative politics in general, a finding now clear for scandals.

Extending the analysis, figure 3.6 adds two sets of key variables: sensitivity to candidate "bad behavior" and important candidate qualities (according to the respondent). The models here also limit the effects to Republican respondents. Republicans who believe it is not proper for a candidate to call an opposing candidate "stupid" or "anti-American" are less likely to enjoy a scandal befalling their political opponent (the coefficient for those saying it was not OK to shout over an opponent in a debate was in the expected direction but not statistically significant). Important positive candidate traits such as being honest, admitting when wrong, and showing respect for candidates are also positive predictors of a belief that scandals are bad (the variables are coded backward).

These data tell us that the story about receptivity to scandal is as much about some voters, in this case Republicans, holding candidates to good campaign practices and fair campaigning as it is about partisan anger. This is an unheralded solution to lowering the impact of political scandals in a world riven with political strife. Encouraging and enforcing norms of candidate behavior, and instilling them in voters, can minimize how much citizens embrace scandals. The implications for these divides are very real. Affective polarization—viewing opposing partisans negatively and co-partisans positively—undermines support for democratic norms. This outcome can generate biases that motivate voters to prefer restricting the basic constitutional rights of the other party.[24]

Another way that partisan attachments matter in embracing scandal is whether or not an individual has friends in the opposite party. In Figure 3.7,

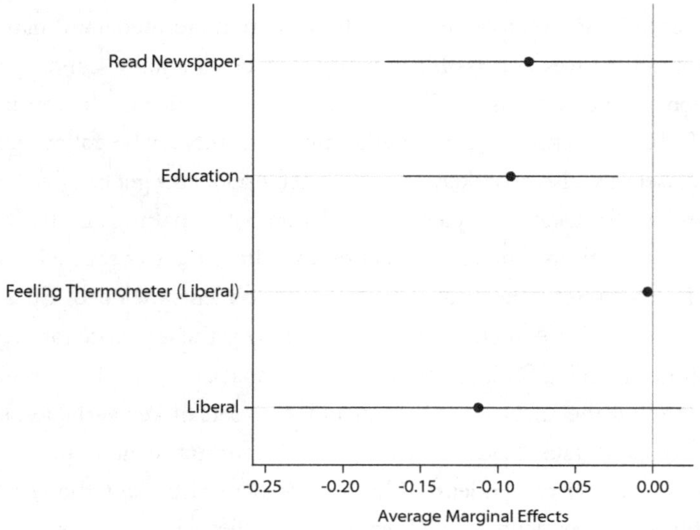

FIGURE 3.5 Republican moderates less likely to enjoy scandal.

Source: Pew survey 2019.

Note: Marginal effects estimated from logistic regression ("enjoy when opponent caught in scandal" is dependent variable), Republican respondents only.

using the same estimates as prior models but including interaction terms for Republicans who have one to four friends who are Democrats, we see a curvilinear pattern for how having one or more friends minimizes a person's desire to see scandals in the opposition party. A Republican who has one Democratic friend is statistically less likely to embrace Democratic politicians caught in scandal. The effect is not strictly linear: the results show that having two or three friends has no effect but having four friends does. This could be the result of a small sample size for having four friends in the opposite party (only 460 total in the dataset), or it could be that having one friend is enough to shift a Republican's mindset to more positively evaluate Democrats. But the pattern is clear: intense partisanship metastasizing into coveting putative political opponents ending up in a scandal is mitigated by association with the opposition party.

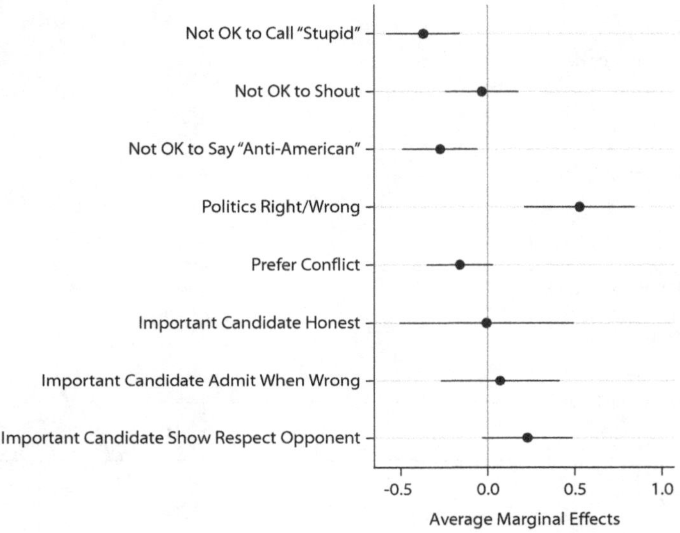

FIGURE 3.6 For Republican partisans, positive candidate traits approval leads to less enjoyment of scandals.

Source: Pew survey 2019.

Note: Marginal effects estimated from logistic regression ("enjoy when opponent caught in scandal" is dependent variable), Republican respondents only.

CONCLUSION

The central theme for why scandals matter less should be clear: partisanship. Partisan extremity plays a significant role in how scandal impact is minimized; extreme partisans are more likely to revel in scandals involving their political "enemies." Democrats who feel warmer toward Republicans are less likely to approve of scandals involving Republicans, while Republicans' feelings towards Democrats have only a minimal effect on their approval of scandals. The findings also highlight the impact of timing on scandal perceptions, with voters showing greater sensitivity to recent scandals compared to older ones. Gender and education also affect scandal sensitivity, with women and more educated individuals being less

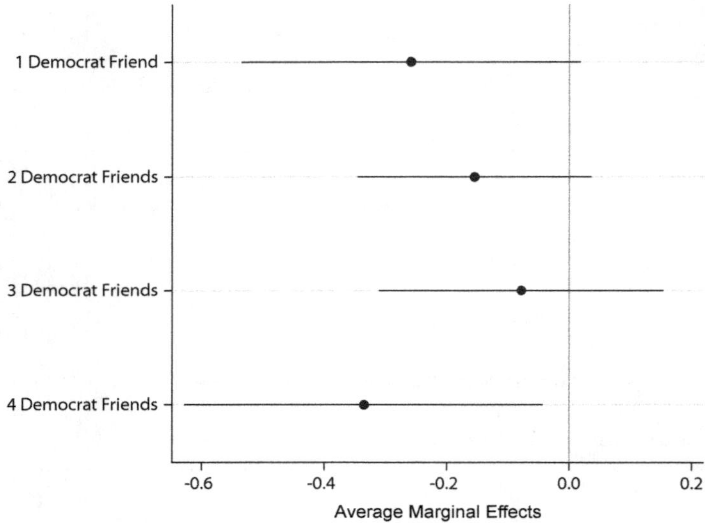

FIGURE 3.7 For Republicans, more friends in other party (Democrats) means less enjoyment of scandal.

Source: Qualtrics survey 2022.

Note: Marginal effects estimated from logistic regression ("enjoy when opponent caught in scandal" is dependent variable), Republicans only; covariates removed for clarity.

tolerant of past scandals. Additionally, having friends in the opposing party can reduce a person's inclination to enjoy seeing political opponents in scandal, indicating that personal connections across party lines may mitigate extreme partisan responses.

While Democrats are generally more likely to say they like to see Republicans in scandal (versus Republicans who liked to see Democrats in scandals), this was likely a product of the survey being in the field during the Trump era. But the differences by party are less interesting than those by ideology. Those with the most extreme ideologies—those in the tails of their parties' ideologies—were not necessarily more likely to like seeing opponents in scandals, but those with extreme dislike of the other party were. This means that affective polarization, more than actual polarization, is the proximate cause of attraction to scandals. Friends are important too. Having friends in the other party smooths over a desire to see putative political opponents caught in crisis. But ideology also matters in a different way: more ideologically moderate candidates were less likely to enjoy seeing opponents in scandals.

4

EVERYTHING IS A SCANDAL THESE DAYS

Scandals can be about just about anything, even the color of a suit. On August 28, 2014, addressing the media from the podium of the press room in the West Wing of the White House, President Barack Obama wore a tan suit with a gray and white striped tie. The internet exploded: more than four thousand tweets, mostly memes, were posted about his sartorial choice. "Yes We Tan," a play on Obama's 2008 rally cry "Yes We Can," became a popular saying ("the audacity of taupe," a play on the president's biography *The Audacity of Hope*, was also popular). Representative Peter King, a conservative Republican from New York, led the charge, seemingly as angry about the suit as that the president had announced a very real and consequential policy change: the United States would escalate military hostilities to combat ISIS in Syria but, according to the President, they "didn't have a strategy yet."[1] The suit showed "a lack of seriousness," despite the fact that several other occupants of the Oval Office have worn taupe-colored suits on duty. The president and military and national security advisers were set to huddle following his statement, but that policy was harder to change than the color of his suit.

Clothes are one thing, food another. Conservative commentators seeking ways to pillory the new president found yet another weapon: mustard. President Obama and Vice President Biden stopped by a local burger joint in northern Virginia in 2009, where he ordered, in his words, "a basic cheddar cheeseburger, medium well, and just mustard, no ketchup, like a spicy mustard or a Dijon mustard." Painting the president as out of touch and "elite," Fox News host Sean Hannity mocked him for claiming to be a "man of the people" while putting fancy mustard on his burger. "I hope you enjoyed that fancy burger, Mr. President," Hannity sneered.[2] Right-wing talk show host Laura Ingraham weighed in: "What kind of man orders a cheeseburger without ketchup but Dijon mustard?" Like where presidents vacation, the length of their ties, or how they eat their pizza, everything has become unnecessarily partisan.

The tan suit episode is perhaps the biggest non-scandal in history but one that shows how minor controversies have been turned into political warfare in this polarized era. This is the origin of outrage politics where people, especially partisans, are just looking for reasons to be outraged—snark over substance. What fuels it? Rampant polarization and the wildfire-fast spread of outrage on social media, structured by affective polarization and motivated reasoning. *Vox*'s Matthew Yglesias makes a similar case that "we're in an age of manufactured nihilism."[3] He argues that political opponents can "short-circuit" the information "receive-accept" model "by saturating the ecosystem with misinformation and overwhelm the media's ability to mediate, then you can disrupt the democratic process." Most Americans say they encounter conflicting reports about the same event, partly because they are seeing partisan media silo information reported as news. In addition, less than half the nation trusts what they read in the media, making factual claims about scandals even harder to convey.[4]

Perhaps this is not surprising. The actual scandal is beside the point. Partisans fill their news diets with a steady peppering of outrage, regardless of the truth or gravity of the events of the day involving politicians or parties they dislike. In fact, both journalists and scholars argue that news vacuums—basically, slow news days—are filled by creating "scandals," a product of opponents' pent-up demand, an erosion of party support, and a rapacious appetite for controversy.[5] The media and partisans "co-produce" news, as "each group has professional incentives to investigate and publicize alleged misconduct"; when both groups promote an allegation, a scandal emerges.[6] It turns out that scandals can be manufactured pretty easily.

CREATING SCANDAL

To simulate a realistic world where a scandal can potentially be manufactured from a small event, we used a survey experiment and created three distinct media stories from the same real event (the fourth treatment, for the control group, was a *New York Times* story about how to make honey-garlic chicken). The first treatment story—the basic, real-life event—was an anodyne, unvarnished press release from the National Park Service. The banner had the National Park Service logo (and a mountain vista), and the title of the press release was "Agencies Announce Decision to Restore Grizzly Bears to North Cascades." This press release was a factual set of discussion points about the importance of grizzly bears in the North Cascades and the scientific justification for their reintroduction:

National Park Service Release

Agencies Announce Decision to Restore Grizzly Bears to North Cascades

The National Park Service and U.S. Fish & Wildlife Service have announced a decision to actively restore grizzly bears to the North Cascades of Washington, where the animals once roamed.

Grizzly bears occupied the North Cascades region for thousands of years as a key part of the ecosystem, distributing native plant seeds and keeping other wildlife populations in balance. Populations declined primarily due to direct killing by humans. The last confirmed sighting of a grizzly bear in the U.S. portion of the North Cascades ecosystem was in 1996.

In the Record of Decision released today, agencies have decided to restore grizzly bears to the North Cascades ecosystem through the translocation of grizzly bears from other ecosystems in the Rocky Mountains or interior British Columbia. The decision is the culmination of an Environmental Impact Statement process that began in 2022.

Agencies will seek to move three to seven grizzly bears per year for a period of five to 10 years to establish an initial population of 25 bears. The U.S. portion of the North Cascades ecosystem is roughly 9,800 square miles in size, larger than the state of New Jersey, and contains some of the most intact wildlands in the contiguous U.S. Roughly 85% of the mountainous region is under federal management.

"We are going to once again see grizzly bears on the landscape, restoring an important thread in the fabric of the North Cascades," said Don Striker, Superintendent of North Cascades National Park Service Complex.

Under the decision, grizzly bears in the North Cascades will be designated as a nonessential experimental population under section 10(j) of the Endangered Species Act. The designation will provide authorities and land managers with additional tools for management that would not otherwise be available under existing Endangered Species Act regulations. The U.S. Fish & Wildlife Service will publish a final 10(j) rule in the Federal Register in coming days.

To simulate a potential scandal from this real event, we then created two additional stories—based on real news reports of the bear reintroduction event from Fox News—that amplify and exaggerate the story. In one treatment, which we label the "regular Fox News treatment," the headline read, "Biden administration accelerates plan to unleash grizzly bears near rural community over widespread local opposition." The brief story highlights local public objection in the region and has a picture of a community meeting where locals protested with homemade signs shaped like bear paws containing the word "NO." The highlight of the story in this treatment was a quote from a representative of the National Cattlemen's Beef Association suggesting that the administration was undertaking these actions without local consensus:

Regular Fox

Biden Admin Accelerates Plan to Unleash Grizzly Bears Near Rural Community Over Widespread Local Opposition

In a joint announcement, the National Park Service and U.S. Fish & Wildlife Service published a final environmental impact statement evaluating its options for grizzly bear management in the region. The filing lists the federal government's preferred course of action as the translocation of grizzly bears from other ecosystems with an "experimental population designation."

The agencies, though, acknowledged the potential impact of the proposal on local communities, livestock and farms. As a result, the plan allows people to injure or kill a grizzly bear that is threatening a person's life or is in the act of attacking livestock, including working dogs on private land, under certain conditions.

Still, the proposal was quickly condemned by the National Cattlemen's Beef Association (NCBA), which represents cattle ranchers, and Rep. Dan Newhouse, R-Wash., who represents local communities in the region.

"The status included in today's announcement may be the administration's attempt to placate the state, but we continue to stand with the ranchers and rural families in northwest Washington who do not want this proposal to move forward at all," said NCBA Government Affairs Director Sigrid Johannes. "Dropping new apex predators into rural Americans' backyards is not something that the federal government should undertake without consensus."

The final treatment, called the "extreme treatment," had a title that read "Biden Administration Recklessly Releases Bears—Why You and Your Family Might Be in Danger." The subhead was a real quote from a local official who said, "If any grizzly bear comes around my place, I'm shooting it." The body of the story is similar to the standard Fox News story but includes a quote from Representative Dan Newhouse, Republican of Washington, who, in addition to implying that the administration disregarded public opinion in favor of "the whims of extreme environmentalists," concluded that these actions violated state law and federal procedure, claiming that "this is the kind of blatant overreach that gets president impeached." The story also included a screenshot of *The Five*, a public affairs show hosted by Janine Perro, next to a dangerous-looking grizzly bear with its mouth wide open:

Extreme Fox

Biden Administration Recklessly Releases Bears—
Why You and Your Family Might Be in Danger

In a joint announcement, the National Park Service and U.S. Fish & Wildlife Service published a final environmental impact statement evaluating its options for grizzly bear management in the region. The filing lists the federal government's preferred course of action as the translocation of grizzly bears from other ecosystems with an "experimental population designation."

The agencies, though, acknowledged the potential impact of the proposal on local communities, livestock and farms. As a result, the plan allows people to injure or kill a grizzly bear that is threatening a person's life or is in the act of attacking livestock, including working dogs on private land, under certain conditions.

Still, the proposal was quickly condemned by the National Cattlemen's Beef Association (NCBA), which represents cattle ranchers, and

Rep. Dan Newhouse, R-Wash., who represents local communities in the region, who pointed out the actions run contrary to state law.

"Their voices have been shut out of this entire process," he continued. "This administration's disregard for public opinion and following the whims of extreme environmentalists, many of whom don't live anywhere near where the bears will be, is proven by the announcement today."

He ended by saying, "These actions violate state laws and the federal government's own procedure for relocation. This is the kind of blatant overreach that gets presidents impeached."

Obviously, partisanship should prime Republicans to see this event as a "scandal" more than Democrats or Independents. If so, we should find that Republican identifiers are more likely to (1) disapprove of President Biden, (2) agree that the Biden administration is more scandal-plagued than past administrations, and (3) say that Biden should resign.

SURVEY AND METHODS

A randomly drawn public online sample of 1,700 adults (sourced through Cloud Research) was the pool of respondents used for this analysis (in the field June 20 to 22, 2024, just before the fateful debate performance that precipitated Joe Biden's exit from the 2024 presidential race and well before the November election). The respondents were assigned randomly to one of four treatments just described, enabling us to compare those individuals who received the control treatment to those given the three scandal treatments. This design also allows us to test any partisan ideological effect—that is, our expectation that scandals do not affect partisans much.

The theme of this book is that scandals matter less in a polarized era, with the host of conditions that attend to that political world. The results conform to that expectation. In attempting to prime respondents to see the

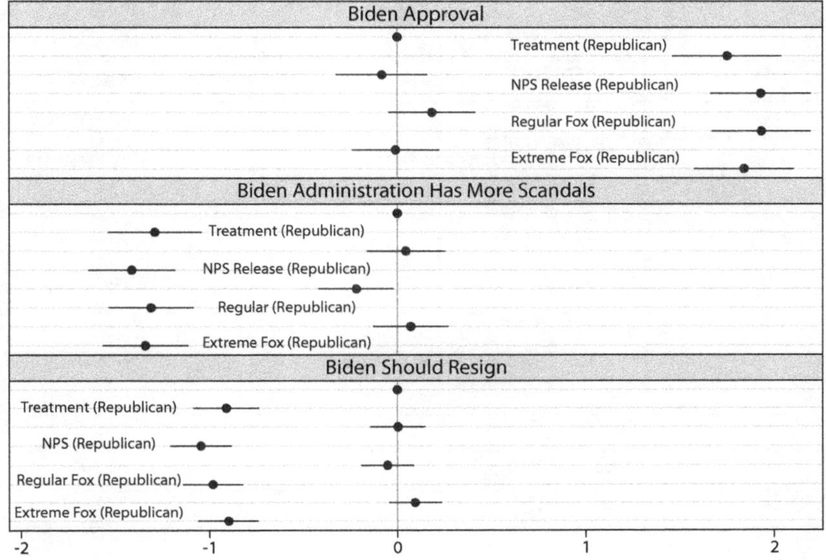

FIGURE 4.1 Experimental treatment by party.

Source: Cloud Research poll 2024, fielded by the author.

Note: Marginal effects estimated from logistic regression. Dependent variables are Biden approval (five-point scale), Biden administration has more scandals (1 if yes), Biden should resign (1 if yes).

release of the grizzlies as a scandal, the difference between the control condition and the very stylized scandals represented in the Fox News fake treatments (conditions 3 and 4; see figure 4.1) was present but very small. For example, in the Biden approval question (panel 1), the difference between Republicans (dot on far right) who saw the control cooking treatment and those who got the full double-barreled scandal treatment was about .25 (on a five-point scale). Similarly, Republicans who got the cooking treatment and the extreme scandal treatment differed by only .01 in their belief that the Biden administration had more scandals than past administrations.

In figure 4.2, we estimate the same comparisons across self-reported ideologies. In this case we have collapsed people who said they were somewhat liberal or very liberal into one group and people who said they were

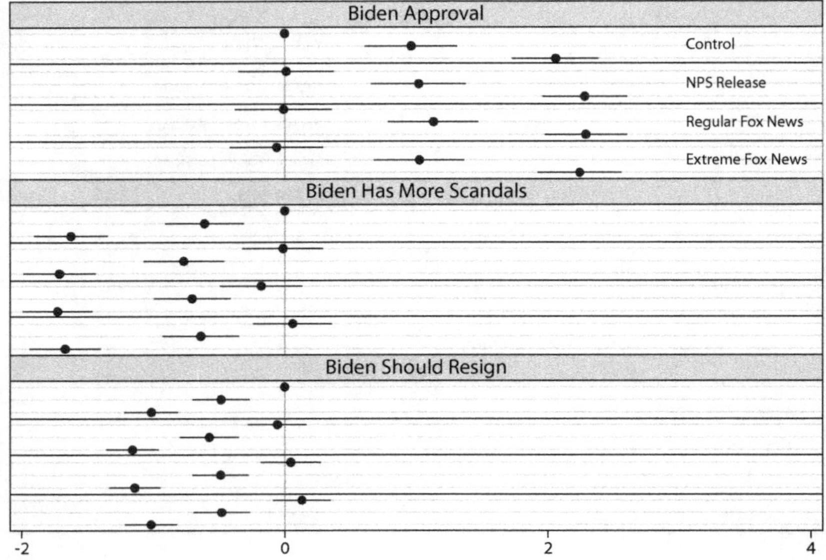

FIGURE 4.2 Experimental treatment by ideology.

Source: Cloud Research poll 2024, fielded by the author.

Note: Marginal effects estimated from logistic regression. Dependent variables are Biden approval (five-point scale), Biden administration has more scandals (1 if yes), Biden should resign (1 if yes). Panels show estimates for ideology (liberal, moderate, conservative) by each treatment.

somewhat conservative or very conservative into another group. The results are substantively larger but still modest when comparing the control group to the extreme scandal treatment group. For example, very conservative respondents who got the highly scandalized treatment were about a third of a point more likely to disapprove of Joe Biden (on a five-point scale). Those very conservative respondents who received the scandalized treatments were equally likely to respond as those in the control that Joe Biden should resign. As figure 4.2 shows, the third condition, the regular Fox News scandal treatment, was among the stronger motivators of conservatives: these respondents were about a quarter of a point more likely (on a three-point scale) to say Joe Biden should resign than those who received the cooking control treatment.[7]

The results indicate a somewhat unexpected outcome: even when presented with an event as a potential scandal, partisans—in this case Republicans and self-identified conservatives—were only slightly more willing to disapprove of Joe Biden, to suggest his administration is more scandal plagued than past administrations, and to hold that Joe Biden should resign. The two "scandalized" treatments of the event were only moderately likely to prime partisans' negative opinions about the incumbent president. In fact, even the simple mention of the name of the president and his grizzly bear policy was enough to evoke negative feelings about Biden, as seen in the "regular Fox News treatment," results that were strikingly similar to the scandal conditions where additional (albeit stylized) evidence implied a full-blown scandal. But even those partisan respondents who were asked to read the cooking treatment were almost as likely to say that Joe Biden should resign.

Examining the results in a slightly different way, figure 4.3 considers the treatments by the feeling thermometer for Democrats. Lower scaled scores indicate less liking for Democrats on a 100-point scale (the dependent variable). This is a simple measure of affective polarization, in which dislike of a party should enhance a respondent's belief that a "scandal" is an impeachable offense. The models also included whether a respondent "enjoyed scandals" (described earlier), as well as age, race, and education. The results indicate that all of the treatments produced bigger drops in approval and a greater willingness to embrace Biden's resignation among those respondents who disliked Democrats. The increasingly extreme treatments appear to work, albeit modestly: respondents exposed to the most extreme treatment were slightly more likely to disapprove of Biden or to believe he should resign.

Table 4.1 amplifies these findings. The results here compare the means for the various treatments for each of two categories of interest: those respondents with low positive feelings for Democrats and liberals. Again, the results are modest but telling in a small, manufactured scandal in the context of the Biden presidency: those with low feelings for Democrats and liberals who were exposed to the extreme treatments were more likely to claim that Biden should resign his office. The results are small but

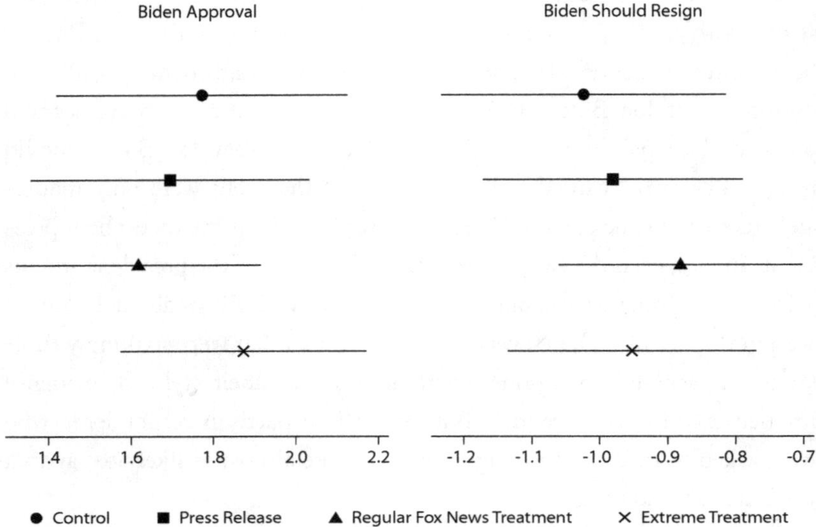

FIGURE 4.3 Experimental treatment by Democratic feeling thermometer.

Note: Regression models with controls. Dependent variables are Biden approval (left) and Biden should resign (right), both on a five-point scale.

TABLE 4.1 Differences in treatment means for Biden to resign, by condition and feeling thermometer

	LOW FEELINGS FOR DEMOCRATS	LOW FEELINGS FOR LIBERALS
CONTROL	1.22	1.38
PRESS RELEASE	1.21	1.36
REGULAR FOX NEWS TREATMENT	1.24	1.42
EXTREME TREATMENT	1.36	1.53

Note: Mean estimation for each treatment. "Low" feelings are measured by a score of less than 10 on a 100-point scale.

informative. Even one modest scandal in the span of a presidency can move the needle a little for partisans.

CONCLUSION

Most people have forgotten about the tan suit episode, although every few years on the anniversary there is a media story about it. There are also Reddit threads inquiring about the history. The suit even has its own Wikipedia page. In 2021, seven years to the month after that fateful day, President Biden wore a tan suit. On the fifth anniversary of suit-gate, *The Hill* noted that "droves of people are taking to social media to recognize what some have referred to as a 'simpler time' when juxtaposed with" contemporary scandals. "Remember when Obama's tan suit was considered a presidential scandal? Sigh."[8] This "scandal" seems quaint compared to, well, actual scandals but underscores an important point about scandal warfare in a polarized America: pretty much anything can be a scandal these days. Outrage politics whets the appetite among partisans for controversy involving their opponents.

Political discourse today no longer distinguishes between actual and false outrage, making it hard for voters to determine what to get angry about and what to ignore as unimportant. Everything is fair game for the outrage machine, and politicians prime this to secure partisan support to fundraise and win elections. This is what makes the modest findings about the impact of scandal on partisans so stunning but not surprising. Even presented with direct, bold, and flashy evidence of a scandal, the episode barely registered for partisans, who did not really care whether a real scandal emerged—they just wanted blood. Even so, the findings reinforce the central concept of this book: partisanship, affective polarization, and media silos are magnifying events into scandals. This makes scandals matter less to in-partisans, who see these events as "fake news," but matter more to out-partisans, who are outraged by them.

5

THE EFFECTS OF SCANDALS ON POLITICAL LEGACIES

Political legacies are shaped by a number of factors, including political scandals. Politicians' political lives are often long, varied, and replete with dozens (if not hundreds) of political issues and related controversies. But how much do scandals affect a legacy?

History's judgment can be harsh. Take the infamous case of Warren G. Harding. When the favorite son of Ohio died in office in 1923 during a cross-country speaking tour in a suite in San Francisco's Palace Hotel, he was a generally popular figure. A symbol of opportunity as he rose from modest means in a small town in Ohio to become president, he embodied the aspirational American "log cabin" myth. But after his death, several major scandals emerged that implicated him and his administration, including Teapot Dome (an infamous bribery scandal) and an extramarital affair, that sullied his reputation.[1] These scandals lowered the public esteem he had worked so hard to craft. In *Dead Last*, the historian Phillip G. Payne paints Harding as "an icon of presidential failure." The tarnish of scandals may also diminish young people's opinion of the president's "benevolence," a change from before the age of scandal.[2] Younger voters' opinions of presidents in the more polarized era are "decidedly more negative" than even in the Watergate period, especially as they come to accept that scandalous behavior is normal for politicians.[3]

But, as we have seen, scandals do not hit the way they used to. Polarization and an unrelenting media cycle have blunted the impact of scandals, making them less potent. Voters, especially partisan voters, care more about other features of electoral politics than their candidates or party being trapped in scandals. But aside from electoral or legal consequences (if any), do scandals have a long-term effect on public perception of the political legacies of those involved?

PRESIDENTIAL LEGACY

Significant social science research has sought to explain presidential greatness, using a growing body of surveys conducted among both experts and the mass public. Famed historian Arthur M. Schlesinger pioneered the practice of surveying intellectual elites about their attitudes toward our greatest presidential leadership. In 1948, *Life* magazine published the results of his study of fifty-five historians, which asked them to assign each president to one of five categories: great, near great, average, below average, and failure. Abraham Lincoln was the unanimous victor and, indeed, the only president to receive a "great" vote from every respondent.[4] Fourteen years later, Schlesinger conducted another survey, this time featuring seventy-five historians, which was published in the *New York Times Magazine*. The results across these two studies were largely consistent, with the majority of 1962 presidential rankings remaining within a couple places of their 1948 counterparts.

In 1996, the *New York Times Magazine* recruited Arthur M. Schlesinger Jr. to conduct another expert poll. He also published an extended report in *Political Science Quarterly*.[5] His method differed slightly departed from his father's, decreasing the number of respondents to thirty-two and expanding the pool to include politicians Governor Mario Cuomo and U.S. Senator Paul Simon. This makes a comparison imperfect, but it provides insight into shifting perspectives on presidential greatness, how impressions of presidents have changed, and how (or if) scandals define legacies. Although the results of Schlesinger Jr.'s survey were largely consistent with the two conducted by his father, several presidents experienced significant changes in reputation in the half-century since the first Schlesinger poll. Presidents whose rankings dropped by more than five places included John Tyler (from 22 to 32), James Buchanan (from 29 to 38), Andrew Johnson (from 23 to 37), Ulysses S. Grant (from 28 to 34), Rutherford B. Hayes (from 14 to 23), Chester A. Arthur (from 17 to 26), William Howard Taft (from 16 to 22), Warren Harding (from 31 to 39), and Herbert Hoover (from 19 to 35). Several of these presidents confronted scandals in their administrations that loomed large after fifty years of scrutiny.

What effect do political scandals have on assessments of presidential greatness? How do these assessments change in light of historical migration in the norms and issues confronted by later presidents? Since scandals continue to shape American politics, how do newer incidents change perceptions of presidential greatness based on past presidential scandals?

SURVEY METHODOLOGY

Two expert presidential greatness surveys help explore the role of scandal in presidential legacy. The first was conducted online from December 22, 2017 to January 16, 2018. Respondents were members of the Presidents & Executive Politics Section of the American Political Science Association, the foremost organization of social science experts in presidential politics. Of 320 respondents invited to participate, 170 provided usable responses, yielding a response rate of 53 percent.[6] A second survey was conducted online from November 19 to December 31, 2023. Respondents were scholars and authors who had published work on the presidency in the past five years in several top political science journals (*American Political Science Review*, *American Journal of Political Science*, *Journal of Politics*, *Legislative Studies Quarterly*, and *Political Research Quarterly*) and specialty journals that focus on the presidency (*Presidential Studies Quarterly*, *Congress & the Presidency*, *White House Studies*). Of 531 respondents invited to participate, 243 provided usable responses, yielding a response rate of 46 percent.[7] The primary purpose of the survey was to analyze the rankings of presidential greatness for all presidents from George Washington to Joe Biden.

Presidential greatness was assessed in two ways. First, we asked respondents to rate each president's overall greatness on a scale from 0 to 100 (0 = failure, 50 = average, and 100 = great). No details about what makes a "great" president were provided; respondents were expected to formulate their own criteria for rating and comparing presidents. Second, we asked survey respondents to indicate how much knowledge they had of each president, on a scale from 1 to 4 (1 = nothing, 2 = some, 3 = a little, and 4 = a lot). This allows us to control for information about individual presidents and scandals, many of them from decades earlier.

The scores from the 2017 survey were averaged across all respondents. Abraham Lincoln had the highest overall greatness ranking, followed by George Washington and Franklin Delano Roosevelt. The next tier of greatness included Theodore Roosevelt, Thomas Jefferson, Harry Truman, and Dwight Eisenhower. The least great president was James Buchanan, followed by Warren Harding, Andrew Johnson, Franklin Pierce, and William Henry Harrison. Of the modern presidents, Bill Clinton earned the highest overall rating and George W. Bush earned the lowest. Between these two were Ronald Reagan (no. 11 with 67.5 percent), Lyndon Baines Johnson (no. 12 with 67.3 percent), John F. Kennedy (no. 14 with 64.0 percent), George H. W. Bush (no. 17 with 60.8 percent), Barack Obama (no. 18 with 58.2 percent), Gerald Ford (no. 24 with 50.1 percent), Jimmy Carter (no. 26 with 44.2 percent), and Richard Nixon (no. 34 with 37.3 percent).

In addition to raw measures of presidential greatness, we investigated the role of scandal in relation to presidential legacy. To capture the dynamics of scandals in American politics, we posed two questions in the 2023 survey about past and current presidential scandals. First, we asked respondents to rank the importance of eleven scandals (1 = most important, 11 = least important).[8] Second, we asked how important each scandal was relative to Watergate (not as important, equally important, or more important).[9] These scandals ranged from famous historical scandals to more recent personal ones: the Clinton Lewinsky affair, the Valerie Plame leak, the Trump-Ukraine connection, Iran-Contra, Teapot Dome, the Trump–Stormy Daniels affair, the Whiskey Ring, Andrew Johnson's impeachment, Andrew Jackson's marriage, and the Whitewater land deal. We also asked about respondents' political preferences (coded "1" if a respondent leaned toward the Democratic Party) and gender (coded "1" if a respondent identified as male).

SCANDALS DO NOT DEFINE PRESIDENTIAL LEGACIES

What do presidency scholars want from presidents? The character, broadly defined, of executives is consequential to American politics, especially modern politics, and can inform us about the governing style and public accountability of an elected executive. According to Pfiffner, "there is a widespread consensus in American politics that presidential character is just as important as intellect, organizational abilities, television presence, or effective public speaking."[10] Variations and violations of the implicit oath of reasonable harmony and clean governing are not tolerated by voters. Fousek and Wasserman argue that "the public has continued to demand ethical leadership from its elected representatives. This is particularly true of the president, who sits at the pinnacle of government and sets the moral tone for the executive branch."[11] To that end, several scholars have explored the issues of corruption and character in elected officials. Pfiffner describes presidential character as "a person's personal behavior, particularly sexual" as it applies to "an official's public behavior, particularly with respect to truthfulness and consistency."[12] Such character issues are associated with political responsiveness to the public, political judgments, fidelity to one's convictions, and democratic legitimacy.[13]

Presidential greatness is traditionally captured by several variables that define strong presidential legacies: economic strength, years in office, intellectual "brilliance," if the president was in office when a war was won, assassinations, and, of course, scandals. Economic strength is measured by the average growth in real gross domestic product over a president's term or terms in office. Years in office is a simple count of the number of years a president served. Assassinations are measured by whether a president's term was ended by an assassin. "Winning" a war (like the Civil War or World War II) is another factor that traditionally predicts presidential greatness. Intellectual brilliance is a factor analysis of rater assessments of a president's intelligence.[14]

Considering the importance of character to assessments of presidential legacy, we might expect to see scandals confronted in an administration drag down a president's greatness assessment. One simple way to test this is to examine the factors that make up greatness assessments plus respondent factors such as information about a president, party affiliation, and gender, in addition to the number of scandals in an administration. We use Morris and Curry's count of scandals until Nixon, then use our own measure of scandals, identified in chapter 1. Finally, we include control measures for how much a respondent knows about a president (scaled 0 = no knowledge to 100 = highest knowledge).[15]

Do scandals affect presidential legacies? Only a little. Table 5.1 displays four OLS (ordinary least squares) regression models testing the effect of the characteristics on the legacy of presidents across two waves of the expert survey on presidential greatness—one full, including all variables described above, and one stripped down to just respondent knowledge of each president and the number of scandals each president faced. In the 2017 "skinny" models, both knowledge and scandal are statistically significant and in the predicted direction. Greater knowledge of a president leads to higher greatness scores, and more scandals in an administration leads to slightly lower greatness ratings. In the 2017 full models, the coefficients are in the same expected direction, but after controlling for all other variables, the importance of scandal decreases and becomes less statistically significant. In addition, the summary measure of goodness of

TABLE 5.1 Full and "skinny" models of scandals and greatness measures

	2017 (SKINNY)	2017 (FULL)	2023 (SKINNY)	2023 (FULL)
KNOWLEDGE	23.6 *** (4.27)	15.7 *** (4.33)	26.7 *** (3.97)	16.6 *** (4.01)
SCANDALS	–.588 ** (.285)	–.418 * (.230)	–.912 *** (.204)	–.655 *** (.164)
CONTROLS	NO	YES	NO	YES
R^2	.419	.655	.524	.728

Source: Expert presidential surveys, fielded by the author.

Note: OLS modeled (dependent variable is presidential "greatness" rating).

*** indicates statistical significance at p <. 01.

** p <. 05.

* p <. 10. Robust standard errors in parentheses.

fit—a traditional statistical way to determine how well the model works—is larger, suggesting that including more variables better captures the story of presidential greatness. The same effect occurs for the 2023 ratings, with scandals having less impact in the full model (but the statistical significance is similar). The takeaway is that scandals are less important to ratings of presidential greatness when all other relevant factors are considered.

Expanding the analysis, figure 5.1 shows the estimated effects on expert ratings of presidential greatness from the full models. The story is the same. Presidential experts with more knowledge about an individual president will rate that president higher. Factors such as real GDP growth, number of years served, and intellectual brilliance all have sizable effects. In the 2017 models (left), the number of years the country is at war has a negative impact on greatness ratings, but winning a war has no strong statistical effect (although the coefficient just misses conventional statistical significance). Assassination of the president has no effect in either model. Scandals do have a negative effect for both the 2017 and 2023 survey models, but the effect is small—for a one unit increase in scandal, a respondent's rating of a president declines by about .41 (2017) or .47 (2023). In contrast, for a one unit increase in years spent in office,

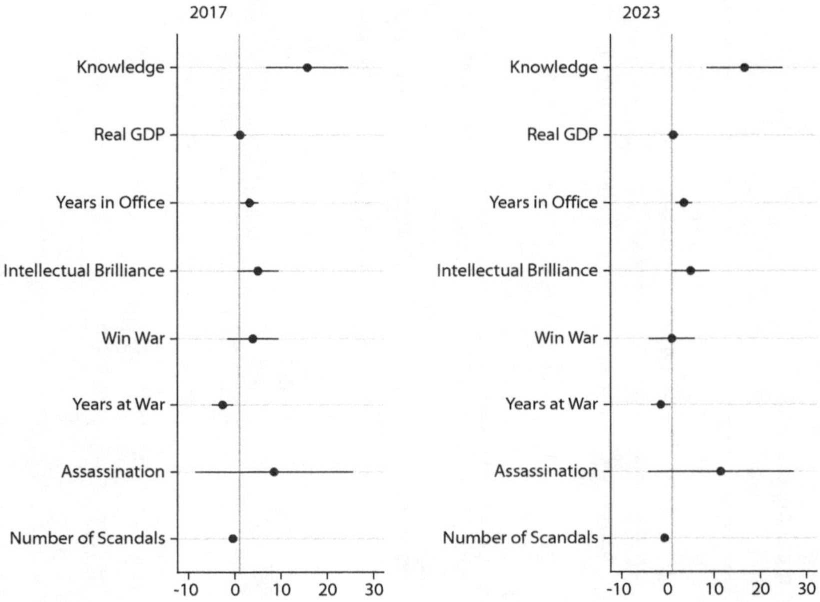

FIGURE 5.1 Scandal has minimal effects on presidential greatness. The impact of scandal on greatness assessments is small—and diminishes over time.

Source: Expert presidential surveys, fielded by the author.

Note: OLS modeled (dependent variable is presidential "greatness" rating).

an individual president's rating, holding all other variables at their mean, rises by 3.3 (2017) or 3.6 (2023) (on a scale of 100). Intellectual brilliance and winning a war produce even higher ratings increases. Controlling for other variables reduces or eliminates the importance of scandal, and this effect is stronger as time passes between surveys.

To capture the dynamics of scandals in American politics, the surveys also asked about specific past and current presidential scandals. First, we asked respondents to rank—in terms of their impact on American politics—the importance of eleven scandals (1 = most important, 11 = least important). Table 5.2 displays results from several OLS regression models using the importance of each scandal as the dependent variable. The

TABLE 5.2 Predicting the importance of each presidential scandals on greatness

	CLINTON-LEWINSKY	PLAME	TRUMP-UKRAINE	WATERGATE	IRAN-CONTRA	TEAPOT DOME	WHISKY RING
PRESIDENTIAL GREATNESS RATING FOR PRESIDENT INVOLVED	–.020(.013)	.009(.007)	.055 ***(.012)	–.001(.003)	.001(.004)	.013 *(.008)	–.006(.008)
INFORMATION ABOUT PRESIDENT	.370(.545)	.065(.470)	–1.07 **(.558)	–.036(1.60)	.087(.283)	–.041(.175)	–.079(.215)
DEMOCRAT	.200(.399)	–.349(.322)	.209(.405)	.063(.151)	–.401 *(.221)	.264(.317)	.846(.332)
MALE	–.467(.510)	1.39(.401)	–.447(.492)	–.176(.189)	.739 ***(.281)	–.584(.411)	.336(.436)
N	172	172	165	171	174	158	165
R^2	.021	.090	.147	.008	.067	.035	.041
PROB > F	.447	4.1	0.00	.360	.019	.241	.142

Source: Expert presidential surveys, fielded by the author.

Note: Dependent variable is the importance of the scandal (coded 1 = most important, 11 = less important).

*** indicates statistical significance at $p < .01$.

** $p < .05$.

* $p < .10$. Robust standard errors in parentheses.

models also include as covariates the rater's assessment of the "greatness" of each president and the amount of information each rater has about each president. The results suggest that the higher the respondents' rating of a president, the less likely that a scandal associated with this president was assessed as important. But on only two of the scandals are these results statistically significant: the Trump-Ukraine scandal and the Teapot Dome scandal. These results make sense: experts who believe a scandal to be less important give a higher rating to the president involved, essentially minimizing the impact of the scandal. This suggests that character matters for individual experts, but those ratings are nuanced by a respondent's sense of the greatness of that president.

CLINTON LEGACY

Experts often have a different view of the presidency than the public such that controversies may be more or less important in evaluating legacies. Bill Clinton is a good test subject. He wrestled the presidency away from the Republicans, who had held it for the previous twelve years, rebuilt the Democratic Party, erased a large federal budget deficit, accelerated globalization of free trade, and helped stabilize Europe after a bloody civil war. Concerns about his overly aggressive crime policy, lack of attention to crises in Africa like Darfur, and lack of support for gay marriage were blind spots in his legacy. Indeed, his time in office was born of controversy—from accusations of extramarital affairs during his 1992 race for the White House to accusations of personal financial malfeasance in Whitewater, accusations of abuse of authority in Travelgate, and an affair (and cover-up) with a White House intern. He spent much of his second term struggling for survival, leading to concerns about the distractions and "what might have been" affecting his historical stature. According to one historian, "the damage done to Clinton's place in history" was "pronounced and probably permanent."[16] The reach of the Clinton administration's scandals also affected the

2016 election. "Nobody in this country was worse than Bill Clinton with women. He was a disaster," President Trump claimed at a 2016 rally in Oregon, after his own record on women was challenged by his opponent, Hillary Clinton.

The *New York Times* White House correspondent Peter Baker observed: "After the terrorist attacks of September 11, 2001, many felt the obsession with Mr. Clinton's sex life and legal misconduct had been ludicrously misdirected. In a later era, with another president accused of instigating an insurrection to overturn an election, lying about extramarital romps in the West Wing hardly seems serious."[17] In retrospect, however, the power imbalance between the former president and Monica Lewinsky filtered through the lens of modern harassment problems and other accusations of sexual assault against Clinton (charges he denies) is seen differently. Even so, the "emerging revisionism may influence a historical legacy" of Bill Clinton even as allies have spent decades framing the "national memory of his presidency as a time of peace and prosperity."[18]

Assessing the public's perspective on Bill Clinton's legacy can help explain the role of scandals on presidential legacy. Two surveys asked similar questions about Bill Clinton's legacy as president—one before the Lewinsky scandal broke (1997) and one as his presidency was ending (2001). The first survey was a Time Magazine/CNN Poll in the field from June 4 to 5, 1997. The question was "All things considered, 25 years from now, do you think Bill Clinton will be remembered for his accomplishments as president, controversies over his personal and financial dealings, both equally, or neither." The second survey was a Gallup/CNN/USA Today poll in the field from January 5 to 7, 2001. The question was "In your view, will Clinton mostly be remembered as president for his accomplishments or for his involvement in personal scandal or something else." In neither poll were these scandals or accomplishments listed specifically, leaving respondents to decide. These questions, though not identically worded, give very similar response types and capture the same dichotomy of whether Bill Clinton's legacy was influenced more by his scandals and controversies or his accomplishments in office.

Over the four years surveyed in these two polls, the public's assessment was fairly stable: the consensus was broadly that the president's scandals would be more important in defining his legacy than his accomplishments. In the 1997 polling, before the Lewinsky scandal broke, 64 percent of the public believed that Bill Clinton would be remembered for his controversies more than his accomplishments in office. In 2001, following the Lewinsky scandal and a grueling battle for the White House in 2000, 69 percent of the public agreed that the president would be remembered more for his involvement in personal scandals than for his accomplishments. This represents only about a 2 percent change after four years that included many small scandals and one near career-ending scandal. The public certainly saw the president's legacy as tarnished a little by scandal, but there was not much malice against him. In the same 2001 poll, 65 percent of respondents did not believe the independent counsel should charge Bill Clinton with a crime after he left office and 52 percent thought President George W. Bush should pardon him if there was a criminal indictment.

Legacy for presidents also has a partisan flavor. Scholars have found that presidential greatness, like presidential approval, is shaped by partisan opinions among the public and experts.[19] A similar divide is evident for the Clinton legacy survey questions from 1997 and 2001. Table 5.3 displays the responses, four years apart, according to self-identified partisanship. Generally, as one would expect, Democrats were more likely to agree that Bill Clinton's accomplishments in office would be his legacy over his controversies. These findings were stable over time, but both those saying his accomplishments and his controversies rose slightly (although this might be accounted for by slightly different questions). Independents were similarly stable over time but tended to see the controversies as more prominent. Republicans were much more likely in both 1997 and 2001 to see Clinton's controversies as his legacy, and those figures rose significantly over the period from 78 percent to 85 percent.

Despite more critical coverage in the year following the end of his term, when legacies are often defined, the perception of Clinton's legacy was

TABLE 5.3 President Clinton known for his accomplishments or controversies

	ACCOMPLISHMENTS (PERCENT)	CONTROVERSIES (PERCENT)	BOTH EQUALLY (PERCENT)
DEMOCRATS			
1997	44	47	5
2001	47	49	3
INDEPENDENTS			
1997	20	71	3
2001	24	72	3
REPUBLICANS			
1997	15	78	2
2001	13	85	2

Source: Time Magazine/CNN poll in the field from June 4–5, 1997. The second survey was a Gallup/CNN/USA Today poll in the field from January 5–7, 2001.

similar before and after the most legacy-defining scandal (Lewinsky) broke. Asked whether Clinton should have resigned because of the affair with former White House intern Monica Lewinsky, Democratic senator Kirsten Gillibrand said, "Yes, I think that is the appropriate response."[20] Donald Trump continually referenced charges against Bill Clinton in the 2016 presidential race against Hillary Clinton, especially after Trump faced his own accusers. Attempting to control the narrative, before the first presidential debate the Trump campaign even brought three women who accused Bill Clinton of inappropriate sexual behavior (Kathleen Willey, Juanita Broaddrick, Paula Jones) and another woman (Kathy Shelton) whose rapist was defended by Hillary Clinton when she was a young lawyer. "Mr. Trump may have said some bad words, but Bill Clinton raped me and Hillary Clinton threatened me," Ms. Broaddrick said. "I don't think there's any comparison."[21] In the greatness rankings, Bill Clinton actually rose two places (to no. 12) from 2017 to 2023.

A NATURAL EXPERIMENT

Presidential greatness is a bulky evaluation, involving issues, controversies, national tragedies, jubilant celebrations, and more. But what about legacies of local politicians, about whom many people have less information? Local scandals matter. New York City mayor Eric Adams was indicted in 2024 on five federal charges of accepting straw man donations and taking bribes in the form of upgraded seats on Turkish Airlines flights around the world. A headline in the Atlantic screamed: "Don't Assume That Eric Adams Is Going Anywhere."[22] Because less is known about local candidates, the impact of scandal might be greater. These episodes may be one of the few things voters know about these public officials. In a natural experiment set in 2023, focusing on a different mayor, we can test how a late-breaking scandal in the long political life of a mayor of the nation's fourth largest city affected his political legacy.

Sylvester Turner's political journey began in the Acres Homes section of Houston, propelling him to Harvard Law School and the Texas House of Representatives and culminating in his tenure as mayor of Houston. During his time in the House, Turner established himself as a pragmatic and influential lawmaker, advocating for a wide range of issues including health care, education, and civil rights. In 2015 Turner ran for the office of mayor of Houston, for which he had previously run in 1991. Facing a crowded field of candidates, Turner emerged victorious in a runoff election, securing a decisive mandate to lead the city forward, especially on fiscal issues. His campaign focused on addressing key issues facing Houston, including infrastructure, environmental justice (especially dumping issues), public safety, economic development, and, of course, traffic. Turner's message ("If you can dream it, you can do it") resonated with voters, who saw in him a leader capable of confronting the city's challenges with pragmatism and vision. But his personal style sometimes got in the way—the *Houston Chronicle* noted "his my-way-or-the-highway approach toward negotiation and his penchant for holding grudges well beyond what good governance allows."[23]

Upon assuming office in January 2016, Turner wasted no time in addressing the city's pension crisis, brokering reforms to stabilize the city's ailing $5.6 billion pension system in crisis and alleviate financial strain on the city budget. In addition to these issues, public safety remained a top concern, with efforts to implement community policing strategies, combat violent crime, and improve police-community relations. The administration worked to promote affordable housing initiatives—serving as a national model—and enhance transportation infrastructure to address the city's growing population and urban development needs. One of the most unexpected challenges of his tenure came in the form of Hurricane Harvey, a catastrophic natural disaster that devastated the city in August 2017. Turner's response to the crisis was widely praised for its effectiveness and coordination. Covid and Winter Storm Uri—a freeze that knocked out power to most of the state for days, leading to more than a hundred deaths—also tested the mayor. In addition to his handling of disasters, Turner prioritized infrastructure investment as a cornerstone of his administration. Recognizing the importance of modernizing Houston's transportation network and improving flood control measures, Turner championed ambitious initiatives aimed at enhancing the city's resilience to future disasters and fostering sustainable growth.

Yet Turner's administration was far from scandal free. His eight years in office saw several corruption and ethics charges, some pointing to what they called a "culture of corruption" at city hall.[24] Tom McCasland, the director of the city's Housing and Community Development Department, was fired in 2021, accusing the mayor of allocating money to a favored developer to secure $15 million in federal disaster recovery funds meant to replace housing lost during Hurricane Harvey.[25] What looked like a competitive award process, McCasland claimed, was actually a predetermined outcome designed to bankroll "a certain developer to the detriment of working families who need affordable homes." "There is no charade," Turner said. "Comments made by the former Director of the City of Houston Housing and Community Development Department are puzzling, inflated, and wrong"—but the mayor's former longtime law partner was among those who benefited from the deal. In another scandal, William-Paul Thomas, the mayor's liaison to the city council, pled guilty to a federal public corruption charge in which Thoams was offered thousands of dollars to use his city government position to help a Houston business owner reclassify a bar as a restaurant so he could circumvent Covid-19 restrictions. The mayor denied knowing any details of the matter.[26]

The Turner administration, it seemed, saved the biggest scandal for last. As his term as mayor was drawing to a close, Mayor Turner used his final state of the city address in September 27, 2023 to distribute to attendees a ninety-page autobiography and administrative lookback called "A Winning Legacy—the Power of Vision, Collaboration, Resilience and Transformation." The book was supposed to burnish his legacy before his second term ended on December 31, 2023, but the distribution drew unwelcome attention when a former political rival alleged that the mayor had pressured Houston First Corporation, a city-affiliated local government corporation that serves as the city's convention and marketing agency and whose directors are appointed by the mayor, to pay the production costs of six hundred copies of the book. The board chair and chief executive officer admitted he requested that the agency pay the cost of the book but denied any "arm-twisting" from Turner—no public funds were to be used, he said, and he was not initially sure if the agency had agreed to cover the cost of the book from the start. A budget provided by Houston First suggested, however, that even without the cost of the book, the $602,0000 in event expenses had already exceeded revenues.[27] By January 2024, the mayor reported he paid $124,000 in campaign funds to pay for production of the book.

In a real-time experiment, a survey that included a question about the mayor's legacy was in the field at the time the scandal broke. SurveyUSA conducted the survey, interviewing 1,120 adults from the city of Houston November 13 to 18, 2023. The survey was conducted online, using a blended sample, mixed mode approach.[28] Because Houston is a diverse city, we oversampled both Latino and Asian voters by 123 percent and

406 percent, respectively, to provide greater fidelity to these groups of respondents.[29] The legacy question asked, "As Mayor Sylvester Turner leaves office after 8 years, do you have a favorable or an unfavorable opinion of his time in office?" The answer was coded from "strongly favorable" (1) to "strongly unfavorable" (5).

The story broke on a local television station November 15, 2023, after the poll was in the field for two days.[30] The timing of the public revelations cleanly split the sample, with 717 respondents completing the survey before the story broke and 720 respondents completing the survey from the day the scandal broke to the close of the survey. Key independent variables include party (Democrat = 1); race (Black = 1); marital status (married = 1); education (some high school = 1, graduate degree = 6); income (less than $30,000 = 1, more than $100,000 = 5); and age (continuous variable). The mean support of Turner's tenure in office was 2.8 on a scale of 5; 22 percent had a strongly favorable opinion of his time in office, compared to 13 percent strongly unfavorable. Democrats (31 percent strongly favorable) and Black respondents (37 percent strongly favorable) had the most favorable opinions, compared to Republicans (13 percent strongly favorable) and white respondents (10 percent strongly favorable). Using standard regression models to test the impact of various characteristics on legacy assessments, including the scandal by itself and together with other demographic factors, we estimate three models, shown in table 5.4.

By itself, the effect of the scandal on respondents' opinions of the mayor's time in office is statistically significant but small. On a five-point scale, respondents in model 1 were .147 points more likely to register an unfavorable opinion after the scandal broke. However, in model 2, when key demographic characteristics—party and race—are included, the effect of scandal disappears. Only being a Democrat or Black mattered in predicting approval of the mayor's time in office. The coefficients are negative (since the variable is coded with 1 as very favorable) and both substantively and statistically strong: self-identified Democrats are the most favorable toward the mayor, followed by Black respondents. In the full

TABLE 5.4 Predictors of Mayor Turner's legacy

	MODEL 1 SCANDAL ONLY	MODEL 2 SCANDAL + DEMOGRAPHICS	MODEL 3 FULL MODEL
SCANDAL BREAK	.147 ** (.077)	.031 (.074)	.028 (.076)
DEMOCRAT	—	-.666 *** (.075)	-.665 *** (.075)
BLACK	—	-.526 *** (.086)	-.538 *** (.089)
MARRIED	—	—	.098 (.079)
EDUCATION	—	—	-.025 (.029)
INCOME	—	—	.031 (.030)
AGE	—	—	-.002 (.002)
N	1,025	1,025	1.025
R^2 (ADJUSTED)	.002	.120	.119

Source: SurveyUSA survey, 2023.

Note: OLS regression. Dependent variable: favorable opinion of Mayor Turner's time in office.

model (model 3), none of the expanded demographic characteristics is statistically significant in predicting favorable legacy except Democratic and Black respondents.

In his book *Marked Men*, Nyron Crawford finds that Black political leaders survive scandals because of Black voters' suspicions about law enforcement actions against the African American community. He concludes that "their behavior is less about forgiveness or tolerance of malfeasance than an effort to protect Black representation from state actors who may have ulterior motives for their actions."[31] This racialized suspicion leads Black voters to suspect that government is acting in bad faith in prosecuting Black leaders, resulting in politicians from African American communities surviving scandals. These forces—along with partisanship—seem to be at play in this case as Turner, only the second Black mayor of Houston, was well liked in the Black community, providing a buffer of support.

CONCLUSION

By itself, none of the evidence presented in this chapter provides definitive proof that scandals have little effect on political legacies. The evidence shows some small effects in isolation, under particular conditions, and in different institutional settings. And legacies are always changing, reshaped by the passage of time, issues, personalities, culture, and norms. But, taken as a whole, the evidence is clear: scandals have only a modest effect on the body of a politician's legacy. Why? People generally tend to forget scandals, and partisans misremember scandals affecting the politicians they support.

CONCLUSION

Why Scandals Are Good (and Why We Need Them)

Who is he [Arnold Rothstein] anyhow, an actor?

No.

A dentist?

". . . No, he's a gambler." Gatsby hesitated, then added cooly: "He's the man who fixed the World Series back in 1919."

"Fixed the World Series?" I repeated.

The idea staggered me. I remembered, of course, that the World Series had been fixed in 1919, but if I had thought of it at all I would have thought of it as something that merely *happened*, the end of an inevitable chain. It never occurred to me that one man could start to play with the faith of fifty million people—with the singlemindedness of a burglar blowing a safe.

"How did he happen to do that?" I asked after a minute.

"He just saw the opportunity."

"Why isn't he in jail?"

"They can't get him, old sport. He's a smart man."

—F. SCOTT FITZGERALD, *THE GREAT GATSBY*

The 1919 baseball World Series saw the heavily favored Chicago White Sox fall to the Cincinnati Reds in an improbable 10–5 win in game eight (of a best-of-nine series) of the final annual American League–National League clash. After the series ended, rumors flew that gamblers had paid off several White Sox players (derisively termed Black Sox thereafter), including the slugger "Shoeless" Joe Jackson and the star pitcher Eddie Cicotte. The eight accused big leaguers were indicted by a grand jury and tried for conspiracy; they confessed to the crime but were found not guilty on nine counts of conspiracy after the official records of their grand jury confessions mysteriously vanished. But the scandal had done its damage. Capturing public sentiment about the heartbreaking scandal, called the "Big Fix" at the time, was an article in the *Chicago Daily News* with the headline "Say, It Ain't So, Joe."

One day after the acquittal, Judge Kenesaw "Mountain" Landis, recently appointed as baseball's first commissioner, permanently banned the accused eight "Black Sox" from baseball for life for "selling out baseball."[1] Commissioner Landis was appointed to lead baseball through its roughest inning: accusations of price fixing in 1919 shocked the public and crippled faith in the nation's nascent sports pastime. Baseball's National League president John Heydler expressed at the time a desire for a chairman to "rule with an iron hand," proclaiming that "baseball has lacked a hand like that for years. It needs it now worse than ever."[2] The scandal, and the actions of the former federal judge known for taking on corporations turned firebrand commissioner, helped to cleanse the young sport in the darkest moment. Over the next several years, the shock-of-white-hair commissioner made it his mission to rid the game of crooks and gamblers who had found their way into the pockets of players and owners, including increasing accountability of the major league teams' association with minor league teams and the process for funneling up-and-coming players to the big leagues.[3]

The indelible effect of baseball's first major scandal was a pivot point in how scandals were handled by major league sports and had ramifications for similar future events. Scandals in the political world, especially in the United States, are no different. Political scandals are frequently treated as a stain on the political system, resulting from poor personal judgment, lax rule enforcement, or bald political corruption. Media coverage treats these as unwelcome hiccups in an otherwise routine series of events. Partisans treat them as a nuisance. Yet, as a forest fire germinates and renews a field, political scandals may help the public and the media enhance accountability, renew trust in government, and focus on key issues of concern. In this concluding chapter, I review the literature on the legacy and impact of political scandals and underscore the ways in which scandals have a potentially positive effect on institutional accountability and voter attentiveness. Finally, I outline an agenda for renewing our study of political scandals as an instrument of media and institutional systemic recalibration and offer some guidance on how to find accountability in the aftermath of political scandals.

WHAT HAVE WE LEARNED?

Partisan political change and polarized fragmentation of the media landscape have created divisions in American politics even on moral or ethical transgressions assumed sacrosanct. The literature has been divided about the effects of scandals: some argue that scandals affect politicians negatively while others suggest polarization minimizes the deleterious effects of scandals on incumbents. With extensive survey evidence and five decades of comprehensive data on scandals, this book finds that political scandals still matter, but the effects vary across institutions and individuals. Partisanship is often the culprit. Extreme partisans are significantly more likely than less partisan respondents to embrace joy in scandals hitting political opponents. Democrats are more aggressive in their embrace of scandals, but Republicans are more permissive of bad political behavior, especially by political leaders of their own party. Partisan party attachments drive scandal forgiveness. Independents are much more likely than Republicans or Democrats to stop supporting candidates who trade favors for financial gain, have committed major criminal acts in the past or while in office, or commit financial fraud at their workplace. Followers of the two major parties are more likely to give leeway to their own partisan public officials when they engage in bad behavior than to their opponents.

Politicians in earlier eras faced greater negative consequences of scandals than those of later eras. For members of Congress specifically, the negative consequences of scandals remained high in the Watergate era but has since dissipated with time. Scandals in the Watergate era led to more resignations in Congress but fewer resignations of White House officials in the 1990s. For presidents, typically robust survival of scandal while in office has diminished since the Lewinsky era, despite a polarized political world protecting partisan politicians. During the Trump administration, White House officials did not survive in office at rates greater than in past eras, demonstrating only modest support for the "Trump effect." However, politicians generally survived scandal more in the polarized era, hinting at the changing role of political scandals. Governors hardly faced scandals in the past decade, partly because of increasingly unified government at the state level. These findings underscore the unique dynamics for each institution and highlight potential differences between elected officials. Discussion of the impact of political scandals should assess the unique institutional arrangements of each political figure as well as the politics of the time in which they serve.

At the core of this is the fact that, as with so many complications in American politics today, partisan politics buffers the impact of scandals. These results suggest support for the notion that partisanship reduces the negative impact of scandal on some incumbent politicians. As *Vox*'s Matthew Yglesias argues, referencing affective polarization, "there's 'us' and 'them,' " and the possibility of persuasion is off the table."[4] The scandal "breaking point" for the most partisan respondents is higher than for nonpartisan respondents: the most partisan publics are more tolerant of scandals involving their own party's politicians than less ideologically motivated publics. Higher scores on an affective partisan scale and greater tolerance for partisan bickering ("bare-knuckle politics") predict respondents enjoying scandals more involving a political opponent. Attraction to scandals is strongly associated with dislike of the other party. And, as our experimental evidence shows, partisan respondents can easily be primed to see controversy—whether it is a real scandal or not.

MAKE SCANDALS GREAT AGAIN: THE POTENTIALLY POSITIVE EFFECTS OF SCANDALS ON DEMOCRACY

Although scandals have various consequences—not all negative—for the individual players and scuff up the integrity of the political system, the aftermath of scandals can have potentially positive effects on the political system. Take the most infamous political scandal in American history: Watergate. This caper had it all—slush funds, hush money, wiretaps, burglaries, and dozens of "dirty tricks," all in the name of national security and keeping political enemies at bay. As the dust settled, calls for greater campaign finance regulation, stricter ethics codes, and limits on government surveillance were front-page news. The system responded. Congress passed the 1974 Federal Election Campaign Act to regulate donations and limit the effect of large donors. The Ethics in Government Act of 1978 created mandatory public disclosure of financial and employment histories for public officials and their families. The Presidential Records Act systematized the collection and preservation of White House records. The Foreign Intelligence Surveillance Act set limits on government spying on U.S. citizens.[5]

The Watergate caper, considered the most noxious scandal in U.S. history, serves as a good example of a scandal that corrected the system in multiple ways.[6] The consequences of Watergate—beyond the needed policy changes—included a range of ethos changes in American politics, including the birth of investigative journalism, closer judicial scrutiny of presidential power (especially related to extraconstitutional matters not associated with national security), and expanded congressional oversight. These institutional and policy changes, in addition to the political changes that turned over a significant number of elected representatives at the state and federal levels, made Watergate the standard by which all other political scandals are judged. While Watergate is generally seen as a negative, the upshot to the scandal that rocked the world is that it ushered in an era of accountability. Do modern scandals do the same? Scandals' loss of impact means a loss of accountability; in short, politicians are getting away with it, and we are letting them. How are scandals, usually used a raw material for explosive charges against opponents, good for democracy?

DIRECTING ATTENTION TO CANDIDATES AND ISSUES

The American public is notoriously inattentive to politics, often being unable to answer even basic questions about the players, politics, or the process. Scandals change that in a good way. Public attentiveness to some accused public wrongdoing is heightened during scandals. Scandals direct attention to an issue otherwise off most people's radar, such as how the Iran-Contra scandal inadvertently spurred voters to think about foreign policy in the 1988 election.[7] The author of the podcast *Fiasco* investigated the Iran-Contra scandal four decades after it took place and found the lessons were still important: "It makes you think about the porous boundary between the government and contractors, and you see the downsides of farming out foreign policy to people who aren't accountable to voters."[8] Even normally hidden institutions in government get attention during scandals, such as when extrajudicial events hit the courts. When media reports broke stories about Supreme Court justice Clarence Thomas taking gifts from big-money Republican donors, the usual scant attention people paid to the Supreme Court (about 3 percent seeking information) surged more than 300 percent, including both Republicans and Democrats.[9]

Scandals may also help to change public discourse about issues and candidates. Scandals increase the quality of discourse in the media about issues or about the role of citizens.[10] Governors and president are more likely to address issues of concern to the public, including pocketbook issues such as health care, the economy, and welfare.[11] Media critic Schudson argues that major scandals like Watergate offer a language and a framework for public discourse that helps to set in motion an understanding about future scandals.[12] These corrections are necessary in democracies that "encourage distrust of authority." The description of the public as blind to anything except scandal is incorrect. The political scientist Beth Miller found that when subjects were exposed to a fictitious candidate through five sequential phony articles, in which one group got five policy articles and a second group got four policy articles and one article about an extramarital affair, the group exposed to the scandal were more likely to remember the candidate's policy positions. She concludes that respondents "appear to have thought more carefully about the candidate after hearing such negative information."[13]

SYSTEMIC CORRECTIONS

The system as a whole is attentive to political scandals, even small ones. This is true of both external and internal actors and actors over whom public officials have varying degrees of control. The executive branch internally responds to scandals by looking for manifestations of corruption in other parts of government, causing a larger footprint of scandal than just the specific office or individual.[14] The U.S. Congress responds to national scandals by holding additional hearings to investigate malfeasance, wrongdoing, or corruption.[15] At the state level, economic growth, government spending, or looser ethics laws signal more gubernatorial scandals.[16] This is consistent with how states react legislatively to scandal: Witko finds that initiative at the state level, a liberal government, strong good-government groups, legislative professionalism, and scandal increase the likelihood of a state increasing the stringency of its regulations.[17] Each of these reactions is meaningful and reasonable: there are both internal and external checks in the aftermath of political scandals, allowing the system to recalibrate.

This makes it more important than ever that the system be allowed to function with proper guardrails. Federal watchdogs took a hard hit during the Trump years, reeling from firings and pressure campaign from the White House and its allies. In 2025 the White House halted FBI background checks for senior staff members.[18] In his first term, in 2020, Trump fired the inspector general (IG) for the intelligence community after the whistleblower forwarded a complaint to Congress that figured in the president impeachment. Another IG for the State Department was dismissed, and a third was demoted after leading efforts on pandemic oversight. The IG at the Transportation Department was switched out when he began a probe into whether Secretary Elaine Chao, who was married to Republican Senate majority leader Mitch McConnell, had directed money to Kentucky to help her husband's reelection effort.[19] President Trump summarily fired seventeen inspectors general in 2025 within days of taking office. Presidents are allowed to remove these IGs (after notifying Congress) and Trump is not the first president to tangle with these officials; President Obama was accused of firing the IG for the Corporation for National Community Service for political reasons.[20] But these politically motivated demotions or firings threaten the independence of the system, which is designed to sniff out corruption or conflicts of interest. The law professor Saikrishna Prakash argues that "we ought to strengthen these crucial officials" who help the government "function properly and legally."[21]

In prosecuting corrupt officials, it has been found that prosecutors are more willing to initiate additional cases when there are higher-level executive scandals in the White House (especially involving federal officials) and the governor's mansion (especially involving state and local officials).[22] These findings suggest that a rise in prosecutions occurred only after a record number of executive scandals at the national level, suggesting a high threshold before concerns about systemic corruption arise. Inspectors general also increase their audits and overall investigatory activity in the wake of more administration scandals, responding positively to signals about possible systemic corruption. The ripple effect of scandals, then, has a longer-term effect than presumed, one that is often unseen but creates a favorable outcome for accountability.

CONCLUSION

SCANDAL SALVATION

If scandals are unavoidable and the impact is minimized in a polarized political world—one that does not look to be much different for the foreseeable future—are we destined to just accept wrongdoing from politicians and the loss of accountability that comes with it? Political science has some answers that might mitigate the frequency and severity of scandals.

CIVIC EDUCATION

Understanding the system, both the players and the rules, is critical to an informed and engaged electorate. Decades of scholarship shows that civic education promotes healthy public discussion and enhances community activism.[23] With scandals, understanding the context of a candidate's background and the policy ramifications of their issue positions will make a politician's actions more prominent for voters. For instance, politicians who are seen as more hypocritical (for instance, running on family values but being caught in an extramarital affair) are more likely to be seen negatively in general and as incompetent in office.[24] We also know from chapter 3 that education—having attended or graduated from college—mitigates the blood sport of scandal. Those with more education are less likely to revel in an opponent's scandals.

Voters can be primed to consider welcome traits in their candidates. Important positive candidate traits, such as being honest, admitting when wrong, and showing respect for candidates, were positive predictors of a belief that scandals were unwelcome. The implication is that the public can be trained on the norms of positive, high-quality campaigning, which in turn reduces the appetite for scandals. Partisans accept greater negative campaigning if their side (not their opponents) are engaging in it, and Independents are less willing to accept this type of campaigning because of fewer partisan attachments, as we saw in chapter 3. Most Independents have ideological preferences, but the absence of strong partisan attachments reduces their blood lust for scandals. In general, then, efforts to lower the temperature of the partisan battles that are rife in modern politics will help mitigate the divisive impact of political scandals.

But the state of civics education is at a nadir—a "civics education crisis," according to the *Washington Post*.[25] Only nine states and the District of Columbia require one year of U.S. government or civics, and those curricula are heavy on knowledge and light on building civics skills.[26] Not surprisingly, according to the Annenberg Public Policy Center of the University of Pennsylvania, civic knowledge is alarmingly low, with a bare majority of Americans (56 percent) able to identify the three branches of government and nearly one in five (20 percent) unable to identify any. Concurrent with these trends, according the American Bar Association, confidence in our democratic institutions has cratered. Only 5, 13, and 16 percent of Americans have a "great deal" of confidence in Congress, the Supreme Court, and the presidency, respectively. Civic ignorance and distrust "fuel political polarization, registering at the highest levels in the modern era."[27] Adapting curriculum to changing patterns can make a big difference in how people see scandals.

ADAPTING LAWS

Not every misuse of public funds is a scandal. In Ohio, four members of a local school board attending a conference in the state capital stayed at a hotel that charged three times the rate of a neighboring hotel. In another case, a superintendent's contract enabled him to receive more than $170,000 in public funds to pay off his college loans. Neither was illegal, but both were errors in judgment furthering public perception of corruption. The Ohio state auditor Dave Yost took action. In 2023 he implemented a new policy allowing for findings of "abuse" of financial office, actions that were not illegal but also not acceptable. "We would see isolated instances where people were not breaking the law, but were treating the public purse as their own ATM," said Yost, who emphasizes that most public employees are well intentioned. "There was a need for us to make a public record of it."[28] The voters should know, he reasoned, and such efforts to improve transparency in government minimizes scandals.

In fact, we know that these reporting laws have an effect on reducing the number of scandals. In other nations, such as Romania, anticorruption efforts systematically reduce electoral manipulation through a backlash against corrupt politicians.[29] But these reforms are not a silver bullet. The tally of sexual harassment charges has grown despite the vast majority of state legislative chambers requiring lawmakers to undergo training about sexual harassment. At least two thirds of all legislatures have enacted some new law in the MeToo era, including clear channels for reporting allegations, expanded legal protections for whistleblowers, and more sunlight on secret settlements. "Training doesn't guarantee that harassment will stop," said Debbie Walsh, director of the Center for American Women and Politics at Rutgers University.[30] The political scientists Justin Kirland and Jeffrey Harden, in their book *The Illusion of Accountability*, find that open meetings laws do not alter legislators' behavior, but an expanded system of organized interests—as James Madison argued in *Federalist* 10—can help hold politicians accountable by engaging the public.

But ethics and disclosure laws do limit scandals: those states that have more disclosure requirements (such as reporting income, gifts, or honorariums) are less likely to have state-level scandals.[31] More stringent ethics laws, requiring elected officials to disclose their financial, ethical, or employment activities, lead to fewer scandals in states that have them. Tougher ethics legislation (especially client and honorarium disclosure legislation) reduces the emergence or revelation of scandals. The implication is that ethics legislation in general limits the number of revealed scandals. Why? States that pass and enforce such legislation are more likely to be states where effective and efficient government is valued. Certain types of individuals, then, are more likely to run and win in these states. Alternatively, governors and their staff may act more ethically and avoid any appearance of impropriety, reducing the number of scandals.

THE MEDIA MUST STEP UP

The role of the media as gatekeepers has narrowed since the dawn of the internet. The media served as arbiters of information, referees, calling out lies, fact-checking misleading claims, and more. They could set the flow of information and set the terms of the conversation.[32] But not anymore. Media sources have multiplied, leaving the mainstream media playing defense instead of offense, having to respond to news out of a myriad of sources. For instance, Alabama secretary of state John Merrill had a secret: he was carrying on an affair with a staff member, which he was sure would remain secret. It did, until a self-described New Right political blog published recordings of the woman. The impact killed Merrill's career. A married father of two, admitting the affair, kept his position as secretary of state but did not make an anticipated run for U.S. Senate that year. Intraparty politics were to blame. The woman claimed she was tricked to talk on a recording by the son of Alabama chief justice Roy Moore, who had a long-held political grudge against Merrill dating back to a Senate race in which Merrill, as secretary of state, had certified the election for Moore's Democratic opponent despite Moore's claims of voter fraud.[33]

Clarity of responsibility is necessary for the media. The greater the clarity, the more difficult time politicians have in shifting blame because voters have an easier time monitoring public officials and holding them accountable.[34] In Italy, incumbent renominations are negatively associated with the number of press mentions that link the incumbent to corruption—but only when corruption is salient.[35] That is where the media come in. Coverage of financial scandals involving banks in the United States increases the public's appetite for regulation.[36] Corporate accounting scandals at Enron and WorldCom led to the speedy passage of the Sarbanes-Oxley law on corporate governance, a law the Republican majority had opposed only months before.

Other scholars challenge the assertion that scandals enhance the media's protective role in American politics. Williams and Delli Carpini argue that the Clinton-Lewinsky scandal represented the virtual elimination of the gatekeeping role of the mainstream media because there are no "gates" through which information passes. If there are no gates, there can be no gatekeepers.[37] Today's influencers can easily (even unknowingly) spread lies or propaganda because the "engagement-fueled logic of social media has bequeathed us a world in which what's trending is a yardstick for what's true."[38] Happily, scholars have found that being exposed to hypothetical cheating and corruption in government had no effect on the likelihood of a person cheating, suggesting limited contagion effects.[39] Even so, exposure to scandal, especially among out-partisans, helps shed light on events a partisan audience may not otherwise see. For example, when Republicans were exposed to headlines about the Trump-Russia scandal from 2017, they reacted more negatively than Democrats or Independents, rating Trump's performance as lower and expressing more negative emotions about him.[40] Counterprogramming can work at influencing even hardened political preferences.

(RE)DEFINING "BRIBERY"

In the Commonwealth of Virginia, former governor Robert McDonnell and his wife were charged with illegally accepting gifts, luxury vacations, and large loans from a wealthy Richmond businessman who sought in return special treatment from state government for his dietary supplement business.[41] It was argued that the former governor and his wife were in financial trouble and willing to trade personal favors for access to top state government officials. In September 2014, a federal jury found them guilty of public corruption.[42] But that is not the end of the story. The Supreme Court took the case. At issue was whether the definition of "official act" in the federal statute used to convict the McDonnells was properly applied and whether the jury had been properly instructed on this definition at trial. The Court ruled that merely setting up a meeting, hosting an event, or calling another public official does not constitute an "official act." Lawyers for the former governor argued that the government could prove bribery only if the governor formally exercised governmental power in exchange for the Rolex watch he took from a benefactor.[43] The effect was to narrow the legal definition of public corruption, making it harder for prosecutors to prove that a public official had engaged in bribery. As a Georgetown Law School professor put it, the courts must now allow behavior that "looks, to any reasonable observer, sketchy as hell."[44]

Some politicians, of course, cheered. Since the decision, the courts have overturned four other convictions in public corruption cases.[45] Former Democratic speaker of the New York House Sheldon Silver had his conviction for corruption charges (extortion, wire fraud, and mail fraud stemming from a bribe the politician was said to have taken from real estate developers) overturned because of the Supreme Court's ruling in *McDonnell v. United States*. Former Republican New York state senate majority leader Dean Skelos and his son had their federal bribery convictions overturned as well. Louisiana Democratic representative William J. Jefferson, who was caught with $90,000 in his freezer, also had his 2012 conviction overturned. Lawyers for New Jersey senator Bob Menendez used similar arguments to try to dismiss the bribery case against him; the case was not dismissed but ended in a mistrial in 2017 (he was, however, tried and convicted on new charges in 2024). Prosecutors must be given proper tools to combat scandals related to corruption or ethical breaches, especially since scholarship suggests that pending criminal cases are more likely to be dropped for politicians who win reelection to the majority party. In addition, a code of conduct for the judiciary—and maybe all public officials—would hold individuals to a higher ethical standard.

"LORDY, I HOPE THERE ARE TAPES"

The Oval Office meeting in May 2017 between FBI director James Comey and President Trump did not go well. The FBI investigation (called "Crossfire Hurricane") investigated potentially illegal activity involving Russia's efforts to meddle in the 2016 election—and the Trump campaign's involvement. Comey documented his White House conversations in memoranda after the encounters. In one such meeting, Comey recalled, Trump hinted that Comey should drop the FBI's investigation into Trump's first national security adviser, Michael Flynn, who eventually pled guilty to lying to investigators about his contact with the Russian ambassador.[46] Flynn was the only member of the Trump administration charged as part of special counsel Robert Mueller's Russia investigation (Trump would pardon Flynn in 2020).[47] Trump tweeted, "Comey better hope there are no 'tapes' of our conversations before he starts leaking to the press!" "Lordy, I hope there are tapes," Comey responded, using the "kitschiest of colloquialisms" when he testified in front of a Senate Intelligence Committee hearing after being fired by President Trump, implying that he would welcome a full transcript of the meeting.[48]

Politicians may try to wiggle out of scandal—a natural response when caught. But in a digital age when everything is caught on camera, are politicians' evasion strategies still useful? Scholars find that politicians who are caught red-handed (so to speak) on video are held accountable when that video evidence is available. That is, politicians nailed in scandal by text evidence can successfully make misinformation claims, but these claims are ineffective when there is video evidence.[49] Politicians' claims that video content is faked are generally not believed. Increased monitoring, available public records, and fact-checking (especially in real time) are critical to transparency.

PARTY LEADERS MUST STEP UP

Voters are not always particularly good at holding politicians accountable. The politicization of the two-party system and rising partisanship—stoking distrust and retreat to each party's camp—yields a political system that in many cases limits accountability at the ballot box. Leaders have the oversight capacity to restrain politicians in their own party—oversight that might make these members take fewer risks.[50] In other countries, where party leaders have more say over which incumbents are renominated, those leaders play a larger role in maintaining a positive party reputation and enhancing the odds of winning a legislative majority.[51] This highlights the role of party leaders in forcing scandalized politicians out of office to enforce democratic accountability. This is good for the political system, democratic integrity, and the party's reputation alike.

One way leaders can sidestep the partisan fray is to engage in constructive arguments and lead with positive politics. Partisans of both stripes hold leaders to a higher standard, and leaders are often judged harshly for negative comments about opposition politicians. Most people want political leaders to "cultivate positive working relationships to govern effectively and pursue policy objectives—incivility undermines this primary aim."[52] A positive approach is healthy for leader reputation too. Incivility makes the name-caller seem less warm and does less for perceptions of dominance or honesty; this "warmth deficit" is the reputational cost of nasty politics.[53] Calling out bad behavior can be electorally beneficial. In Europe, among voters who are positive toward multiculturalism, exposure to a news story about persecution of ethnic or racial minorities boosts support for free speech and perceived visibility and support for the opposition party.[54]

Parties that do not learn the lesson about party orientation and partisan blame, especially after a scandal, may find themselves struggling politically. The scandal involving Republican Massachusetts representative Mark Foley's improper behavior toward several congressional pages contributed substantially to the Democratic tide in the 2006 midterm elections. Disapproval of the Republican leadership's seeming indifference to Foley's immorality aided not only Democrats running for Congress but also Democrats running for governor.[55] Specific reform proposals following scandals are often mired in partisan conflict. Congress has shown a willingness to engage in institutional maintenance when necessary, but even nonideological issues like "good government" reforms become mired in ideological and partisan conflict in a polarized era. In the United Kingdom in 2009, dozens of members of Parliament were nabbed claiming expenses such as second homes, overclaiming for meals, and evading taxes. The majority party speaker of the House of Commons resigned, six cabinet members resigned, and several members of Parliament decided not to run again or were barred from representing Labour in the upcoming local elections. The scandal broke only a week before the 2009 elections, causing an already unpopular Labour government to take brutal losses at the ballot box. Party commonality and careful gatekeeping allows the public to understand more easily and (potentially) to punish a party for wrongdoing. This improves accountability.

THE PUBLIC MUST DO ITS PART

Scandals rest at the feet of politicians who got themselves into trouble, but how we as the public react to these events is on us. We know there is often lessen accountability for scandals in a polarized age because partisans overly punish opposition politicians and overlook misdeeds by their own. Making friends across the partisan divide can help. Having friendships that cross party lines is associated with warmer feelings toward the opposing party, especially among Republicans. But few such friendships exist: just 7 percent of Republicans and 6 percent of Democrats report having "a lot" of friends in the other party.[56] Theories of civic friendship show that interparty friendships work by "catalyzing empathy, reducing prejudice, furthering justice, and even restoring democracy."[57] The empathy created by these cross-partisan friendships can foster connection and a reduction in political tensions.[58] This smoothing of friction can establish better boundaries for political wrongdoing by public officials and give people of all ideologies a rounder perspective.

The public is also reflexively less likely to hold officials in their own party accountable for mistakes, reserving harsh judgments for the opposition party.[59] This partisan polarization creates artificial divides with no nuance or room for compromise, limiting accountability. I have provided a series of questions citizens should ask themselves when a politician is caught in scandal, designed to encourage self-reflection and reduce partisan animosity. These questions are without judgment; they do not require agreement about wrongdoing but seek to produce a realistic assessment of the effect of wrongdoing on the politicians and the system. The goal is to repair trust and focus on systemic integrity, trust in democracy, and faith in political leaders.

If the scandal involves a member of the opposition party:

- Looking past the reflexive political combat, how important is this scandal to the politician's ability to do their job?
- Is your outrage about the scandal driven by political combat or by the nature of the scandal itself?

- Are you seeking source material about the scandal that reflects a neutral assessment of the events?

If the scandal involves a member of your party:

- Assess the importance of the scandal and its impact.
  - Did the scandal break any laws or campaign promises?
  - Did the scandal violate any professional norms or ethical standards?
  - Would you have trouble explaining this scandal to a child?
- Trust in politicians is important, as is taking off partisan blinders to understand the impact of a scandal.
  - How does the scandal affect the image of the person or the party?
  - Has your trust in that person fallen?
- Systemic health means voters must police who runs government.
  - What does the scandal do to the reputation of the institution or democracy?
  - Has the scandal increased your cynicism about politics or about politicians?
  - Can this person still do their job despite the scandal?
  - Can you see another candidate or public official better suited to serve in this role?

CONCLUSION

Just over a hundred years after the "Black Sox" scandal rocked the south side of Chicago and Major League Baseball, twelve miles north across the Illinois prairie along the shores of Lake Michigan, the Chicago Cubs signed a ten-year, hundred-million-dollar partnership deal with Draft-Kings to allow legal sports betting at a restaurant and bar connected to historic Wrigley Field.[60] The club was the first major league team to open a sports book at their home stadium. This partnership between an online betting site and a major league team is an ignominious coda to gambling in baseball and a stark reminder: yesterday's scandals are tomorrow's opportunity. Even Pete Rose—banned from baseball for betting on the Reds team he was managing at the time—had his lifetime ban from the sport posthumously lifted, making him eligible for the Hall of Fame.

The media, executive branch officials, legislators, prosecutors—and we!—all have a responsibility to protect their interests and the political system. In the aftermath of scandals, the media investigate charges of corruption, malfeasance, or lying. Politicians often withstand scandal by expanding their political muscle. Legislators probe individuals and events, evaluate the evidence, and use this information in political ways to sanitize the system or, if necessary, to impeach or remove an official. Prosecutors and other investigators determine whether laws have been broken and the severity of these infractions. Thus, while the public may quickly tire of scandal, forgive the participants, and return to routine political activity, the system plays a longer game. The extent of the impact, especially positive effects as the system attempts to recover, is less well understood. This book has provided a clear road map for exploring the beneficial aspects of scandals for the political system—and a warning about what happens if scandals do not matter.

NOTES

INTRODUCTION: THE DEATH OF SCANDAL?

The epigraphs are taken from Colin Dwyer, "Donald Trump: 'I Could . . . Shoot Somebody, and I Wouldn't Lose Any Voters," National Public Radio, January 23, 2016; and Zachary Basu, "Never Back Down: Rich and Powerful Exploit Post-Shame Society," *Axios*, June 18, 2023.

1. Peter Baker, "For Trump, a Lifetime of Scandals Heads Toward a Moment of Judgment," *New York Times*, October 21, 2024.
2. Sam Levine, "George Santos Admits to Being a 'Terrible Liar,'" *Guardian*, February 21, 2023, https://www.theguardian.com/us-news/2023/feb/21/george-santos-piers-morgan-terrible-liar.
3. Matt Stieb and Margaret Hartmann, "Here's Every Single Lie Told by George Santos," *New York Magazine*, March 8, 2024, https://nymag.com/intelligencer/article/guide-george-santos-lies.html.
4. Steven Shepard, "The 'Scandal Penalty' That George Santos Could Impose on NY-03," *Politico*, February 18, 2024, https://www.politico.com/news/2024/02/13/george-santos-scandal-new-york-election-00141174.
5. Jon Levine, "George Santos to Announce Reelection Campaign Monday," *New York Post*, April 15, 2023, https://nypost.com/2023/04/15/george-santos-to-announce-reelection-campaign-monday/.
6. Tamara Keith, "When Politicians Have No Shame, the Old Rules Don't Apply," National Public Radio, February 15, 2023, https://www.npr.org/2023/02/15/1157049312/george-santos-politics-of-shame.

INTRODUCTION

7. Benjamin Ginsberg and Martin Shefter, *Politics by Other Means: Politicians, Prosecutors, and the Press from Watergate to Whitewater* (Norton, 1999).
8. Marion T. Doss and Robert North Roberts, *From Watergate to Whitewater: The Public Integrity War* (ABC-CLIO, 1997).
9. Suzanne Garment, *Scandal: The Culture of Mistrust in American Politics* (Anchor, 1991).
10. Larry Sabato, Feeding Frenzy: How Attack Journalism Has Transformed American Politics (Free Press, 1993); Aeron Davis, "Investigating Journalist Influences on Political Issue Agendas at Westminster," Political Communication 24, no. 2 (2007): 181–199.
11. Bob Woodward, *Five Presidents and the Legacy of Watergate* (Simon & Schuster, 1999); Robert Dallek, "Presidential Fitness and Presidential Lies: The Historical Record and a Proposal for Reform," *Presidential Studies Quarterly* 40, no. 1 (2010): 9–22.
12. Richard Barberio, *Presidents and Political Scandal: Managing Scandal in the Modern Era* (Palgrave Macmillan, 2020).
13. Beth Miller, "The Effects of Scandalous Information on Recall of Policy Related Information," *Political Psychology* 31, no. 6 (2010): 887–914.
14. Miller, "Effects of Scandalous Information."
15. Logan Dancey, "Reform on My Terms: Partisan and Ideological Responses to a Corruption Scandal," *PS: Political Science and Politics* 47, no. 2 (2014): 367–371.
16. Michael Romano, "Tuning In to Scandal: Television News Coverage of Congressional Scandals," *PS: Political Science and Politics* 47, no. 2 (2014): 386–390; Gary C. Jacobson and Michael A. Dimock, "Checking Out: The Effects of Bank Overdrafts on the 1992 House Elections," *American Journal of Political Science* 38, no. 3 (1994): 601–624.
17. Brandon Rottinghaus, "What Causes Gubernatorial Scandals?," in *Power, Constraint, and Leadership in the U.S. States*, ed. David P. Redlawsk (Palgrave, 2015); Brandon Rottinghaus, *The Institutional Effect of Executive Scandals* (Cambridge University Press, 2015).
18. C. von Sikorski, "Political Scandals as a Democratic Challenge: The Aftermath of Political Scandals—A Meta-Analysis," *International Journal of Communication* 12 (2018): 25.
19. James N. Druckman, Erik Peterson, and Rune Slothuus, "How Elite Partisan Polarization Affects Public Opinion Formation," *American Political Science Review* 107, no. 1 (2013): 57–79.
20. Amber E. Boydstun, Alison Ledgerwood, and Jehan Sparks, "A Negativity Bias in Reframing Shapes Political Preferences Even in Partisan Contexts," *Social Psychological and Personality Science* 10, no. 1 (2017): 53–61, https://doi.org/10.1177/1948550617733520.
21. Jeffrey Lazarus, "Incumbent Vulnerability and Challenger Entry in Statewide Elections," *American Politics Research* 36, no. 1 (2008): 108–129; Rodrigo Praino, Daniel Stockemer, and Vincent G. Moscardelli, "The Lingering Effects of Scandals in Congressional Elections: Incumbents, Challengers, and Voters," *Social Science Quarterly* 94, no. 4 (2013): 1045–1061.
22. Brandon Rottinghaus, "Surviving Scandal: The Institutional and Political Dynamics of National and State Executive Scandals," *PS: Political Science and Politics* 47, no. 1 (2013): 131–140.

23. Joshua Boston, Benjamin J. Kassow, Ali S. Masood, and David R. Miller, "Your Honor's Misdeeds: The Consequences of Judicial Scandal on Specific and Diffuse Support," *PS: Political Science and Politics* 56, no. 2 (2023): 195–200.
24. Dancey, "Reform on My Terms."
25. Francis F. Lee, "The Spillover Effects of Political Scandals: The Moderating Role of Cynicism and Social Media Communications," *Journalism and Mass Communication Quarterly* 95, no. 3 (2017): 101–123.
26. Dhavan V. Shah, Mark D. Watts, David Domke, and David P. Fan, "News Framing and Cueing of Issue Regimes: Explaining Clinton's Public Approval in Spite of Scandal," *Public Opinion Quarterly* 66, no. 3 (2002): 339–370; Joshua P. Darr, Nathan P. Kalmoe, Kathleen Searless, Mingxiao Sui, Raymond J. Pingree, Brian K. Watson, Kirill Bryanov, and Martina Santia, "Collision with Collusion: Partisan Reaction to the Trump-Russia Scandal," *Perspectives on Politics* 17, no. 3 (2019): 772–787; Adam D. Wolsky, "Scandal, Hypocrisy, and Resignation: How Partisanship Shapes Evaluations of Politicians' Transgressions," *Journal of Experimental Political Science* 9, no. 1 (2020): 74–87; Daniel Stockemer and Rodrigo Praino, "The Good, the Bad and the Ugly: Do Attractive Politicians Get a 'Break' When They are Involved in Scandals?," *Political Behavior* 41 (2019): 747–767.
27. Douglas L. Kriner and Eric Schickler, "Investigating the President: Committee Probes and Presidential Approval, 1953–2006," *Journal of Politics* 76, no. 2 (2014): 101–123; Abby K. Wood and Christian R. Grose, "Campaign Finance Transparency Affects Legislators' Election Outcomes and Behavior," *American Journal of Political Science* 66, no. 2 (2022): 516–534; Kayla S. Canelo, Brent D. Boyea, and Danielle N. Myers, "Facing the Public: Voter Assessments of Judicial Scandal." *Journal of Law and Courts* (2025): 1–17, https://doi.org/10.1017/jlc.2025.9.
28. "Mo. House Speaker Resigns Amid Texting Scandal," KSDK, May 15, 2015, https://www.ksdk.com/article/news/politics/mo-house-speaker-resigns-amid-texting-scandal/63-205922675; Reid Wilson, "Tennessee House Speaker to Resign Amid Scandal," *The Hill*, May 21, 2019, https://thehill.com/homenews/state-watch/444748-tennessee-house-speaker-to-resign-amid-scandal/; Morgan Watkins, "Jeff Hoover Resigns as House Speaker Amid Sexual Harassment Scandal," *Courier Journal*, January 8, 2018, https://www.courier-journal.com/story/news/politics/2018/01/08/jeff-hoover-submits-letter-resignation-house-speaker/1008744001/; John O'Connor, "Ex-Illinois House Speaker Michael Madigan to Resign Seat," AP News, February 18, 2021, https://apnews.com/article/legislature-illinois-michael-madigan-chicago-8e7c4a259cb6d0652562877a3b8b3044.
29. Praino, Stockemer, and Moscardelli, "The Lingering Effects of Scandals."
30. Scott J. Basinger, "Scandals and Ethics Reform in the U.S. House of Representatives," *Public Integrity* 18, no. 4 (2016): 359–375.
31. Shepard, "The 'Scandal Penalty.'"
32. Collin Paschall, Tracy Sulkin, and William Bernhard, "The Legislative Consequences of Congressional Scandals," *Political Research Quarterly* 73, no. 2 (2020): 293–307.

33. Arthur H. Miller, "Sex, Politics, and Public Opinion: What Political Scientists Really Learned from the Clinton-Lewinsky Scandal," *PS: Political Science and Politics* 32, no. 4 (1999): 721–729; Virginia A. Chanley, Thomas J. Rudolph, and Wendy M. Rahn, "The Origins and Consequences of Public Trust in Government: A Time Series Analysis," *Public Opinion Quarterly* 64, no. 3 (2000): 239–256, https://doi.org/10.1086/317987; Tiffany D. Barnes, Emily Beaulieu, and Gregory W. Saxton, "Sex and Corruption: How Sexism Shapes Voters' Responses to Scandal," *Politics, Groups, and Identities* 8, no. 1 (2020): 103–121.
34. Alberto Chong, Ana L. De La O, Dean Karlan, and Leonard Wantchekon, "Does Corruption Information Inspire the Fight or Quash the Hope? A Field Experiment in Mexico on Voter Turnout, Choice, and Party Identification," *Journal of Politics* 77, no. 1 (2015): 55–71.
35. John Fousek and David Wasserman, "Ethical Issues in U.S. Presidential Leadership," *Presidential Studies Quarterly* 40, no. 1 (2010): 2.
36. Molly W. Andolina and Clyde Wilcox, "Public Opinion: The Paradoxes of Clinton's Popularity," in *The Clinton Scandals and the Future of American Government*, ed. Mark J. Rozell and Clyde Wilcox (Georgetown University Press, 2000); Brian Newman and Andrew Forcehimes, "'Rally Around the Flag' Events for Presidential Approval Research," *Electoral Studies* 29, no. 1 (2010): 18–34.
37. Scott R. Meinke and William D. Anderson, "Influencing Impaired Administrations: Presidents, White House Scandals, and Legislative Leadership," *Legislative Studies Quarterly* 26, no. 4 (2001): 639–659; Rottinghaus, "What Causes Gubernatorial Scandals?"
38. Amy S. Funck and Katherine T. McCabe, "Partisanship, Information, and the Conditional Effects of Scandal on Voting Decisions," *Political Behavior* 44 (2022): 1389–1409.
39. Robert Williams, *Political Scandals in the USA* (Edinburgh University Press, 1998), 4.
40. Robert M. Entman, *Scandal and Silence: Media Responses to Presidential Misconduct* (Polity Press, 2012); Wioletta Dziuda and William G. Howell, "Political Scandal: A Theory," *American Journal of Political Science* 65 (2021): 197–209; Wolsky, "Scandal, Hypocrisy, and Resignation"; Funck and McCabe, "Partisanship, Information."
41. Seth C. McKee, Heather K. Evans, and Jennifer Hayes Clark, "The 'PERFECT' Call: Congressional Representation by Tweet in the Midst of the Ukraine Whistleblower Scandal," *American Politics Research* 50, no. 1 (2022): 30–44; Brian T. Hamel and Michael G. Miller, "How Voters Punish and Donors Protect Legislators Embroiled in Scandal," *Political Research Quarterly* 72, no. 1 (2019): 117–131.
42. Regina G. Lawrence, W. Lance Bennett, and Valerie Hunt, "Toward a Fuller Model of Mediated Political Communication: Public Engagement with the Lewinsky Scandal," paper presented at the annual meeting of the American Political Science Association, 1999; Rodney Tiffen, *Scandals: Media, Politics, and Corruption in Contemporary Australia* (UNSW Press, 1999).

43. Marc J. Hetherington, "Resurgent Mass Partisanship: The Role of Elite Polarization," *American Political Science Review* 95, no. 3 (2001): 619–631; Druckman, Peterson, and Slothuus, "How Elite Partisan Polarization Affects Public Opinion Formation."
44. Matthew S. Levendusky, "Clearer Cues, More Consistent Voters: A Benefit of Elite Polarization," *Political Behavior* 32 (2010): 111–131.
45. Adam Wren, Mia McCarthy, Megan Messerly, and Eli Stokols, "Trump Bets He Can Scandal-Proof His Most Controversial Cabinet Picks," *Politico*, November 20, 2024.
46. Toby Bolsen, James N. Druckman, and Fay Lomax Cook, "The Influence of Partisan Motivated Reasoning on Public Opinion," *Political Behavior* 36 (2014): 235–262.
47. Miller, "Sex, Politics"; John Zaller, *A Theory of Media Politics: How the Interests of Politicians, Journalists, and Citizens Shape the News* (University of Chicago Press, 1999); Robert Busby, *Scandal and American Politics in the Twenty-First Century* (Palgrave Macmillan, 2022).
48. Beth Miller Vonnahme, "Surviving Scandal: An Exploration of the Immediate and Lasting Effects of Scandal on Candidate Evaluation," *Social Science Quarterly* 95, no. 5 (2014): 1308–1321; Miguel M. Pereira and Nicholas W. Waterbury, "Do Voters Discount Political Scandals Over Time?," *Political Research Quarterly* 72, no. 3 (2019): 584–595.
49. Pereira and Waterbury, "Do Voters Discount Political Scandals Over Time?"
50. Steven P. Nawara and Mandi Bailey, "Scandal-Ridden Campaigns: The Relationship Between Cognitive Load and Candidate Evaluation," *Social Science Journal* 62, no. 1 (2021): 57–74.
51. Funck and McCabe, "Partisanship, Information."
52. Tiffany D. Barnes, Emily Beaulieu, and Gregory W. Saxton, "Restoring Trust in the Police: Why Female Officers Reduce Suspicions of Corruption," *Governance* 31 (2018): 143–161; Tiffany D. Barnes and Emily Beaulieu, "Gender Stereotypes and Corruption: How Candidates Affect Perceptions of Election Fraud," *Politics and Gender* 10, no. 3 (2014): 365–391.
53. David Doherty, Conor M. Dowling, and Michael G. Miller, "Are Financial or Moral Scandals Worse? It Depends," *PS: Political Science and Politics* 44, no. 4 (2011): 749–757; David Doherty, Conor M. Dowling, and Michael G. Miller, "Does Time Heal All Wounds? Sex Scandals, Tax Evasion, and the Passage of Time," *PS: Political Science and Politics* 47, no. 2 (2014): 357–366.
54. Basinger, "Scandals and Ethics Reform."
55. Gregory S. Schneider, "'A Wounded Healer': Ralph Northam Wraps Up Term in Office, Forged by Scandal Into a Governor of Lasting Consequence," *Washington Post*, January 9, 2022, https://www.washingtonpost.com/dc-md-va/2022/01/09/governor-northam-blackface-scandal-legacy/.
56. Barnes, Beaulieu, and Saxton, "Restoring Trust in the Police"; Catherine Reyes-Housholder, "A Constituency Theory for the Conditional Impact of Female Presidents," *Comparative Politics* 51, no. 3 (2019): 101–123.

57. Elizabeth S. Smith, Ashleigh Smith Powers, and Gustavo A. Suarez, "If Bill Clinton Were a Woman: The Effectiveness of Male and Female Politicians' Account Strategies Following Alleged Transgressions," *Political Psychology* 26, no. 1 (2005): 115–134.
58. Marie Courtemanche and Joanne Connor Green, "A Fall from Grace: Women, Scandals, and Perceptions of Politicians," *Journal of Women, Politics, and Policy* 41, no. 2 (2020): 219–240; Costa et al., "How Partisanship and Sexism Influence Voters' Reactions."
59. Barnes, Beaulieu, and Saxton, "Sex and Corruption."
60. Zaller, *A Theory of Media Politics*.
61. Mark Fischle, "Mass Response to the Lewinsky Scandal: Motivated Reasoning or Bayesian Updating?," *Political Psychology* 21, no. 1 (2000): 151–175.
62. Kriner and Schickler, "Investigating the President."
63. Annemarie S. Walter and David P. Redlawsk, "Voters' Partisan Responses to Politicians' Immoral Behavior," *Political Psychology* 40, no. 5 (2019): 1075–1097.
64. James N. Druckman and Matthew S. Levendusky, "What Do We Measure When We Measure Affective Polarization?," *Public Opinion Quarterly* 83, no. 1 (2019): 114–122.
65. Shanto Iyengar, Yphtach Lelkes, Matthew Levendusky, Neil Malhotra, and Sean J. Westwood, "The Origins and Consequences of Affective Polarization in the United States," *Annual Review of Political Science* 22 (2019): 129–146.
66. Alex Isenstadt, "Senate GOP Rallies to Herschel Walker," *Politico*, October 25, 2021, https://www.politico.com/news/2021/10/25/senate-gop-rallies-herschel-walker-517048.
67. Natalie Allison, "Walker's Christian Fans Unfazed by Abortion Revelations," *Politico*, October 6, 2022, https://www.politico.com/news/2022/10/06/walkers-christian-fans-unfazed-by-abortion-revelations-00060589.
68. Yosef Bhatti, Kasper M. Hansen, and Asmus Leth Olsen, "Political Hypocrisy: The Effect of Political Scandals on Candidate Evaluations," *Acta Politica* 48 (2013): 10–19; Eva Anduiza, Aina Gallego, and Jordi Muñoz, "Turning a Blind Eye: Experimental Evidence of Partisan Bias in Attitudes Toward Corruption," *Comparative Political Studies* 46, no. 12 (2013): 1664–1692; Walter and Redlawsk, "Voters' Partisan Responses"; Mia Costa, Trevor Briggs, Ajaipal Chahal, Jonathan Fried, Rijul Garg, Sophia Kriz, Leo Lei, Anthony Milne, and Jennah Slayton, "How Partisanship and Sexism Influence Voters' Reactions to Political #MeToo Scandals," *Research and Politics* 7, no. 3 (2020): 1–15.
69. Omer Yair and Brian F. Schaffer, "Response Decoupling and Partisans' Evaluations of Politicians' Transgressions," *Political Behavior* 45 (2023): 1198–1209; Jeronimo Cortina and Brandon Rottinghaus, "Does Partisanship Stop at Scandal's Edge? Partisan Resiliency and the Survival of Political Scandal," *American Review of Politics* 36, no. 1 (2017): 2–29.
70. Samara Klar and Alexandra McCoy, "Partisan-Motivated Evaluations of Sexual Misconduct and the Mitigating Role of the #MeToo Movement," *American Journal of Political Science* 65, no. 4 (2021): 777–789.

71. Paul Goren, "Character Weakness, Partisan Bias, and Presidential Evaluation," *American Journal of Political Science* 46, no. 3 (2002): 56–77.
72. Stephanie Stark and Sofía Collignon, "Sexual Predators in Contest for Public Office: How the American Electorate Responds to News of Allegations of Candidates Committing Sexual Assault and Harassment," *Political Studies Review* 20, no. 3 (2022): 329–352.
73. Rottinghaus, "Surviving Scandal."
74. Shah, Watts, Domke, and Fan, "News Framing."
75. Mark Murray, "Majority of Iowa Caucusgoers Say Trump Conviction Wouldn't Affect Their Support," NBC News, January 14, 2024, https://www.nbcnews.com/meet-the-press/meetthepressblog/majority-iowa-caucusgoers-say-trump-conviction-wouldnt-affect-support-rcna133876.
76. Lauren Sforza, "A Fifth of People Who Plan to Vote for Trump Think He Committed Serious Federal Crimes: Poll," *The Hill*, March 4, 2024, https://thehill.com/homenews/campaign/4507968-a-fifth-of-people-who-plan-to-vote-for-trump-think-he-committed-serious-federal-crimes-poll/.
77. Niall Stanage, "The Memo: Poll Points to Deep Trouble for Trump If He Gets Convicted," *The Hill*, February 1, 2024, https://thehill.com/homenews/campaign/4441241-trump-poll-convictions-deep-trouble/.
78. Busby, *Scandal and American Politics*.
79. Shepard, "The 'Scandal Penalty.'"
80. Wolsky, "Scandal, Hypocrisy, and Resignation."
81. Nicholas Fandos and Katie Glueck, "Cuomo Portrays Himself as a Victim in a Six-Figure TV Ad Blitz," *New York Times*, February 28, 2022, https://www.nytimes.com/2022/02/28/nyregion/andrew-cuomo-tv-ad.html.
82. Donald P. Green, Adam Zelizer, and David Kirby, "Publicizing Scandal: Results from Five Field Experiments," *Quarterly Journal of Political Science* 13, no. 3 (2018): 237–261.
83. Matthew C. Woessner, "Scandal, Elites, and Presidential Popularity: Considering the Importance of Cues in Public Support of the President," *Presidential Studies Quarterly* 35, no. 1 (2005): 94–115; Gabor Simonovits, Jennifer McCoy, and Levente Littvay, "Democratic Hypocrisy and Out-Group Threat: Explaining Citizen Support for Democratic Erosion," *Journal of Politics* 84, no. 3 (2022): 1806–1811.
84. Jon Kingzette, James N. Druckman, Samara Klar, Yanna Krupnikov, Matthew Levendusky, and John Barry Ryan, "How Affective Polarization Undermines Support for Democratic Norms," *Public Opinion Quarterly* 85, no. 2 (2021): 45–89.
85. Dziuda and Howell, "Political Scandal."
86. Hamel and Miller, "How Voters Punish and Donors Protect."
87. Ginsberg and Shefter, *Politics by Other Means*.
88. Raphael Small and Robert M. Eisinger, "Whither Presidential Approval," *Presidential Studies Quarterly* 50, no. 4 (2020): 845–863; Matthew J. Lebo and Daniel Cassino, "The Aggregated Consequences of Motivated Reasoning and the Dynamics of Partisan Presidential Approval," *Political Psychology* 28, no. 6 (2007): 719–746.

89. Simonovits, McCoy, and Littvay, "Democratic Hypocrisy."
90. Meena Bose and Craig M. Burnett, "Public Approval, Policy Issues, and Partisanship in the American Presidency: Examining the 2019–2020 Trump Impeachment and Acquittal," *PS: Political Science and Politics* 55, no. 2 (2021): 266–274.
91. Darr et al., "Collision with Collusion."
92. Michael D. Shear, "No Guide to Survive a Scandal," *New York Times*, June 11, 2011; Miller, "The Effects of Scandalous Information"; Jody C. Baumgartner and Naoko Kada, *Checking Executive Power: Presidential Impeachment in Comparative Perspective* (Praeger, 2003).
93. Michael A. Dimock and Gary C. Jacobson, "Check and Choices: The House Bank Scandal's Impact on Voters in 1992," *Journal of Politics* 57, no. 4 (1995): 1143–1159.
94. Victor J. Hinojosa and Aníbal S. Pérez-Liñán, "Presidential Survival and the Impeachment Process: The United States and Colombia," *Political Science Quarterly* 121, no. 4 (2006): 653–675.
95. Basinger, "Scandals and Ethics Reform."
96. Jon C. Rogowski and Joseph L. Sutherland, "How Ideology Fuels Affective Polarization," *Political Behavior* 38 (2016): 485–508.
97. Jon Kingzette, James N. Druckman, Samara Klar, Yanna Krupnikov, Matthew Levendusky, and John Barry Ryan, "How Affective Polarization Undermines Support for Democratic Norms," *Public Opinion Quarterly* 85, no. 2 (2021): 663–677, https://doi.org/10.1093/poq/nfab029.
98. Gary C. Jacobson, "The Presidential and Congressional Elections of 2020: A National Referendum on the Trump Presidency," 136, no. 1 (2021): 11–45.
99. McKee, Evans, and Clark, "The 'PERFECT' Call."
100. Claire L. Adida, Lauren D. Davenport, and Gwyneth McClendon, "Ethnic Cueing Across Minorities: A Survey Experiment on Candidate Evaluation in the United States," *Public Opinion Quarterly* 80, no. 4 (2016): 815–836; Nyron N. Crawford, *Marked Men: Black Politicians and the Racialization of Scandal* (NYU Press, 2024), 9.
101. Peter Grier, "Rick Perry Puts Mug Shot on T-Shirts: What That Says About 2016," *Christian Science Monitor*, August 25, 2014, https://www.csmonitor.com/USA/Politics/Decoder/2014/0825/Rick-Perry-puts-mug-shot-on-T-shirts-what-that-says-about-2016.
102. Jessica Piper and Natalie Allison, "Trump Turns His Legal Woes Into a Campaign Fundraising Machine," *Politico*, April 14, 2024, https://www.politico.com/news/2024/04/19/trump-trial-campaign-fundraising-00153185.
103. Maeve Reston and Clara Ence Morse, "Trump's Conviction Fueled Donation Surge That Could Reshape Contest," *Washington Post*, June 21, 2024, https://www.washingtonpost.com/politics/2024/06/20/trump-conviction-fundraising-campaign-donations/.
104. Rebecca Falconer, "Trump Campaign's Donation Site Crashes After Guilty Verdict," *Axios*, May 30, 2024, https://www.axios.com/2024/05/31/trump-donation-site-crashes-trial-conviction.

105. Kaylyn Jackson Schiff, Daniel S. Schiff, and Natália S. Bueno, "The Liar's Dividend: Can Politicians Claim Misinformation to Evade Accountability?," *American Political Science Review* 119, no. 1 (2025): 71–90.
106. Will Weissert and Adriana Gomez Licon, "Gaetz Vows to Fight, Tries to Stay on Offensive Amid Scandal," AP News, April 9, 2021, https://apnews.com/article/politicians-in-crisis-refuse-to-resign-16046aff55900e97f59aec9aa5153df6.
107. Weissert and Gomez Licon, "Gaetz Vows to Fight."
108. Sean Illing, "'Flood the Zone with Shit': How Misinformation Overwhelmed Our Democracy," *Vox*, February 6, 2020, https://www.vox.com/policy-and-politics/2020/1/16/20991816/impeachment-trial-trump-bannon-misinformation.
109. Matthew S. Levendusky, "Why Do Partisan Media Polarize Viewers," *American Journal of Political Science* 57, no. 3 (2013): 611–623; Darr et al., "Collision with Collusion."
110. Ángela Fonseca Galvis, James M. Snyder, and B. K. Song, "Newspaper Market Structure and Behavior: Partisan Coverage of Political Scandals in the United States from 1870 to 1910," *Journal of Politics* 78, no. 2 (2016): 368–380.
111. Green, Zelizer, and Kirby, "Publicizing Scandal."
112. Lawrence, Bennett, and Hunt, "Toward a Fuller Model."
113. Carolyn L. Funk, "The Impact of Scandal on Candidate Evaluations: An Experimental Test of the Role of Candidate Traits," *Political Behavior* 18 (1996): 1–24.
114. Seth B. Warner, "Analyzing Attention to Scandal on Twitter: Elites Sell What Supporters Buy," *Political Research Quarterly* 76, no. 2 (2023): 841–856.
115. Galvis, Snyder, and Song, "Newspaper Market Structure."
116. Sara Fischer, "Conservative Trust in Media Has Cratered," *Axios*, August 31, 2021, https://www.axios.com/2021/08/31/conservative-trust-in-media-has-cratered.
117. Darr et al., "Collision with Collusion."
118. Jerry Clayton, "Republicans and Democrats Are Living in Separate Realities, New Study Suggests," Texas Public Radio, July 9, 2023, https://www.tpr.org/news/2023-07-09/republicans-and-democrats-are-living-in-separate-realities-new-study-suggests.
119. Danny Hayes, "Local News Coverage of Political Scandals Is Disappearing," Good Authority, October 4, 2023, https://goodauthority.org/news/local-news-coverage-of-political-scandals-is-disappearing/.
120. Hayes, "Local News Coverage of Political Scandals Is Disappearing."
121. Matthew Yglesias, "The Hack Gap: How and Why Conservative Nonsense Dominates American Politics," *Vox*, October 23, 2018, https://www.vox.com/2018/10/23/18004478/hack-gap-explained.
122. Matthew Yglesias, "Media Obsession with a Bullshit Email Scandal Helped Trump to the White House," *Vox*, November 9, 2016, https://www.vox.com/policy-and-politics/2016/11/9/13570724/media-obsession-emails.
123. Illing, "'Flood the Zone with Shit.'"
124. Steven W. Webster, *American Rage: How Anger Shapes Our Politics* (Cambridge University Press, 2020).

125. S. W. Webster, A. N. Glynn, and M. P. Motta, "Partisan Schadenfreude and Candidate Cruelty," *Political Psychology* 45 (2024): 259–277, https://doi.org/10.1111/pops.12922.
126. Carey E. Stapleton and Ryan Dawkins, "Catching My Anger: How Political Elites Create Angrier Citizens," *Political Research Quarterly* 75, no. 3 (2022): 1–12.
127. Seo-young Silvia Kim, Jan Zilinsky, and Brian Brew, "Donate to Help Us Fight Back: Political Fundraising and Toxic Rhetoric Online," *Party Politics*, March 11, 2024, https://doi.org/10.1177/13540688241235901.
128. Illing, "'Flood the Zone with Shit.'"
129. Darr et al., "Collision with Collusion."
130. Amy E. Lerman and Daniel Acland, "United in States of Dissatisfaction: Confirmation Bias Across the Partisan Divide," *American Politics Research* 48, no. 2 (2020): 227–237.
131. Jennifer Medina and Reid J. Epstein, "Do Americans Have a 'Collective Amnesia' About Donald Trump?," *New York Times*, March 5, 2024, https://www.nytimes.com/2024/03/05/us/politics/trump-presidency-election-voters.html.
132. Diana Zulli, "Socio-Mediated Scandals: Theorizing Political Scandals in a Digital Media Environment," *Communication Theory* 31, no. 4 (2021): 862–883.
133. Weissert and Gomez Licon, "Gaetz Vows to Fight."
134. Alexander Mallin, "Comey Defends Russia Investigation as 'Essential' in Testimony to Senate Panel," ABC News, September 30, 2020, https://abcnews.go.com/Politics/comey-defends-russia-investigation-essential-testimony-senate-panel/story?id=73338331.
135. Matthew DeBell, Michelle Amsbary, Ted Brader, Shelley Brock, Cindy Good, Justin Kamens, Natalya Maisel, and Sarah Pinto, "Methodology Report for the ANES 2020 Time Series Study," 2022, University of Michigan and Stanford University, https://electionstudies.org/wp-content/uploads/2022/08/anes_timeseries_2020_methodology_report.pdf.
136. Glenn Kessler, Scott Clement, and Emily Guskin, "Which Trump Lies Stick? Republicans Believe Some Falsehoods More Than They Did Six Years Ago, Our Poll Finds," *Washington Post*, April 9, 2024, https://www.washingtonpost.com/politics/2024/04/09/some-trump-falsehoods-stick-more-than-others-fact-checker-poll-finds/.
137. Adam Wren, Mia McCarthy, Megan Messerly, and Eli Stokols, "Trump Bets He Can Scandal-Proof His Most Controversial Cabinet Picks," *Politico*, November 20, 2024.

1. STUDYING SCANDAL

1. Nancy Marion, *The Politics of Disgrace: The Role of Political Scandal in American Politics* (Carolina Academic Press, 2010).
2. Russ Witcher, "The Media," in *Watergate and the Resignation of Richard Nixon: Impact of a Constitutional Crisis*, ed. Harry P. Jeffrey and Thomas Maxwell-Long (CQ Press, 2004).

1. STUDYING SCANDAL

3. Kim Long, *The Almanac of Political Corruption, Scandals, and Dirty Politics* (Delacorte Press, 2007).
4. Jeff Zeleny, "Now It's Democrats Who Feel Sting of Scandal," *New York Times*, March 4, 2010, https://www.nytimes.com/2010/03/05/us/politics/05memo.html.
5. David A. Leib, "Over 100 State Lawmakers Accused of Misconduct in 3 Years," AP News, January 23, 2020, https://apnews.com/article/10aedac91ac64f7e05daacad97408eeb.
6. Paul Apostolidis and Juliet Williams, *Public Affairs: Politics in the Age of Sex Scandals* (Duke University Press, 2004), 1.
7. Kristi Keck, "Surviving a Political Sex Scandal," CNN, July 7, 2009, www.cnn.com/2009/POLITICS/07/14/political.sex.scandal.survival/index.html.
8. Marion, *The Politics of Disgrace*, 11.
9. John B. Thompson, *Political Scandal: Power and Visibility in the Media Age* (Wiley, 2000).
10. Theodore Lowi, foreword to *The Politics of Scandal: Power and Process in Liberal Democracies*, ed. Andrei S. Markovits and Mark Silverstein (Holmes & Meier, 1988), vii.
11. Robert Williams, *Political Scandals in the USA* (Edinburgh University Press, 1998).
12. Ari Adut, *On Scandal: Moral Disturbances in Society, Politics, and Art* (Cambridge University Press, 2008).
13. Robert M. Entman, *Scandal and Silence: Media Responses to Presidential Misconduct* (Polity Press, 2012).
14. Andrei S. Markovits and Mark Silverstein, "Power and Process in Liberal Democracies," in *The Politics of Scandal: Power and Process in Liberal Democracies* (Holmes & Meier, 1988).
15. Larry J. Sabato, *Feeding Frenzy: How Attack Journalism Has Transformed American Politics* (Free Press, 1991).
16. Kathleen Hall Jamieson, *Dirty Politics: Deception, Distraction, and Democracy* (Oxford University Press, 1992).
17. David Rose, *Sex Scandal America: Politics and the Ritual of Public Shaming* (Key Publishing House, 2009); Scott Basinger and Brandon Rottinghaus, "Skeletons in the White House Closets: An Empirical Investigation into Modern Presidential Scandals," *Political Science Quarterly* 127, no. 2 (2012): 213–239.
18. Using newspapers and official sources to determine when scandals broke (and hence whether or not they existed) minimized the presence of false or malicious rumors in the data.
19. We opted not to code individuals below this level because our interest was in the relationship between an individual involved in the scandal and the president. "Scandal" is rarely applied to longtime civil service employees who may engage in tomfoolery or financial corruption. Their cases are handled at lower levels; the implications are generally minimal and certainly not associated with the president. In short, we desired to collect information on political scandals that had implications for governance.
20. The dataset collected by Basinger runs through 2013; Scott J. Basinger, "Scandals and Ethics Reform in the U.S. House of Representatives," *Public Integrity* 18, no. 4 (2016):

35–375. The present dataset has been updated to 2021. Brian T. Hamel and Michael G. Miller, "How Voters Punish and Donors Protect Legislators Embroiled in Scandal," *Political Research Quarterly* 72, no. 1 (2019): 148–159.

21. Charlie Savage, "Sex, Drug Use, and Graft Cited in Interior Department," *New York Times*, September 10, 2008, https://www.nytimes.com/2008/09/11/washington/11royalty.html.
22. Jack W. Germond and Jules Witcover, *Wake Us When It's Over: Presidential Politics of 1984* (Macmillan, 1985).
23. Seanna Adcox, "Nikki Haley Hacking: Governor Admits Errors, Revenue Chief Jim Etter Resigns," Associated Press, November 20, 2012.
24. Katherine Gregg, "Credit Card Use Next Target of Carcieri Audit," *Providence Journal-Bulletin*, February 14, 2003.
25. Young Hun Kim and Donna Bahry, "Interrupted Presidencies in Third Wave Democracy," *Journal of Politics* 70, no. 3 (2008): 807–822; Riccardo Puglisi and James M. Snyder Jr., "Newspaper Coverage of Political Scandals," *Journal of Politics* 73, no. 3 (2011): 931–950.
26. The search term strings employed are listed in the appendix to this book (available on the author's website). Using Lexis-Nexis Academic and searching by individual years for national scandals, this search string was used to search in the "All News" (English) section (which included major newspapers in the United States) for the archives of the Associated Press. For state scandals, the state Associated Press wire and all state media (which included most major newspapers from each state) were used.
27. Alan Rosenthal, *The Best Job in Politics: Exploring How Governors Succeed as Policy Leaders* (CQ Press, 2013).
28. See Paul Apostolidis and Juliet A. Williams, "Sex Scandals and Discourses of Power," in *Public Affairs: Politics in the Age of Sex Scandals*, ed. Paul Apostolidis and Juliet A. Williams (Duke University Press, 2004); Wesley O. Hagood, *Presidential Sex: From the Founding Fathers to Bill Clinton*, rev. and updated ed. (Citadel Press, 1998).
29. Lanny J. Davis, *Truth to Tell: Tell It Early, Tell It All, Tell It Yourself* (Free Press, 1999).
30. Scott Charton, "Use of Closed State Library by Governor's Family Draws Ridicule," Associated Press, 1990.
31. Adut, *On Scandal.*
32. Tanjev Schultz, "Interactive Options in Online Journalism: A Content Analysis of 100 U.S. Newspapers," *Journal of Computer-Mediated Communication* 5, no. 1 (1999).
33. Benjamin Ginsberg and Martin Shefter, *Politics by Other Means: Politicians, Prosecutors, and the Press from Watergate to Whitewater* (Norton, 1999).
34. Richard J. Ellis, *Lightning Rods: The Politics of Blame Avoidance* (University of Kansas Press, 1994).
35. We generated the list of scandals using a multistep process. As a first step, two research assistants generated lists of "events" that fit one or more elements of our definition of scandal. The list was drawn from books that claim to be "encyclopedias" and "almanacs" of scandals, supplemented by analytical books and other commentaries on

White House or gubernatorial scandals. The main sources relied on were Suzanne Garment, *Scandal: The Culture of Mistrust in American Politics* (Anchor Books, 1992); Kim Long, *The Almanac of Political Corruption, Scandals, and Dirty Politics* (Delacorte, 2007); Nancy E. Marion, *Politics of Disgrace: The Role of Political Scandal in American Politics* (Carolina Academic Press, 2010); Larry Sabato, *Feeding Frenzy: How Attack Journalism Has Transformed American Politics* (Free Press, 1993); Tanjev Schultz, "Interactive Options in Online Journalism: A Content Analysis of 100 U.S. Newspapers," *Journal of Computer-Mediated Communication* 5, no. 1 (1999).

As a third step, the list of events plus all resources—newspaper articles, books, and articles—were given to a third research assistant, along with a rubric for deciding whether each event was a scandal. As a fourth and final step, one of the original two research assistants collected data on the individuals allegedly involved in each of the scandals.

36. Puglisi and Snyder, "Newspaper Coverage"; Kim and Bahry, "Interrupted Presidencies."
37. "Serious" scandals are illegal activities that, if proved, would be criminally registered as multiple felonies for a single individual, or the events threatened the institution. This excludes some scandals, such as driving under the influence of alcohol, which do not meet that legal or significance threshold. This also excludes cases in which a single law was broken. For instance, Watergate and the Lewinsky affair both threatened the presidency and involved multiple charges against multiple individuals.
38. Basinger and Rottinghaus, "Skeletons in the White House Closets"; Brandon Rottinghaus, "What Causes State-Level Executive Scandals?," in *The American Governor*, ed. David P. Redlawsk (Palgrave Macmillan, 2015).
39. Katy O'Donnell, "Ben Carson Cleared of Misconduct in Furniture Episode," *Politico*, September 12, 2019, https://www.politico.com/story/2019/09/12/ben-carson-misconduct-furniture-1729914.
40. "Trump Impeachment: The Short, Medium, and Long Story," BBC, February 5, 2020, https://www.bbc.com/news/world-us-canada-49800181.
41. Alexandra Petri, "David Wu Resigns—Never Trust a Man in a Tiger Suit," Opinion, *Washington Post*, July 26, 2011, https://www.washingtonpost.com/blogs/compost/post/david-wu-resigns--never-trust-a-man-in-a-tiger-suit/2011/07/26/gIQAl4u8aI_blog.html.
42. Arthur H. Miller, "Sex, Politics, and Public Opinion: What Political Scientists Really Learned from the Clinton-Lewinsky Scandal," *PS: Political Science and Politics* 32, no. 4 (1999): 721–729.
43. Joe Biesk, "Top Fletcher Adviser Resigns, Says He's Going to Private Sector," Associated Press, September 12, 2005; Mark Chellgren, "Fletcher Sacks Administration Member Over Personnel Problems," Associated Press, September 14, 2005.
44. Ian Urbina, "Indictment for Governor of Kentucky," *New York Times*, May 12, 2006.
45. Long, *The Almanac of Political Corruption.*
46. Robert E. Pierre, "Ill. Governor's Campaign, 2 Former Aides Indicted," *Washington Post*, April 3, 2002.

47. Robert E. Pierre, "Former Governor Ryan Is Indicted in Illinois," *Washington Post*, December 18, 2003.
48. Randal C. Archibold, "Governor of Nevada Is Cleared in an Inquiry on Gifts, His Lawyer Says," *New York Times*, November 2, 2008.
49. Gail Collins, "Is Yours More Corrupt Than Mine?," *New York Times*, May 11, 2013.
50. Bill Kramer, "There Are More States Under One-Party Control Than at Any Other Time in Modern History," Multistate, May 9, 2023, https://www.multistate.us/insider/2023/5/9/there-are-more-states-under-one-party-control-than-at-any-other-time-in-modern-history.
51. Philip Bump, "The Rise of the State-Level Supermajority," *Washington Post*, April 28, 2023, https://www.washingtonpost.com/politics/2023/04/28/supermajority-state-legislatures/.
52. Jenna Portnoy and Laura Vozzella, "McDonnell Verdict Will Test VA's Political Self-Image, and Perhaps Change Ethics Laws," *Washington Post*, September 5, 2014, https://www.washingtonpost.com/local/virginia-politics/mcdonnell-trial-will-test-virginias-political-self-image--and-perhaps-change-its-laws/2014/09/05/52a2749a-3392-11e4-8f02-03c644b2d7d0_story.html.
53. Charlie Savage, "The Scandal of Michigan's Emergency Managers," *Nation*, March 5–12, 2012.
54. Alessandra Stanley, "Where Political Comebacks and Celebrity Comebacks Meet," *New York Times*, September 26, 2009, https://www.nytimes.com/2009/09/27/weekinreview/27stanley.html.
55. Lindsey Boerma, "Eliot Spitzer's New Ad for Comptroller: 'I Failed, Big Time,'" CBS News, July 22, 2013, https://www.cbsnews.com/news/eliot-spitzers-new-ad-for-comptroller-i-failed-big-time/.
56. John O'Connor, "Quoting Dr. Seuss, 'Just Go, Go, GO!' Federal Judge Dismisses Blagojevich Political Comeback Suit," AP News, March 21, 2024, https://apnews.com/article/rod-blagojevich-lawsuit-c8fd9a13510c470004566cec7357c44c.
57. Alex Isenstadt, "'Clear and Present Danger': Republicans Fret About Greitens' Comeback," *Politico*, March 15, 2021, https://www.politico.com/news/2021/03/15/republicans-fret-eric-greitens-comeback-475737.
58. Natalie Allison, "Disgraced Former Governor Is Recast as MAGA Warrior in Senate Bid," *Politico*, October 25, 2021, https://www.politico.com/news/2021/10/25/former-governor-greitens-maga-warrior-senate-bid-517051.
59. Jonathan Miller, "Congressional Scandals Ain't What They Used to Be," Roll Call, January 22, 2019.
60. Jeff Gulati and Lara M. Brown, "The Personal Is Political: Reconsidering the Impact of Scandals on Congressional Incumbents," *Congress & the Presidency* 48, no. 1 (2021): 25–49; Robert Busby, *Scandal and American Politics in the Twenty-First Century* (Palgrave Macmillan, 2022).
61. John Harris, "Cuomo Tries the Trump Strategy for Surviving Scandal," *Politico*, March 18, 2021, https://www.politico.com/news/magazine/2021/03/18/andrew-cuomo-donald-trump-scandal-survival-476923.

2. WEATHERING THE STORM: HOW TO SURVIVE A SCANDAL

1. Evan Andrews, "8 Early American Political Scandals," History.com, October 18, 2023, https://www.history.com/news/8-early-american-political-scandals.
2. U.S. Senate, "Expulsion Case of William Blount of Tennessee" (1797), https://www.senate.gov/about/powers-procedures/expulsion/Blount_expulsion.htm#:~:text=In%20an%20apparent%20effort%20to,those%20territories%20to%20Great%20Britain.
3. Howard Kurtz, "Scandal," *Washington Post*, September 21, 1991; Benjamin Ginsberg and Martin Shefter, *Politics by Other Means: Politicians, Prosecutors, and the Press from Watergate to Whitewater* (Norton, 1999).
4. Kurtz, "Scandal."
5. Michael D. Shear, "No Guide to Survive a Scandal," *New York Times*, June 11, 2011.
6. John Zaller, *A Theory of Media Politics: How the Interests of Politicians, Journalists, and Citizens Shape the News* (University of Chicago Press, 1999).
7. Molly W. Andolina and Clyde Wilcox, "Public Opinion: The Paradoxes of Clinton's Popularity," in *The Clinton Scandals and the Future of American Government*, ed. Mark J. Rozell and Clyde Wilcox (Georgetown University Press, 2000).
8. Suzanne Garment, *Scandal: The Culture of Mistrust in American Politics* (Anchor Books, 1991).
9. John B. Thompson, *Political Scandal: Power and Visibility in the Media Age* (Wiley, 2000).
10. Michael R. Kagay, "Presidential Address: Public Opinion and Polling During Presidential Scandal and Impeachment," *Public Opinion Quarterly* 63, no. 3 (1999): 449–463.
11. Some states have only one chamber, but since there were no recorded scandals in these states for this period, this was not an issue.
12. Jeffrey L. Bernstein and Amanda C. Shannon, *Vital Statistics on American Politics 2017–2020* (CQ Press, 2022).
13. Klarner Politics, "Data Made Publicly Available," https://www.klarnerpolitics.org/datasets-1, accessed June 1, 2022.
14. Morris P. Fiorina and Samuel J. Abrams, "Political Polarization in the American Public," *Annual Review of Political Science* 11 (2008): 563–588; Geoffrey C. Layman, Thomas M. Carsey, and Juliana Menasce Horowitz, "Party Polarization in American Politics: Characteristics, Causes, and Consequences," *Annual Review of Political Science* 9 (2006): 83–110.
15. Ginsberg and Shefter, *Politics by Other Means*.
16. Tiffany D. Barnes, Emily Beaulieu, and Gregory W. Saxton, "Sex and Corruption: How Sexism Shapes Voters' Responses to Scandal," *Politics, Groups, and Identities* 8, no. 1 (2020): 103–121; Brenna Armstrong, Tiffany D. Barnes, Diana Z. O'Brien, and Michelle M. Taylor-Robinson, "Corruption, Accountability, and Women's Access to Power," *Journal of Politics* 84, no. 2 (2022): 1207–1213.
17. Thad Beyle, Richard G. Niemi, and Lee Sigelman, "Gubernatorial, Senatorial, and State-Level Presidential Job Approval: The U.S. Officials Job Approval Ratings (JAR) Collection," *State Politics & Policy Quarterly* 2, no. 3 (2002): 215–229.

18. Survey USA, http://www.surveyusa.com/50statetracking.html, accessed June 1, 2022.
19. Several elements of normality are violated that precede the use of OLS regression, most prominently the presence of data censoring.
20. Mario Cleves, William Gould, Obertto R. Gutierrez, and Yulia V. Marchenko, *An Introduction to Survival Analysis Using Stata* (StatCorp, 2010).
21. David R. Cox, "Regression Models and Life-Tables," *Journal of the Royal Statistical Society* 34, no. 2 (1972): 187–202.
22. Janet M. Box-Steffensmeier and Bradford S. Jones, *Event History Modeling: A Guide for Social Scientists* (Cambridge University Press, 2012); Christopher Zorn, "Modeling Duration Dependence," *Political Analysis* 8, no. 3 (2000): 367–380.
23. D. Y. Lin and L. J. Wei, "The Robust Inference for the Cox Proportional Hazards Model," *Journal of the American Statistical Association* 84, no. 408 (1989): 1074–1078.
24. Cleves, Gould, Gutierrez, and Marchenko, *An Introduction to Survival Analysis.*
25. Frederick J. Boehmke, Daniel S. Morley, and Megan Shannon, "Selection Bias and Continuous-Time Duration Models: Consequences and a Proposed Solution," *American Journal of Political Science* 50, no. 1 (2006): 192–207. The problem emerges in a nonrandom sample if unobserved factors affect the duration of an event and whether the event is observed at all. In this case, the media may be a factor that influences both the reporting of a scandal and its length. However, the start and end of scandals are endogenously determined by an individual's behavior. The role of the media, especially social media, is important because the framing, especially in later eras, is partisan (and therefore predictable) and often gendered. Seth C. McKee, Heather K. Evans, and Jennifer Hayes Clark, "The 'PERFECT' Call: Congressional Representation by Tweet in the Midst of the Ukraine Whistleblower Scandal," *American Politics Research* 50, no. 1 (2022): 30–44.
26. If a politician decided not to run again putatively because of the scandal, it is not counted as a failure. It was often unclear if the scandal was the direct cause of a politician's choosing not to run again. In the end, we erred on the side of empirically capturing when the scandal definitively caused a resignation rather than speculating about the proximate cause.
27. Paul J. Quirk, "Coping with the Politics of Scandal," *Presidential Studies Quarterly* 28, no. 4 (1998): 898–902; Robert Busby, *Reagan and the Iran-Contra Affair: The Politics of Presidential Recovery* (St. Martin's Press, 1999).
28. Scott R. Meinke and William D. Anderson, "Influencing Impaired Administrations: Presidents, White House Scandals, and Legislative Leadership," *Legislative Studies Quarterly* 26, no. 4 (2001): 639–659.
29. Himanshi Raizada, "The Timing of Presidential Scandals: The Dynamics of Economics, the Media and a Divided Government," *Open Journal of Political Science* 3, no. 3 (2013): 98–105.
30. Gladys Engel Lang and Kurt Lang, *The Battle for Public Opinion: The President, the Press, and the Polls During Watergate* (Columbia University Press, 1983).

31. Paul J. Quirk, "Coping with the Politics of Scandal," *Presidential Studies Quarterly* 28, no. 4 (1998): 898–902; Molly W. Sonner and Clyde Wilcox, "Forgiving and Forgetting: Public Support for Bill Clinton During the Lewinski Scandal," *PS: Political Science and Politics* 32, no. 3 (2013): 554–557.
32. Victor J. Hinojosa and Aníbal S. Pérez-Liñán, "Presidential Survival and the Impeachment Process: The United States and Colombia," *Political Science Quarterly* 121, no. 4 (2006): 655.
33. Parameterized models demonstrate similar findings, suggesting robustness to the findings. Alternative models that identify a competing risk of the scandal ending in firing, prosecution, or dismissal and the scandal ending because of a lack of indictment or the executive's term in office ending reveal substantially similar results.
34. D. R. Cox and E. J. Snell, "A General Definition of Residuals," *Journal of the Royal Statistical Society* 30, no. 2 (1968): 248–275.
35. Frank E. Harrell Jr., Robert M. Califf, and David B. Pryor, "Evaluating the Yield of Medical Tests," *Journal of the American Medical Association* 247, no. 18 (1982): 2543–2546; Frank E. Harrell Jr., Kerry L. Lee, and Daniel B. Mark, "Multivariate Prognostic Models: Issues in Developing Models, Evaluating Assumptions and Adequacy, and Measuring and Reducing Errors," *Statistics in Medicine* 15, no. 4 (1996): 461–491. The Harrell's C ranges from 0 to 1 and the Somers' D ranges from –1 to 1. In the Harrell's C in table 2.1, the models correctly identify the order of survival times for more than 70 percent of pairs.
36. Cleves, Gould, Gutierrez, and Marchenko, *An Introduction to Survival Analysis.*
37. An interaction between the size of partisan support and public approval was also not statistically significant.
38. In alternative models a dummy variable was used to indicate whether or not the requisite number of votes was received for impeachment or removal from office. There was no significant effect.
39. Brandon Rottinghaus and Zlata Bereznikova, "Exorcising Scandal in the White House: Presidential Polling in Times of Crisis," *Presidential Studies Quarterly* 36, no. 3 (2006): 493–505.
40. Tiffany D. Barnes, Emily Beaulieu, and Gregory W. Saxton, "Restoring Trust in the Police: Why Female Officers Reduce Suspicions of Corruption," *Governance* 31 (2018): 143–161.
41. Richard J. Ellis, *Lightning Rods: The Politics of Blame Avoidance* (University of Kansas Press, 1994).
42. Lou Cannon, "Lessons of Scandals Past," *Washington Post*, October 31, 2005.
43. Peter Baker, "The Lasting Effects of Political Poison," *New York Times*, December 13, 2008.
44. Kagay, "Presidential Address"; David Doherty, Conor M. Dowling, and Michael G. Miller, "Are Financial or Moral Scandals Worse? It Depends," *PS: Political Science and Politics* 44, no. 4 (2011): 749–757.

45. Thomas E. Sowers II and James P. Nelson, "The Timing of Presidential Scandals: The Role of Economics, Divided Government and the Media," *Open Journal of Political Science* 6, no. 1 (2016): 83–94.
46. Douglas L. Kriner and Eric Schickler, *Investigating the President: Congressional Checks on Presidential Power* (Princeton University Press, 2016).
47. An interaction between the size of partisan support and public approval was also not statistically significant.
48. Young Hun Kim and Donna Bahry, "Interrupted Presidencies in Third Wave Democracy," *Journal of Politics* 70, no. 3 (2008): 807–822.
49. The specification matters here. Cutting the window at a later date (2008) does not have the same statistically significant effect, although including year as a continuous variable does have the same effect.
50. Will Weissert and Adriana Gomez Licon, "Gaetz Vows to Fight, Tries to Stay on Offensive Amid Scandal," AP News, April 9, 2021, https://apnews.com/article/politicians-in-crisis-refuse-to-resign-16046aff55900e97f59aec9aa5153df6.
51. Scott Basinger and Brandon Rottinghaus, "Skeletons in the White House Closets: An Empirical Investigation Into Modern Presidential Scandals," *Political Science Quarterly* 127, no. 2 (2012): 213–239; Scott Basinger and Brandon Rottinghaus, "Stonewalling: Explaining Presidential Behavior During Scandal," *Political Research Quarterly* 65, no. 2 (2012): 290–302.
52. Scott J. Basinger, "Scandals and Ethics Reform in the U.S. House of Representatives," *Public Integrity* 18, no. 4 (2016): 359–375.
53. "Voters Enraged Over House Bank Abuses," in *CQ Almanac 1992*, 48th ed. (Congressional Quarterly, 1993), 23–42.
54. Guy Gugliotta, "Foley Saw House Bank Problems as Correctable," *Washington Post*, March 31, 1992, https://www.washingtonpost.com/archive/politics/1992/04/01/foley-saw-house-bank-problems-as-correctable/3b02fb17-1a51-4c04-a1ca-5246886e7aa8/.
55. Gugliotta, "Foley Saw House Bank Problems."
56. "Voters Enraged Over House Bank Abuses."
57. David Baumann, "Nussle and the Paper Bag," *Credit Union Times*, October 6, 2017, https://www.cutimes.com/2017/10/06/nussle-and-the-paper-bag/?slreturn=20240304124551.
58. "Voters Enraged Over House Bank Abuses."
59. "Voters Enraged Over House Bank Abuses."
60. "Voters Enraged Over House Bank Abuses."
61. Gary C. Jacobson and Michael A. Dimock, "Checking Out: The Effects of Bank Overdrafts on the 1992 House Elections," *American Journal of Political Science* 38, no. 3 (1994): 601–624.
62. "Voters Enraged Over House Bank Abuses."
63. Michael S. Schmidt, Katie Benner, and Nichoals Fandos, "Matt Gaetz Is Said to Face Justice Dept. Inquiry Over Sex with an Underage Girl," *New York Times*, May 17, 2021,

https://www.nytimes.com/2021/03/30/us/politics/matt-gaetz-sex-trafficking-investigation.html.

64. Gary Fineout and Jordain Carney, "Matt Gaetz Had a Hell of a Month: What's Next for the Florida Republican?," *Politico*, February 16, 2023, https://www.politico.com/news/2023/02/16/matt-gaetz-florida-governor-00083366.
65. Jose Pagliery, "These Text Messages Pointed the Feds to Matt Gaetz," *Daily Beast*, April 2, 2021, https://www.thedailybeast.com/these-text-messages-led-the-feds-to-matt-gaetz.
66. Katie Benner and Michael S. Schmidt, "Justice Dept. Inquiry Into Matt Gaetz Said to Be Focused on Cash Paid to Women," *New York Times*, April 1, 2021, https://www.nytimes.com/2021/04/01/us/politics/matt-gaetz-justice-department.html.
67. Benner and Schmidt, "Justice Dept. Inquiry."
68. Evan Perez, David Shortell, Paula Reid, and Pamela Brown, "Feds' Investigation of Matt Gaetz Includes Whether Campaign Funds Were Used to Pay for Travel and Expenses," CNN, April 2, 2021, https://www.cnn.com/2021/04/01/politics/matt-gaetz-campaign-funds-investigation/index.html.
69. Benner and Schmidt, "Justice Dept. Inquiry."
70. Lexi Lonas, "McCarthy Says Gaetz Won't Be Punished Unless Charges Filed," *The Hill*, April 15, 2021, https://thehill.com/homenews/house/548511-mccarthy-says-gaetz-wont-be-punished-unless-charges-filed/.
71. Eric Tucker, Michael Balsamo, and Lisa Mascaro, "Gaetz Faces House Ethics Probe; Federal Investigation Widens," AP News, April 10, 2021, https://apnews.com/gaetz-faces-house-ethics-probe-federal-investigation-widens-c64f9142f20f15701ea50d5de79f600b.
72. Alayna Treene, "Scoop: Matt Gaetz Eyes Early Retirement to Take Job at Newsmax," *Axios*, March 30, 2021, https://www.axios.com/2021/03/30/matt-gaetz-retirement-congress-newsmax.
73. Melanie Zanona and Olivia Beavers, "Gaetz's Glare Stings House GOP—But His Future's Safe for Now," *Politico*, April 13, 2021, https://www.politico.com/news/2021/04/13/matt-gaetz-political-future-481241
74. Zanona and Beavers, "Gaetz's Glare Stings House GOP."
75. Christine Mui, "Controversy Equals Cash for Greene," *The Hill*, July 18, 2021, https://thehill.com/homenews/campaign/563609-controversy-equals-cash-from-greene-gaetz/.
76. Fineout and Carney, "Matt Gaetz Had a Hell of a Month."
77. Scott Wong and Frank Thorp V, "Inside the Most Bizarre Congress in Recent Memory," NBC News, December 31, 2024, https://www.nbcnews.com/specials/118th-congress-craziest-speaker-races-mccarthy-johnson-gaetz/index.html.
78. Paula D. McClain, "Arizona's 'High Noon': The Recall and Impeachment of Evan Mecham," *PS: Political Science and Politics* 21, no. 3 (2013): 628–638.
79. Associated Press, "Evan Mecham, Ousted Governor, Dies at 83," *New York Times*, February 23, 2008, https://www.nytimes.com/2008/02/23/us/23mecham.html.

80. Jon D. Hill, "Evan Mecham, Please Go Home," *Time*, November 9, 1987, https://content.time.com/time/subscriber/article/0,33009,965917,00.html.
81. McClain, "Arizona's 'High Noon.'"
82. "Gov. Evan Mecham Says He Finds Nothing Funny About . . .," UPI, September 2, 1987, https://www.upi.com/Archives/1987/09/02/Gov-Evan-Mecham-says-he-finds-nothing-funny-about/2957557553600/.
83. Don Harris, "The Colorful and Tumultuous Political Career of Evan Mecham," *Arizona Capitol Times*, November 29, 2011, https://azcapitoltimes.com/news/2011/11/29/the-colorful-and-tumultuous-political-career-of-evan-mecham/.
84. Steve Goldenstein, "Music Writer Recalls U2's History with Arizona's Political Scene," KJZZ, September 17, 2017, https://kjzz.org/content/538784/music-writer-recalls-u2s-history-arizonas-political-scene.
85. Hill, "Evan Mecham, Please Go Home."
86. Richard Ruelas, "Doonesbury: Trump Was Worse Than Past Arizona Gov. Evan Mecham, *The Republic*, July 21, 2016, https://www.azcentral.com/story/news/politics/elections/2016/07/21/doonesbury-trump-worse-than-past-az-gov-ev-mecham/87383506/.
87. Arizona Archives Online, "Governor Evan Mecham Impeachment Papers, 1986–1988," http://azarchivesonline.org/xtf/view?docId=ead/dfc/AzULawGovernorEvanMechamImpeachmentPapers.xml;query=;brand=default.
88. McClain, "Arizona's 'High Noon.'"
89. Arizona Archives Online, "Governor Evan Mecham Impeachment Papers."
90. Associated Press, "Evan Mecham, Ousted Governor, Dies at 83," *New York Times*, February 23, 2008.
91. McClain, "Arizona's 'High Noon.'"
92. McClain, "Arizona's 'High Noon.'"
93. Melissa Rigg and Susan R. Carson, "Mecham Convicted; Recall Status in Doubt," *Arizona Daily Star*, April 5, 1988, https://tucson.com/1988-gov-evan-mecham-impeached/article_c7c7d61a-ceab-11e5-9cb4-e36cafcf4cfc.html.
94. Rigg and Carson, "Mecham Convicted."
95. Associated Press, "Evan Mecham, Ousted Governor, Dies at 83."
96. Nick Niedzwiadek and Anna Gronewold, "'Bullying, Screaming': In Albany, Cuomo Wields Phone as a Weapon," *Politico*, February 19, 2021, https://www.politico.com/news/2021/02/19/andrew-cuomo-phone-bullying-screaming-470025.
97. Nathanial Rakich, "4 Ways Andrew Cuomo's Political Future Could Play Out," FiveThirtyEight, March 8, 2021, https://fivethirtyeight.com/features/4-ways-andrew-cuomos-political-future-could-play-out/.
98. Jesse McKinley and Luis Ferre-Sadurni, "New Allegations of Cover-Up by Cuomo Over Nursing Home Virus Toll, *New York Times*, February 21, 2021, https://www.nytimes.com/2021/02/12/nyregion/new-york-nursing-homes-cuomo.html.
99. Max Greenwood, "Cuomo Takes Heat from All Sides on Nursing Home Scandal," *The Hill*, February 19, 2021, https://thehill.com/homenews/campaign/539475-cuomo-takes-heat-from-all-sides-on-nursing-home-scandal.

100. Zach Budryk, "Former Cuomo Aide Says Governor Kissed Her Without Consent," *The Hill*, February 24, 2021, https://thehill.com/homenews/state-watch/540423-former-cuomo-aide-says-governor-kissed-her-without-consent/?rl=1.
101. Jessie McKinley, "Cuomo Is Accused of Sexual Harassment by a 2nd Former Aide," *New York Times*, February 27, 2021, https://www.nytimes.com/2021/02/27/nyregion/cuomo-charlotte-bennett-sexual-harassment.html.
102. Rakich, "4 Ways Andrew Cuomo's Political Future Could Play Out."
103. Rakich, "4 Ways Andrew Cuomo's Political Future Could Play Out."
104. Chris Cillizza, "35 Words That Almost Certainly Will End Andrew Cuomo's Political Career," CNN, August 3, 2021, https://www.cnn.com/2021/08/03/politics/andrew-cuomo-sexual-harassment-governor/index.html.
105. Jesse McKinley and Luis Ferre-Sadurni, "Uprising Grows Over Cuomo's Bullying and 'Brutalist Political Theater,'" *New York Times*, February 22, 2021, https://www.nytimes.com/2021/02/22/nyregion/cuomo-new-york-covid.html.
106. Rakich, "4 Ways Andrew Cuomo's Political Future Could Play Out."
107. Rakich, "4 Ways Andrew Cuomo's Political Future Could Play Out."
108. McKinley and Ferre-Sadurni, "Uprising Grows Over Cuomo's Bullying." https://www.nytimes.com/2021/02/22/nyregion/cuomo-new-york-covid.html.
109. Caroline Vakil, "Top Aide to Cuomo Resigns," *The Hill*, August 8, 2021, https://thehill.com/homenews/state-watch/566937-top-aide-to-cuomo-resigns/.
110. Chris Cillizza, "Andrew Cuomo Just Isn't Sorry," CNN, August 23, 2021, https://www.cnn.com/2021/08/23/politics/cuomo-resignation-sorry/index.html.
111. "Andrew Cuomo Refuses to Resign: 'I Never Touched Anyone Inappropriately,'" *Axios*, August 3, 2021, https://www.axios.com/2021/08/03/cuomo-governor-new-york-sexual-misconduct.
112. Geoffrey Skelley, "Andrew Cuomo Had Nowhere to Go but Out," FiveThirtyEight, August 10, 2021, https://fivethirtyeight.com/features/andrew-cuomo-had-nowhere-to-go-but-out.
113. Thomas Catenacci, "Top Donors Halt Support for Andrew Cuomo Amid Sexual Harassment Scandal," *Daily Caller*, March 1, 2021, https://dailycaller.com/2021/03/01/donors-financial-contributions-andrew-cuomo-new-york-sexual-harassment/
114. Lechlan Markay, "Scoop: Dem Fundraising Platform ActBlue Boots Cuomo," *Axios*, August 5, 2021, https://www.axios.com/2021/08/05/democratic-fundraising-platform-actblue-boots-cuomo.
115. John Bowden, "Cuomo and De Blasio Trade Jabs Through Media: 'Serial Sexual Assaulter Says What?,'" *The Hill*, April 29, 2021, https://thehill.com/homenews/state-watch/551044-cuomo-and-de-blasio-trade-jabs-through-media-serial-sexual-assaulter/.
116. Cillizza, "Andrew Cuomo Just Isn't Sorry."
117. John F. Harris, "Cuomo Tries the Trump Strategy for Surviving Scandal," *Politico*, March 18, 2021, https://www.politico.com/news/magazine/2021/03/18/andrew-cuomo-donald-trump-scandal-survival-476923.

2. WEATHERING THE STORM

118. Arthur Schlesinger Jr., "Jimmy Carter, an Original," *New York Times*, June 5, 1977, https://www.nytimes.com/1977/06/05/archives/jimmy-carter-an-original-a-government-as-good-as-its-people-carter.html.
119. Schlesinger, "Jimmy Carter, an Original."
120. Jonathan Alter, *His Very Best: Jimmy Carter, a Life* (Simon & Schuster, 2021).
121. Jimmy Carter, *Keeping Faith: Memoirs of a President* (Bantam Books, 1982).
122. Carter, *Keeping Faith*, 135.
123. Andie Tucher, *Not Exactly Lying: Fake News and Fake Journalism in American History* (New York: Columbia University Press, 2023).
124. Carter, *Keeping Faith.*
125. Alter, *His Very Best.*
126. James Poniewozik, "For Ex-President's Trials, the Recriminations Will Be Televised," *New York Times*, February 18, 2024.
127. Weissert and Gomez Licon, "Gaetz Vows to Fight."
128. Juliet Eilperin, Josh Dawsey, and Darryl Fears, "Interior Secretary Zinke Resigns Amid Investigations," *Washington Post*, December 15, 2018, https://www.washingtonpost.com/national/health-science/interior-secretary-zinke-resigns-amid-investigations/2018/12/15/481f9104-0077-11e9-ad40-cdfd0e0dd65a_story.html.
129. Ben Lefebvre, "Interior Secretary Zinke Traveled on Charter, Military Planes," *Politico*, September 28, 2017, https://www.politico.com/story/2017/09/28/ryan-zinke-charter-military-planes-interior-243280.
130. Lefebvre, "Interior Secretary Zinke Traveled on Charter, Military Planes."
131. Ben Lefebvre, "Zinke Booked Government Helicopters to Attend D.C. Events," *Politico*, December 7, 2017, https://www.politico.com/story/2017/12/07/ryan-zinke-helicopters-dc-212730.
132. Eilperin, Dawsey, and Fears, "Interior Secretary Zinke Resigns Amid Investigations."
133. Emily Holden and Oliver Milman, "Embattled Interior Secretary Ryan Zinke Steps Down After Series of Scandals," *Guardian*, December 15, 2018, https://www.theguardian.com/us-news/2018/dec/15/ryan-zinke-interior-secretary-steps-down.
134. Adiel Kaplan, "Ryan Zinke Knowingly Misled Federal Investigators as Interior Secretary, Inspector General Finds," NBC News, August 24, 2022, https://www.nbcnews.com/politics/2022-election/ryan-zinke-knowingly-misled-federal-investigators-interior-secretary-i-rcna44614.
135. Eilperin, Dawsey, and Fears, "Interior Secretary Zinke Resigns Amid Investigations."

3. HOW POLARIZATION MINIMIZES SCANDALS

1. Larry M. Bartels, "Beyond the Running Tally: Partisan Bias in Political Perception," *Political Behavior* 24, no. 2 (2002): 117–150.
2. Michael A. Dimock and Gary C. Jacobson, "Check and Choices: The House Bank Scandal's Impact on Voters in 1992," *Journal of Politics* 57, no. 4 (1995): 1143–1159.

3. Annemarie S. Walter and David P. Redlawsk, "Voters' Partisan Responses to Politicians' Immoral Behavior," *Political Psychology* 40, no. 5 (2019): 1075–1097.
4. Samara Klar and Alexandra McCoy, "Partisan-Motivated Evaluations of Sexual Misconduct and the Mitigating Role of the #MeToo Movement," *American Journal of Political Science* 65, no. 4 (2021): 777–789.
5. Ho-Chun Herbert Chang, James Druckman, Emilio Ferrara, and Robb Willer, "Liberals Engage with More Diverse Policy Topics and Toxic Content Than Conservatives on Social Media," OSF Preprints, February 15 2023, https://osf.io/preprints/osf/x59qt_v1.
6. Ángela Fonseca Galvis, James M. Snyder, and B. K. Song, "Newspaper Market Structure and Behavior: Partisan Coverage of Political Scandals in the United States from 1870 to 1910," *Journal of Politics* 78, no. 2 (2016): 368–381.
7. Stephan Wojcik and Adam Hughes, "Sizing Up Twitter Users," Pew Research Center, April 24, 2019, https://www.pewresearch.org/internet/2019/04/24/sizing-up-twitter-users/.
8. Adam Edelman, "A Guide to Trump's Nicknames and Insults About the 2020 Democratic Field," NBC News, May 13, 2019, https://www.nbcnews.com/politics/2020-election/everything-trump-has-said-about-2020-field-insults-all-n998556.
9. Thomas Zeitzoff, *Nasty Politics: The Logic of Insults, Threats, and Incitement* (Oxford University Press, 2023).
10. Jeremy A. Frimer and Linda J. Skitka, "The Montagu Principle: Incivility Decreases Politicians' Public Approval, Even with Their Political Base," *Journal of Personality and Social Psychology* 115, no. 5 (2018): 845–866.
11. Jeremy A. Frimer and Linda J. Skitka, "Americans Hold Their Political Leaders to a Higher Discursive Standard Than Rank-and-File Co-Partisans," *Journal of Experimental Social Psychology* 86 (2020), https://doi.org/10.1016/j.jesp.2019.103907.
12. Seo-young Silvia Kim, Jan Zilinsky, and Brian Brew, "Donate to Help Us Fight Back: Political Fundraising and Toxic Rhetoric Online," *Party Politics*, March 11, 2024, https://doi.org/10.1177/13540688241235901.
13. Zeitzoff, *Nasty Politics*.
14. Walter and Redlawsk, "Voters' Partisan Responses."
15. Stephanie Stark and Sofía Collignon, "Sexual Predators in Contest for Public Office: How the American Electorate Responds to News of Allegations of Candidates Committing Sexual Assault and Harassment," *Political Studies Review* 20, no. 3 (2022): 329–352.
16. Megan Messerly, "First Families Are Finally Catching Up to America," *Politico*, September 13, 2024, https://www.politico.com/news/2024/09/13/kamala-harris-donald-trump-divorce-blended-families-00179015.
17. Yosef Bhatti, Kasper M Hansen, and Asmus Leth Olsen, "Political Hypocrisy: The Effect of Political Scandals on Candidate Evaluations, *Acta Politica* 48 (2013): 408–428, https://doi.org/10.1057/ap.2013.6.
18. The Cronbach's alpha is above .75 for each item, signaling that each item contributes strongly to the overall index by measuring the underlying concept. The average interitem

correlation is low for each variable, suggesting that the change as a result of removing the variable would be minimal. Factor analysis shows that variables explain .80 of cumulative variance. Factor loadings show high first-factor dimensionality.

19. The overall scale reliability coefficient is .81, again suggesting the index measures the underlying concept. Alternative specifications were explored, including adding supplemental variables or removing other variables. In each instance, the measure performed worse overall with the inclusion or exclusion of these variables.
20. Adam D. Wolsky, "Scandal, Hypocrisy, and Resignation: How Partisanship Shapes Evaluations of Politicians' Transgressions," *Journal of Experimental Political Science* 9, no. 1 (2020): 74–87.
21. Elizabeth S. Smith, Ashleigh Smith Powers, and Gustavo Suarez, "If Bill Clinton Were a Woman: The Effectiveness of Male and Female Politicians' Account Strategies Following Alleged Transgressions," *Political Psychology* 26, no. 1 (2005): 115–134.
22. Miguel M. Pereira and Nicholas W. Waterbury, "Do Voters Discount Political Scandals Over Time?," *Political Research Quarterly* 72, no. 3 (2019): 584–595.
23. Walter and Redlawsk, "Voters' Partisan Responses."
24. Jon Kingzette, James N. Druckman, Samara Klar, Yanna Krupnikov, Matthew Levendusky, and John Barry Ryan, "How Affective Polarization Undermines Support for Democratic Norms," *Public Opinion Quarterly* 85, no. 2 (2021): 663–677, https://doi.org/10.1093/poq/nfab029.s

4. EVERYTHING IS A SCANDAL THESE DAYS

1. Aris Folley, "Obama's Tan Suit Controversy Hits 5-Year Anniversary," *The Hill*, August 28, 2019, https://thehill.com/blogs/in-the-know/in-the-know/459155-barack-obamas-tan-suit-controversy-hits-5-year-anniversary/.
2. Jeva Lange, "The Big Controversy at This Point in Obama's Presidency Was Over Dijon Mustard," *The Week*, June 9, 2017, https://theweek.com/speedreads/704818/big-controversy-point-obamas-presidency-over-dijon-mustard.
3. Sean Illing, "'Flood the Zone with Shit': How Misinformation Overwhelmed Our Democracy," *Vox*, February 6, 2020, https://www.vox.com/policy-and-politics/2020/1/16/20991816/impeachment-trial-trump-bannon-misinformation
4. Illing, "'Flood the Zone with Shit.'"
5. Brendan Nyhan, "Strategic Outrage: The Politics of Presidential Scandal" (PhD diss., Duke University, 2009).
6. Brendan Nydan, "Scandal Potential: How Political Context and News Congestion Affect the President's Vulnerability to Media Scandal," *British Journal of Political Science* 45, no. 2 (2015): 435–466.
7. Another way to examine the effect of each treatment on the dependent variable is to estimate the average treatment effects (ATE). The results are inconsistent, as explained in the text, but do show modest effects of the treatments on the three dependent

variables of concern. There are statistically significant effects of the "regular Fox News" treatment on Biden's approval and a general effect for the treatment on the belief that the Biden administration had more scandals than other administrations.

8. Lange, "The Big Controversy at This Point in Obama's Presidency."

5. THE EFFECTS OF SCANDALS ON POLITICAL LEGACIES

1. Philip G. Payne, "The Harding Presidency: Scandals, Legacy and Memory," in *A Companion to Warren G. Harding, Calvin Coolidge, and Herbert Hoover*, ed. A. S. Katherine (Sibley Wiley, 2014).
2. Fred I. Greenstein, "The Benevolent Leader Revisited: Children's Images of Political Leaders in Three Democracies," *American Political Science Review* 69, no. 3 (1975): 1371–1398.
3. Diana Owens and Jack Dennis, "Kids and the Presidency: Assessing Clinton's Legacy," *Public Perspective*, April/May 1999.
4. Meena Bose, "Presidential Ratings: Lessons and Liabilities," *White House Studies* 3, no. 1 (2003): 5.
5. Arthur M. Schlesinger Jr., "Rating the Presidents: Washington to Clinton," *Political Science Quarterly* 112, no. 2 (1997): 179–190.
6. Brandon Rottinghaus, Gregory Eady, and Justin S. Vaughn, "Presidential Greatness in a Polarized Era: Results from the Latest Presidential Greatness Survey," *PS: Political Science and Politics* 53, no. 3 (2020): 413–420.
7. Responses from respondents who did not confirm that they officially agreed to participate are excluded from the data. In the event that a respondent completed the survey twice, the submission that the respondent spent the least time completing was dropped, as was any submission in which the respondent did not answer any questions.
8. The question asks: "We'd like to ask you a question about presidential controversies. Rank the following presidential scandals in terms of the impact on American politics."
9. The question asks: "Relative to Watergate, how important are the following presidential scandals?"
10. James P. Pfiffner, *The Character Factor: How We Judge America's Presidents* (Texas A&M University Press, 2004), 6.
11. John Fousek and David Wasserman, "Ethical Issues in U.S. Presidential Leadership," *Presidential Studies Quarterly* 40 (2010): 2.
12. Pfiffner, *The Character Factor*, 6.
13. William Galston, "Commentary: Ethics and Character in the U.S. Presidency," *Presidential Studies Quarterly* 40, no. 1 (2010): 90–101.
14. Jill L. Curry and Irwin L. Morris, "The Contemporary Presidency: Explaining Presidential Greatness: The Roles of Peace and Prosperity," *Presidential Studies Quarterly* 40, no. 3 (2010): 515–530.

15. Curry and Morris, "The Contemporary Presidency: Explaining Presidential Greatness."
16. Russell L. Riley, "Bill Clinton: Impact and Legacy," Miller Center, University of Virginia, https://millercenter.org/president/clinton/impact-and-legacy.
17. Peter Baker, "25 Years Later, Looking for Lessons in the Clinton Scandal," *New York Times*, January 21, 2023, https://www.nytimes.com/2023/01/21/us/politics/25-years-clinton-lewinsky.html.
18. Peter Baker, "'What About Bill?' Sexual Misconduct Debate Revives Questions About Clinton," *New York Times*, November 15, 2017, https://www.nytimes.com/2017/11/15/us/politics/bill-clinton-sexual-misconduct-debate.html.
19. Rottinghaus, Eady, and Vaughn, "Presidential Greatness."
20. Lori Cox Han and Matthew J. Krov, "Out of Office and in the News: Early Projections of the Clinton Legacy," *Presidential Studies Quarterly* 33, no. 4 (2003); Kristen East, "Democrat Gillibrand Says Bill Clinton Should Have Resigned Over Lewinsky Scandal," *Politico*, November 6, 2017, https://www.politico.com/story/2017/11/16/kirsten-gillibrand-bill-clinton-resign-lewinsky-246532.
21. Jonathan Lemire, "Trump, Before Debate, Appears with Bill Clinton's Accusers," AP News, October 9, 2016, https://apnews.com/article/bill-clinton-donald-trump-988a39ec2a8f4429aa23ad220a9d8c14.
22. Russell Berman, "Don't Assume That Eric Adams Is Going Anywhere," *Atlantic*, September 27, 2024.
23. Editorial Board, "Mayor Turner Was Stubborn. Flawed. And Houston's Better Because of Him," *Houston Chronicle,* December 31, 2023, https://www.houstonchronicle.com/opinion/editorials/article/mayor-turner-legacy-disaster-harvey-inequality-18580381.php.
24. B. D. Hobbs, "New Scandals Emerge in Final Days of Mayor Turner's Term," KTRH News, December 11, 2023, https://ktrh.iheart.com/featured/houston-texas-news/content/2023-12-08-new-scandals-emerge-in-final-days-of-mayor-turners-term//
25. Jen Rice, "Houston Housing Director Fired After Accusing Sylvester Turner of Awarding $15 Million to Favored Developer," *Houston Public Media*, September 21, 2021, https://www.houstonpublicmedia.org/articles/news/politics/2021/09/21/409022/city-housing-director-fired-after-making-ethical-allegations-against-turner-administration/.
26. Adam Zuvanich and Haya Panjwani, "Aide to Houston Mayor Resigns After Reportedly Pleading Guilty to Public Corruption," *Houston Public Media*, August 3, 2022, https://www.houstonpublicmedia.org/articles/news/city-of-houston/2022/08/03/429845/aide-to-houston-mayor-resigns-after-reportedly-pleading-guilty-to-public-corruption/.
27. Matt Sledge, "Houston First to Seek Donations to Pay for $124,000 Book Lauding Mayor Sylvester Turner," *Houston Landing*, November 16, 2023, https://houstonlanding.org/houston-first-board-chair-ditches-plan-to-pay-for-124000-book-glorifying-sylvester-turner/.

28. Sixty-three percent of likely voters were online panelists chosen randomly by Lucid; they were shown the survey questions on the display of their smartphone, laptop, or tablet. Thirty-seven percent of likely voters were texted on their cell phones by live operators, who secured the cooperation of each respondent before linking them to an online survey. The pool of adult survey respondents was weighted for gender, age, race, and homeownership.
29. A total of 285 interviews with Latino likely voters and 81 interviews with Asian registered voters.
30. Greg Groogan, "Houston First Asked to Fund $124,000 Book on Mayor's Legacy, Organization Responds," *Fox 26 Houston*, November 16, 2023, https://www.fox26houston.com/news/houston-first-asked-to-fund-124000-book-on-mayors-life-legacy.
31. Nyron N. Crawford, *Marked Men: Black Politicians and the Racialization of Scandal* (NYU Press, 2024), 9.

CONCLUSION: WHY SCANDALS ARE GOOD (AND WHY WE NEED THEM)

1. Evan Andrews, "What Was the 1919 'Black Sox' Baseball Scandal?," History.com, August 24, 2023, https://www.history.com/articles/black-sox-baseball-scandal-1919-world-series-chicago.
2. Major League Baseball Hall of Fame, "Class of 1944," https://baseballhall.org/hof/landis-kenesaw.
3. David Pietrusza, *Rothstein: The Life, Times, and Murder of the Criminal Genius Who Fixed the 1919 World Series* (Basic Books, 2011).
4. Sean Illing, "'Flood the Zone with Shit': How Misinformation Overwhelmed Our Democracy," *Vox*, February 6, 2020, https://www.vox.com/policy-and-politics/2020/1/16/20991816/impeachment-trial-trump-bannon-misinformation.
5. Jack Goldsmith, "Watergate-Era Reforms 50 Years Later," *Harvard Law Today*, June 8, 2022, https://hls.harvard.edu/today/watergate-era-reforms-50-years-later/.
6. Keith W. Olson, *Watergate: The Presidential Scandal That Shook America* (University Press of Kansas, 2003).
7. Jon A. Krosnick and Donald R. Kinder, "Altering the Foundations of Support for the President Through Priming," *American Political Science Review* 84 (1990): 497–512.
8. Emily Berch, "What We Can Learn from the Iran/Contra Scandal," *Nation*, February 12, 2020, https://www.thenation.com/article/politics/leon-neyfakh-interview/.
9. C. N. Krewson, J. A. Schoenherr, and M. Shieh, "Did You Hear About Clarence Thomas? Measuring Public Attention Toward the Supreme Court," *Research and Politics* 11, no. 2 (2024), https://doi.org/10.1177/20531680241263709.
10. John B. Thompson, *The Media and Modernity: A Social Theory of the Media* (Stanford University Press, 1995), 238.

11. Brandon Rottinghaus, "What Causes Gubernatorial Scandal?," in *Power, Constraint, and Leadership in the U.S. States*, ed. David P. Redlawsk (Palgrave, 2015), 71–92.
12. Michael Schudson, "Notes on Scandal and the Watergate Legacy," *American Behavioral Scientist* 47, no. 9 (2004): 1231–1238.
13. Beth Miller, "The Effects of Scandalous Information on Recall of Policy Related Information," *Political Psychology* 31, no. 6 (2010): 887–914.
14. Brandon Rottinghaus, "Surviving Scandal: The Institutional and Political Dynamics of National and State Executive Scandals," *PS: Political Science and Politics* 47, no. 1 (2013): 131–140.
15. Douglas L. Kriner and Eric Schickler, *Investigating the President: Congressional Checks on Presidential Power* (Princeton University Press, 2016).
16. Rottinghaus, "Surviving Scandal."
17. Christopher Witko, "Explaining Increases in the Stringency of State Campaign Finance Regulation, 1993–2002," *State Politics and Policy Quarterly* 7, no. 4 (2007): 369–393.
18. Katherine Faulders and Luis Martinez, " 'Highly Unusual': White House Halts FBI Background Checks for Senior Staff, Shifts Them to Pentagon," ABC News, March 13, 2025, https://abcnews.go.com/Politics/white-house-orders-halt-fbi-background-checks-senior/story?id=119735530.
19. Carrie Johnson, "Reeling from Trump-Era Chaos, Watchdogs Seek Greater Protections," National Public Radio, December 28, 2020, https://www.npr.org/2020/12/28/949202926/with-much-work-to-do-federal-watchdogs-seek-greater-protections.
20. Saikrishna Prakash, "Trump Has Declared War on Inspectors General: The System Can Still Be Saved," *Washington Post*, May 22, 2020, https://www.washingtonpost.com/outlook/inspectors-general-independence-constitution-executive/2020/05/22/bb6be092-9b79-11ea-ac72-3841fcc9b35f_story.html.
21. Prakash, "Trump Has Declared War on Inspectors General."
22. Brandon Rottinghaus, *The Institutional Effects of Executive Scandals* (Cambridge University Press, 2016).
23. James Youniss, "Civic Education: What Schools Can Do to Encourage Civic Identity and Action," *Applied Development Science* 15, no. 2 (2011): 98–103.
24. Monika L. McDermott, Douglas Schwartz, and Sebastian Vallejo, "Talking the Talk but Not Walking the Walk: Public Reactions to Hypocrisy in Political Scandal," *American Politics Research* 43, no. 6 (2015): 952–974.
25. Glenn C. Altschuler and David Wippman, "We Have a Civics Education Crisis—and Deep Divisions on How to Solve It, *Washington Post*, May 31, 2023, https://www.washingtonpost.com/made-by-history/2023/05/31/civics-education-history/.
26. Sarah Shapiro and Catherine Brown, "A Look at Civics Education in the United States," American Federation of Teachers, Summer 2018, https://www.aft.org/ae/summer2018/shapiro_brown.
27. Shawn Healy, "Momentum Grows for Stronger Civic Education Across States," *Human Rights Magazine*, January 4, 2022, https://www.americanbar.org/groups/crsj/publications

/human_rights_magazine_home/the-state-of-civic-education-in-america/momentum-grows-for-stronger-civic-education-across-states/.

28. Mike Maciag, "Ohio's New Ethics Strategy: Public Shaming Politicians," Governing.com, August 28, 2015, https://www.governing.com/archive/gov-ohio-ethics-auditor.html.
29. Marko Klasnja and Grigore Pop-Eleches, "Anticorruption Efforts and Electoral Manipulation in Democracies," *Journal of Politics* 84, no. 2 (2022): 739–752.
30. David A. Leib, "Over 100 State Lawmakers Accused of Misconduct in 3 Years," *SP News*, January 23, 2020, https://apnews.com/article/10aedac91ac64f7e05daacad97408eeb.
31. Rottinghaus, "What Causes Gubernatorial Scandal?"
32. Illing, "'Flood the Zone with Shit.'"
33. Connor Sheets and Kyle Whitmire, "Sex, Lies, and the Alabama Secretary of State: The Fall of John Merrill," Alabama.com, April 16, 2021, https://www.al.com/news/2021/04/sex-lies-and-the-alabama-secretary-of-state-the-fall-of-john-merrill.html.
34. Leslie A. Schwindt-Bayer and Margit Tavits, *Clarity of Responsibility, Accountability, and Corruption* (Cambridge University Press, 2016).
35. Raffaele Asquer, Miriam A. Golden, and Brian T. Hamel, "Corruption, Party Leaders, and Candidate Selection: Evidence from Italy," *Legislative Studies Quarterly* 45, no. 2 (2019): 291–325.
36. Pepper D. Culpepper, Jae-Hee Jung, and Taeku Lee, "Backlash: How Media Coverage of Bank Scandals Moves Mass Preferences on Financial Regulation," *American Journal of Political Science* 68, no. 2 (2024): 427–444.
37. Bruce A. Williams and Michael X. Delli Carpini, "Unchained Reaction: The Collapse of Media Gatekeeping and the Clinton-Lewinsky Scandal," *Journalism* 1, no. 1 (2000): 61.
38. Sander van der Linden, "How Influencers and Algorithms Mobilize Propaganda—and Distort Reality," *Nature*, September 9, 2024, https://www.nature.com/articles/d41586-024-02917-1.
39. Israel Waismel-Manor, Patricia Moy, Rico Neumann, and Moran Shechnick, "Does Corruption Corrupt? The Behavioral Effects of Mediated Exposure to Corruption," *International Journal of Public Opinion Research* 34, no. 1 (2022): 1–22.
40. Joshua P. Darr, Nathan P. Kalmoe, Kathleen Searless, Mingxiao Sui, Raymond J. Pingree, Brian K. Watson, Kirill Bryanov, and Martina Santia, "Collision with Collusion: Partisan Reaction to the Trump-Russia Scandal," *Perspectives on Politics* 17, no. 3 (2019): 772–787.
41. Rosalind S. Helderman, Carol D. Leonnig, and Sari Horwitz, "Former Va. Gov. McDonnell and Wife Charged in Gifts Case," *Washington Post*, January 21, 2014, https://www.washingtonpost.com/local/virginia-politics/former-va-gov-mcdonnell-and-wife-charged-in-gifts-case/2014/01/21/1ed704d2-82cb-11e3-9dd4-e7278db80d86_story.html.
42. Rosalind S. Helderman and Matt Zapotosky, "Ex-Va. Governor Robert McDonnell Guilty of 11 Counts of Corruption," *Washington Post*, September 4, 2014.

43. Zephyr Teachout, "The Menendez Trial Revealed Everything That's Gone Wrong with US Bribery Law," *Vox*, November 17, 2017, https://www.vox.com/the-big-idea/2017/11/15/16656784/menendez-corruption-supreme-court.
44. Adam Liptak, "A Writer Sees Leniency in the Supreme Court's Approach to Public Corruption," *New York Times*, October 21, 2024.
45. Liptak, "A Writer Sees Leniency."
46. Associated Press, "WATCH: Comey Says, 'Lordy, I Hope There Are Tapes,'" PBS News, June 8, 2017, https://www.pbs.org/newshour/politics/comey-lordy-hope-tapes.
47. Ryan Lucas, "Trump Pardons Michael Flynn, Who Pleaded Guilty to Lying About Russia Contact," National Public Radio, November 25, 2020, https://www.npr.org/2020/11/25/823893821/trump-pardons-michael-flynn-who-pleaded-guilty-to-lying-about-russia-contact.
48. Sean Rossman, "Comey's, 'Lordy, I Hope There Are Tapes' Gives Internet the Vapors," *USA Today*, June 8, 2017, https://www.usatoday.com/story/news/nation-now/2017/06/08/comeys-lordy-hope-there-tapes-gives-internet-vapors/380555001/.
49. Kaylyn Jackson Schiff, Daniel S. Schiff, and Natália S. Bueno, "The Liar's Dividend: Can Politicians Claim Misinformation to Evade Accountability?," *American Political Science Review* 119, no. 1 (2025): 71–90.
50. Torun Dewan and David P. Myatt, "Scandal, Protection, and Recovery in the Cabinet," *American Political Science Review* 101, no. 1 (2007): 63–77.
51. Asquer, Golden, and Hamel, "Corruption, Party Leaders, and Candidate Selection.
52. Jeremy A. Frimer and Linda J. Skitka, "Americans Hold Their Political Leaders to a Higher Discursive Standard Than Rank-and-File Co-Partisans," *Journal of Experimental Social Psychology* 86 (2020), https://doi.org/10.1016/j.jesp.2019.103907.
53. Jeremy A. Frimer and Linda J. Skitka, "The Montagu Principle: Incivility Decreases Politicians' Public Approval, Even with Their Political Base," *Journal of Personality and Social Psychology* 115, no. 5 (2018): 845–866.
54. Laura Jacobs and Joost van Spanje, "Martyrs for Free Speech? Disentangling the Effect of Legal Prosecution of Anti-Immigration Politicians on Their Electoral Support," *Political Behavior* 43, no. 3 (2021): 973–996.
55. Michael D. Cobb and Andrew J. Taylor, "Paging Congressional Democrats: It Was the Immorality, Stupid," *PS: Political Science and Politics* 47, no. 2 (2014): 351–356.
56. "3. Partisan Environments, Views of Political Conversations, and Disagreements," *Partisanship and Political Animosity in 2016*, Pew Research Center, June 22, 2016, https://www.pewresearch.org/politics/2016/06/22/3-partisan-environments-views-of-political-conversations-and-disagreements/.
57. Alyssa N. Rockenbach and Tara D. Hudson, "Transforming Political Divides: How Student Identities and Campus Contexts Shape Interpartisan Friendships," *AERA Open* 10 (2024), https://doi.org/10.1177/23328584231222475.
58. Luiza A. Santos, Jan G. Voelkel, and Jamil Zaki, "Belief in the Utility of Cross-Partisan Empathy Reduces Partisan Animosity and Facilitates Political Persuasion," *Psychological Science* 33, no. 9 (2022): 1557–1573, https://doi.org/10.1177/09567976221098594.

59. Tabitha Bonilla, "The Influence of Partisanship on Assessments of Promise Fulfillment and Accountability," *American Political Science Review*, August 5, 2024, https://www.cambridge.org/core/journals/american-political-science-review/article/influence-of-partisanship-on-assessments-of-promise-fulfillment-and-accountability/D563078C0C7658E99223B8300A9F4656.
60. Jon Greenberg, "Is a Wrigley Field Sportsbook a Sign of the Apocalypse or a Sensible Alternative?, *Athletic*, April 10, 2024, https://theathletic.com/5400560/2024/04/10/chicago-cubs-sportsbook-wrigley-field/.

INDEX

INDEX

INDEX

GPSR Authorized Representative: Easy Access System Europe, Mustamäe tee 50, 10621 Tallinn, Estonia, gpsr.requests@easproject.com

www.ingramcontent.com/pod-product-compliance
Lightning Source LLC
Chambersburg PA
CBHW032135020426
42334CB00016B/1167

* 9 7 8 0 2 3 1 2 1 8 8 2 5 *